The Gospel of Luke

The Gospel of
LUKE

JUDITH LIEU

WIPF & STOCK · Eugene, Oregon

Wipf and Stock Publishers
199 W 8th Ave, Suite 3
Eugene, OR 97401

The Gospel of Luke
Epworth Commentaries
By Lieu, Judith M.
Copyright©1997 by Lieu, Judith M.
ISBN 13: 978-1-62032-202-4
Publication date 4/6/2012
Previously published by Epworth Press, 1997

CONTENTS

Contents

Contents

PREFACE

Every book owes its birth to many more people than the author alone. This is particularly true of this Commentary. The absence of footnotes and of appeal to or debate with other scholars hides my very great debt to those who have wrestled with Luke before me. Yet beyond the standard obligations felt by every writer, this volume has some special ones. *Luke* has accompanied my journey from King's College London to Macquarie University, Sydney, and through this Preface I would like to express my deep gratitude to all who have offered support and encouragement on that journey. I owe particular thanks to the Editorial Committee of the Epworth Press both for entrusting me with *Luke* and for their long patience and continued confidence as they awaited its delayed completion. Yet my greatest debt is to my fellow preachers and congregations who have challenged me to hold in a creative tension my commitment to critical study of the New Testament and the call to the proclamation of the gospel, and within whose fellowship I have been nurtured: to the Queen's College Birmingham, and to the Leamington and the Watford Circuits.

INTRODUCTION

Luke's Gospel can be read in many ways. Most obviously it is the story of Jesus of Nazareth, from his birth to his death. Although there is nothing quite like the Gospels in the literature of the world of the time, they come as close to 'biographies' as to anything else, and this is particularly true of Luke who has earned the epithet 'the historian'. Yet his story reaches from before Jesus' birth to its angelic proclamation and beyond his death to the confession 'the Lord has risen'. Although the biographies of other ancient heroes might mark their births with supernatural omens, in Luke these extensions take the story into the realm of faith. The Gospel tells the story of Jesus from the conviction of faith that he was God's means of salvation.

Seen in this way, Luke's Gospel is the climax of a much older story. He himself traces it back to Adam (3.38), for those who knew their scriptures the beginning of the human race. Yet more particularly Luke shows that Jesus was fulfilling the promises made by God long ago to the people of Israel: the Gospel can hardly be understood without some knowledge of or reference to the scriptures Christians know as the Old Testament.

However, Luke's Gospel can also be read as the first episode in a narrative which will continue with the story of the church in the book of Acts, a story which itself closes without a finale. Certainly Acts presupposes the Gospel, to which it refers back (Acts 1.1), although it is, of course, less easy to decide whether when writing the Gospel Luke was already anticipating his second volume. Luke has also earned the epithet 'historian' from his continuing the story into the time of the church; this in turn has prompted heated debates as to how good a historian he is, or as to whether this is how he would want to be read. Such debates are particularly relevant in Acts but they are not irrelevant to the Gospel, or indeed to deciding what any of the Gospels is really about.

Certainly, whether or not 'Acts' was already in Luke's mind as he wrote the Gospel, the church and its needs undoubtedly were. This is true of each of the Gospels: they retell the story of Jesus in the light of the concerns of the church of their own time. Although the broad outline of their accounts may be the same, by different details and emphases, by different ordering of the material, or by the inclusion of different incidents, they reflect those concerns. No doubt this was happening as soon as the story of Jesus was recounted, long before the first evangelist began to write it down, and it has happened ever since. Luke is different from the other Gospels in that he not only does this but also continues with his second volume. Both by reading Acts but also by carefully studying his Gospel we can recover the important issues which faced the church as he saw them. Here 'the church' does not mean only, or perhaps not even primarily, the church throughout the then known world, but the local church among whom Luke wrote and who, presumably, would have been the first and intended readers of his work.

The perspective taken in this commentary is that to study the Gospel is not just to explore the story of Jesus of Nazareth. It is to explore *Luke's* story, to recognize how he sees Jesus both as a climax and as a beginning, to hear the voice of faith which is not the same as the voice of a documentary analysis, and so to understand how he interprets Jesus for his own time.

Therefore this introduction has started with the Gospel and not with its author, about whom we know little more than his writings can tell us. Both the Gospel and Acts were almost certainly originally anonymous. Although their first readers surely knew who the author was, it was more important that he was making known and bringing together the traditions about Jesus as they had been handed down within the life of the church. According to a tradition which first appears towards the end of the second century in the Muratorian Canon and in Irenaeus of Lyons, he was Luke, 'the beloved doctor' and companion of Paul (Col. 4.14; II Tim. 4.11; Philemon 24). In relation to Acts it has sometimes been doubted whether one who knew Paul would present him in a way which often seems quite distant from the Paul of the letters, but this problem cannot arise with the Gospel. The Gospel itself acknowledges that it is not written by an eyewitness, as Luke was not, and would give less reason for us to expect the influence of Paul's thought. The style fits that of a man familiar with the semi-technical literature of the Graeco-Roman world of the time, although that it shows particular affinities with medical literature cannot be demonstrated. However, even if we could be confident about the identity of Luke as the author it would not give us much more insight into understanding the Gospel than can be gathered from the Gospel itself. As just noted, the Gospel itself declares its author to be a 'second generation' Christian, dependent on the reports of earlier witnesses. Its Greek is relatively polished, although at times the author shows himself, or his sources, to be heavily influenced by the Geeek translation of the Hebrew scriptures, the Septuagint (LXX). Although, as we shall see, he is particularly interested in the spread of the gospel to the Gentiles, there is nothing to determine with certainty whether he himself was born a Gentile or a Jew from one of the diaspora communities within the Roman empire.

Despite his general appeal to 'the original eyewitnesses and servants of the Gospel' (1.2), modern scholars have attempted greater precision in determining the sources on which he drew. It is now widely agreed that Luke, like Matthew, was dependent on Mark, for most frequently where all three recount the same episode Mark acts as the common denominator to explain the commonalities and variations between them. Thus the way Luke uses Mark, and the changes he makes, provide one important insight into Luke's particular interests and concerns. There is also a substantial amount of material which Luke has in common with Matthew; because this similarity extends on occasion to actual wording it seems likely that the relationship is a literary one, i.e. at the level of written source(s). Although there are proponents of each of the possibilities, that Luke used Matthew, that Matthew used Luke, or that they used one, or more than one, common source, it is the last view which is adopted here. This source is often referred to as 'Q', but it is assumed here that 'Q' did not exist as a single recoverable source but that it is an umbrella 'title' covering a range of types of material available to both Matthew and Luke, sometimes in the same but sometimes in different forms. Once again Luke's use of this material may offer insights into his own concerns, although without 'Q' with which to compare him, any conclusions must be more tentative than when comparing him with Mark. Beyond this, there are a number of episodes or pieces of teaching which come only in this Gospel. Only by careful analysis of the language and ideas is it possible to guess when he is repeating earlier tradition, when he is rewriting more freely.

Yet the interest of this commentary is not in reconstructing Luke's earlier sources or in remaining at the level of his use of them. The finished Gospel is not a conglomerate of other material but a literary unity in its own right. As already stated it is Luke's story that we read, and as such it invites a sensitivity to the way he brings his material together, leading the reader on as Jesus too makes his journey, and conveying what it means not only through what is said but also through how it is said.

The concerns that Luke addresses will therefore emerge through the commentary, and in some ways it is inappropriate to warn the reader of them and to summarize them before even starting the Gospel. Yet it is the convention of Introductions to attempt some such summary. So here there will some suggestions as to what were the issues which beset the church in Luke's time, while encouraging the reader to explore them in the Gospel, with the help of the commentary, of the special notes which occasionally punctuate its text, and of the index of themes. The additional notes, which are indented in the commentary, are marked * on the Contents page. The text given (in italics) is usually that of the REB; however, on occasion I have used my own translation and have indicated that I differ from the REB and my reasons for doing so.

We have already seen that Luke sets the story of Jesus within a continuum which reaches back into the past history of Israel and forward into the history of the early church. Perhaps this was inevitable as he and others were forced by the passage of time to recognize that Jesus had not brought in the end of time, and were also forced to give meaning to the life of the church and to the experience of the early Christians. Yet this could not lead him to see Jesus' ministry as just one incident within the ongoing course of history. The history writing of Israel in what Christians call the 'Old Testament' already described climactic events as God's activity through history – a view of the meaning of history which is often called 'salvation history'. So was the story of Jesus simply to be set within that pattern, followed by God's continuing purpose through the life of the church? Christian faith, however, saw the time of Jesus as not just another channel of God's purpose but as uniquely so, as different in quality from all God's previous activity, as a time of fulfilment. Luke, therefore, has to mark out the time of Jesus while also fitting it into a continuing pattern.

Earlier Christian tradition had understood Jesus as proclaiming and embodying God's sovereign rule which had long been hoped for at the climax of history. All Christian preaching as we encounter it in the New Testament struggled to hold in tension the certainty that Jesus was God's final word and the continuing hope that God's rule would be fully and visibly manifested in a way that it indubitably was not yet. Luke had to integrate this tension between 'the now and not yet' with his awareness of the life of the church. If he was to encourage believers to take the present with its demands of discipleship seriously, would he have to down-play the sense of the imminence of the kingdom which we find in Mark's Gospel? What was the relationship between the kingdom as Jesus had proclaimed and embodied it and the life of the church? Should Christians continue to scrutinize every upheaval in history as the beginning of the promised end? Luke has to understand the kingdom, present through Jesus and yet to come, in the light of the church, and write that understanding into his retelling of the story of Jesus.

Yet the story of Jesus had to provide the means through which the early believers could also understand their own discipleship. Each of the Gospels, while describing how Jesus summoned followers to himself, also invites readers from subsequent generations to hear that call. For Luke Jesus' ministry was in one sense the foundation of the church and Jesus' first disciples had a unique role which he explores in the early chapters of Acts; but he too was very aware of the needs of his own community. How could he both preserve the unrepeatable position of the first disciples and address those needs through his account of Jesus' teaching?

Noting the themes to which Luke draws special attention or which are peculiar to his Gospel offers, as we have seen, a way into discovering those needs. Prominent among these appear to be issues of wealth and poverty. It has often been noted that in Luke Jesus has a particular concern for the marginalized in society, women, tax-collectors, the poor, and the 'ethnically marginalized' Samaritans. At the same time wealth and the use of wealth constitute a recurring theme; Acts too suggests that a number of prominent early Christians were from the more affluent sections of society, although this may be part of Luke's desire to emphasize the respectability of Christianity. How could the church have room for such without diluting the radical demand which was part of the earliest traditions of Jesus' preaching of the kingdom?

As just suggested, the place of Christianity within society would itself be a pressing issue for reflection. Acts has often been seen as an 'apology', establishing the innocence of Christians in Roman eyes. The death of Jesus by the Roman penalty of crucifixion would provide the obvious focus and provocation for such a concern. Although this was not inevitable, in practice in the telling of the story of Jesus the role of the Jews was bound up with the same issue. If Roman involvement in the death of Jesus was to be down-played, need Jewish involvement be heightened? Other factors could also lead in this direction. The more the early Christians were convinced that Jesus was the intended fulfilment of God's purposes made known to Israel in the past, particularly through the prophets, the more the 'failure' of most Jews to believe in him as the messiah was a source of perplexity or a dangerous potential counter-argument. Jewish unbelief had to be understood, and God's continuing purposes for the Jews in the light of a church which included both former Jews and former Gentiles had to be rethought. Why had Jesus not been believed in his own time? Was his death the work of those who held power or an expression of a universal Jewish unbelief? Was such unbelief part of a pattern fixed for the future or did God have some as yet unrevealed purpose? More particularly, when the Romans destroyed Jerusalem and the Temple in 70 CE following a revolt by the Jewish people, was this again the activity of God, and if so how did it fit into the past and future of God's kingdom?

By the time Luke wrote an increasing number of Gentiles (non-Jews) were entering the church without first converting to Judaism. Paul's letters far more vividly than Luke in Acts witness to the pain and conflict this process had caused. This could only be so if Jesus' own teaching and ministry had given no clear pointers towards the place of the Gentiles. Yet did this mean that there was no true continuity between Jesus' ministry as a Jew among Jews and the church with its growing Gentile membership? Luke undoubtedly has a particular sensitivity towards this problem.

In fact historical analysis suggests that in his own context Jesus was at best an ambiguous figure who made few if any clear claims about his own significance. Modern scholars are undecided whether to see him as a prophet, a preacher of God's imminent kingdom, a wise teacher, a 'charismatic' in one of its many meanings or . . . Luke and his readers were less undecided, and when Luke was writing language of 'messiah' was probably being supplemented or replaced by more developed ideas of Jesus as God's son. From Acts we can see how Christian experience was being interpreted as the activity of God's spirit, and how access to God through the spirit and through prayer played a focal role. Moreover, it was no longer enough to say that Jesus' death was in accordance with God's will: it had to be included within the total understanding of Jesus' purpose and of Jesus himself as the fulfilment of God's promised salvation. These

and other interests are explored by Luke in his telling of the story of
Jesus.

All this does not mean that Luke collapses the distinction between
Jesus and the church; indeed, writing a second volume meant he
need not do this. Yet it does mean that while Luke tells the story of
Jesus, the way he does so owes much to his own experience, to the
past experience of the church whose traditions he passes on, and to
the church's present needs as he understood them. To preach from
Luke's Gospel is indeed to preach Jesus, but it is to preach Jesus as
seen through Luke's eyes, for we cannot 'reconstruct' a 'historical'
Jesus freed from others' perceptions. To understand how and why
Luke crafts the picture he does is therefore an essential part of
understanding 'his' Jesus. To see how he makes Jesus address the
needs of his church is to ask how the story of a figure from another
time, place and culture can address the later needs of the church.
There may be times when Luke's answer may seem an ambiguous
one at best for the modern church: Luke's attitude to the Jews, and
the question whether his sympathies tend towards appeasement of
the state and of the comfortable in society have provoked particular
debate in recent years. Just as Luke did not slavishly repeat the traditions he received but wrestled to re-express them in his context, the
challenge for the preacher is both to receive, to enter into Luke's
understanding of the Gospel, and to make known the offer and
demand of the same Gospel in the world.

Further Reading

There are numerous commentaries and studies of Luke or of
particular aspects of his thought. The following is only a selection of
recent works which develop some of the issues considered here:

1. Commentaries

G.B. Caird, *Saint Luke* (Pelican NT Commentaries), Penguin 1963

C.F. Evans, *Saint Luke* (TPI New Testament Commentaries), SCM
Press, London and Trinity Press International, Philadelphia 1993

J.A. Fitzmyer, *The Gospel according to Luke* (2 vols, Anchor Bible 28,
29) Doubleday, New York 1981

A.R.C. Leaney, *A Commentary on the Gospel according to St Luke*

(Blacks NT Commentaries), A. & C. Black 1958

J. Nolland, *Luke* (3 vols, Word Biblical Commentary 35), Word Books, Dallas 1989–93

2. Studies of Luke's thought

H. Conzelmann, *The Theology of St Luke*, SCM Press 1982

J. Drury, *Tradition and Design in Luke's Gospel. A Study in Early Christian Historiography*, DLT 1976

E. Franklin, *Christ the Lord. A Study in the Purpose and Theology of Luke*, Westminster Press, Philadelphia 1975

I.H. Marshall, *Luke: Historian and Theologian*, Paternoster 1970

C. Talbert, *Literary Pattern. Theological Themes and the Genre of Luke-Acts*, Scholars Press, Montana 1974

R.C. Tannehill, *The Narrative Unity of Luke-Acts. A Literary Interpretation*. Vol. 1, *The Gospel according to Luke*, Fortress Press, Philadelphia, 1986

C.M. Tuckett, *Luke* (New Testament Guides), Sheffield Academic Press 1996

3. Special topics

L. Alexander, *The Preface to Luke's Gospel. Literary Convention and Social Context in Luke 1.1–4 and Acts 1.1* (SNTSMS 78), CUP 1993

K. Bailey, *Poet and Peasant and Through Peasant Eyes: A Literary-Cultural Approach to the Parables in Luke*, Eerdmans, Grand Rapids 1983

R.L. Brawley, *Luke-Acts and the Jews. Conflict, Apology and Conciliation*, Scholars Press, Atlanta 1987

R.J. Cassidy, *Jesus, Politics and Society. A Study of Luke's Gospel*, Orbis, Maryknoll 1978

D. Crump, *Jesus the Intercessor* (WUNT 2.49), J.C.B. Mohr, Tübingen 1992

J.A. Darr, *On Character Building. The Reader and the Rhetoric of Characterization in Luke-Acts*, Westminster John Knox, Louisville 1992

P.F. Esler, *Community and Gospel in Luke-Acts* (SNTSMS 57), CUP 1987

C.A. Evans and J.A. Sanders, *Luke and Scripture. The Function of Sacred Tradition in Luke-Acts*, Fortress Press, Minneapolis 1993

S. Farris, *The Hymns of Luke's Infancy Narrative* (JSNTSup), JSOT Press 1985

C.H. Giblin, *The Destruction of Jerusalem according to Luke's Gospel*, Biblical Institute Press, Rome 1985

D.M. Moessner, *Lord of the Banquet. The Literary and Theological Significance of the Lukan Travel Narrative*, Fortress Press, Minneapolis 1989

H. Moxnes, *The Economy of the Kingdom. Social Conflict and Economic Relations in Luke's Gospel*, Fortress Press, Philadelphia 1988

J. Neyrey (ed), *The Social World of Luke-Acts. Models for Interpretation*, Hendrickson, Massachusetts 1991

T.K. Seim, *The Double Message. Patterns of Gender in Luke-Acts*, T. & T. Clark 1994

J. Squires, *The Plan of God in Luke-Acts* (SNTSMS 76), CUP 1993

J.B. Tyson, *Images of Judaism in Luke-Acts*, University of South Carolina Press, Columbia 1992

The Beginning of the Gospel
1.1–2.52

The Gospels were born from the preaching of the early church. In that preaching the story began with Jesus embarking on his ministry through the preaching and baptism of John (Acts 10.37), as he does still in Mark's Gospel. Luke, however, provides that story with a preface, not only the technical preface of 1.1–4 but a preface to introduce those first 'actors on the stage', Jesus and John. As in contemporary biographies of heroes in the Greek and Roman world, the events surrounding Jesus' birth, and that of John, prepare the reader for the future significance of his life. Yet the reader of these chapters would not find herself or himself in the world of those other heroes but in that of the Jewish scriptures, of the Temple in Jerusalem, of the divine gift of a child against all the limitations of nature, of prophecy, and of humble praise to God. These, as we shall see, act as a sort of prologue, introducing ideas and themes which will be more fully worked out through the Gospel.

The preface
1.1–4

First, however, comes the preface proper, which gives hardly any hint of that other world. Matthew and Mark start their Gospels in very different ways, but both set 'Jesus Christ' firmly in the first line; John reaches far back to 'the word', soon to be made flesh, present in the beginning with God. By contrast Luke introduces his account with a carefully constructed literary introduction – vv. 1–4 are a single sentence – which betrays little of the Gospel's central message. The polished Greek, the acknowledgment of earlier attempts at an account, the claim to careful investigation and to orderly reporting as a foundation for reliable knowledge, would be familiar to his readers not from other sacred writing but from scientific or other semi-technical treatises – more so than from historical writings, with

1

which Luke's work has more often been compared. Only the attentive reader would see in *the events that have been accomplished* (= REB *taken place*) *among us* a pointer to the theme of fulfilment which provides one of the keys to the Gospel: Jesus makes that claim with a related verb in 4.21. Luke's earlier authorities were not only *eyewitnesses*, those with first-hand knowledge, but *servants of the word*, which in Christian parlance meant '*the gospel*' (hence the REB translation, cf. Acts 4.29; 6.2,4): the first disciples are here given a role which was to become increasingly important in the church's understanding of apostleship (cf. Acts 10.39–42). Dependent on the witness they have *handed down* are the *us* of whom he speaks, believers of (a) later generation(s).

What follows, then, is not presented as a preaching of the Gospel. It acknowledges the passage of time and the need for an *orderly*, systematic rather than chronological, account based on a chain of tradition and consistent study where there are no unaccounted for gaps. *Theophilus*, whose name betrays nothing of his background or status, has probably been *instructed* rather than '*informed*' (REB) already. There is nothing to suggest that he was a Roman official investigating this new religion, or that he was Luke's patron and responsible for the dissemination of the book: *your excellency* is over-formal for this conventional compliment. Instead he is probably more of an insider and represents the growing need, felt by the *many* to whom, without disparagement, Luke looks back, for authority and interpretation in a church whose spread is recounted in Acts.

The coming of Christ
1.5–2.52

Against this background the story that follows comes as a double shock. First the style changes dramatically from the literate Greek of the preface to one which resonates with the language and style of the Greek translation of the Jewish scriptures, the Septuagint. Indeed, although proof is not possible, in these two chapters Luke may be dependent at times on sources which have themselves been translated from Hebrew. Secondly, we are plunged into a story of Temple and priestly families; despite the REB's subheading, Jesus will not be mentioned until 1.31 and we must wait until ch. 2 for his birth. Moreover, in contrast to modern readers, for whom these may be among the best-known of the stories about Jesus, Luke's first readers may have been familiar only with his adult ministry. Understanding the message of these stories and understanding why Luke prefaced his account with them go together.

Certainly they introduce Jesus as one marked out from birth and before for future importance. As already noted, accounts of divine intervention in their birth were similarly told for Greek and Roman heroes, but equality with these is not Luke's main purpose. The early church wrestled with the question at what point Jesus was designated Son of God. In some early traditions the resurrection was the focal point (cf. Rom 1.4), but before long it was felt that this only confirmed what was already true in Jesus' ministry. It would be easy to read Mark 1.11 as suggesting that the anointing by the spirit and the divine affirmation at Jesus' baptism inaugurated his sonship. Luke, like Matthew, does not drop the baptism but pushes sonship back to Jesus' conception and birth (1.32, 35; cf. Matt. 2.15), although how Luke understands this is something to which we shall return.

Yet, unlike Matthew, Luke does not start with Jesus but with the birth of John the Baptist, and so invites the question, What is the relationship between John and Jesus? The question would already have been provoked by John's baptism of Jesus (Mark 1.9; Acts 10.37; but cf. Luke 3.21 and the commentary there), and Luke returns to it twice (7.28; 16.16). Here, in these birth narratives, John is very carefully put in his place as a diagram soon makes clear:

John the Baptist	Jesus
Annunciation of birth: 1.5–25	Annunciation of birth:1.26–38
(in the Temple)	*(in the home)*
Mother of Jesus visits mother of John;	
Mother of John greets and blesses mother of Jesus: 1.39–45	
Mary's acclamation of what God has done: 1.46–54	
Birth: 1.57–58	Birth: 2.1–7 (8–20)
Circumcision & Naming: 1.59–66	Circumcision & Naming: 2.21
Inspired prophecy about John's future: 1.68–79	Inspired prophecy about Jesus' future: 2.(25) 29–32 (38)
(in the home)	*(in the Temple)*
Growth: 1.80	Growth: 2.39–40

Both stories follow a similar pattern, and, most significantly, both births are 'miraculous', heralded by an angelic messenger. Yet the parallelism is soon disrupted by Elizabeth's acknowledgment that Mary is *blessed among women* and *mother of my lord*. As we look more closely we discover that whereas the 'miracle' of John's birth was the overcoming of age and barrenness for a married couple, the greater 'miracle' of Jesus' birth is the overcoming of the virginity of a girl who does not have sexual relations with any man. We become all the more aware of this 'weighting' towards Jesus because instead of meeting first John's story and then Jesus', as if they were separate and independent, the two annunciations are brought together, followed by Mary's visit to Elizabeth.

Closer study of the stories will bring this theme even clearer. Yet the table also shows how the whole story begins and ends in the Temple; this would still be true if we added 2.41–52, the account of Jesus' visit to the Temple at the age of twelve. Between, they centre round the home, so that we find ourselves in a world of piety and praise in both Temple and home. Moreover, the stories of a child given to those without hope of a child, and the language of the praise they offer, will take us into the world of the 'Old Testament'. The Temple does not stand for something alien to God, refusing to recognize him (but see 19.41–47 and pp. 156–58); it stands for the faith and experience of Israel from which Jesus is born, and for the faithful there who receive him. In the same way Acts starts with the early Christians regularly meeting in the Temple (Acts 2.46). One of the problems the Gospel seeks to answer is why Israel or the Jews came to reject Jesus, and what is the continuing relationship between them and the Christians.

Annunciation
1.5–25 and 26–38

Luke fits the events he is about to describe firmly in history, in the reign of *Herod* the Great, who ruled from 37–4 BCE as a client king under Roman provision: *Judaea* here refers not just to the southern area (cf. 3.1) but to the whole region. He develops this historical interest in 2.1–2 and 3.1–2, where he extends the stage to that of the Roman Empire; but here his words echo the style of I–II Kings, just as his reference to the *priestly descent* of Zechariah and Elizabeth, and later to the Davidic descent of Joseph (1.27), take us, as we have just seen, into the world of the 'Old Testament'. Zechariah and Elizabeth, without children and now *well on in years*, remind us of Abraham and Sarah and, like Simeon and Anna later (2.25, 36), they are described in terms summarizing the true piety of Jewish tradition, *upright and devout*. We will understand what follows best if we see how it evokes and answers themes and ideas from the Old

Testament; this will already have been true of Luke's sources, but he has put the story together to make it even more unmistakeable.

Luke does not explain, although it would have added to the drama if his readers had known, that although each of the twenty-four *divisions of the priesthood* (cf. I Chron. 24.7–19) served in the Temple for a week twice a year, so great was the number of priests that any one might only do so once in a lifetime. The presence of the *people all assembled* suggests that the *hour of offering* was probably that of the evening (cf. Ex. 30.1–8), but Luke is more interested in the dramatic effect created, just as he ignores the fact that Zechariah would have been alone by the altar of incense in the outer chamber or 'holy place' only for a few moments.

Instead, this scene, and the assumption that Zechariah was also *at prayer* (cf. v.13 and the commentary at 3.21 for this important theme in Luke), recall Dan. 9.20–27, where *Gabriel*, who is only mentioned here and in 8.16 in the Old Testament, tells Daniel in cryptic form of the events to come until 'sin [will be] brought to an end . . . and everlasting right ushered in'. That angels brought messages from God (cf. Acts 10.3; 12.7 etc.) was not just part of the thought-world of Luke's own time, but also part of his biblical heritage; there is both continuity with and fulfilment of the past.

Thus the stories of the angel Gabriel's visits to Zechariah and to Mary follow a pattern which we find in similar stories in the Old Testament (e.g. Gen. 17; Judg. 13):

1) The appearance of the angel	1.11	1.26–28
2) Reaction/fear	1.12	1.29
3) The message: a) address by name	1.13	1.30
b) they are described	1.13	1.30
c) not to fear	1.13	1.30
d) a woman is to bear a (male) child	1.13	1.31
e) his name is given (and interpreted)	1.13	1.31
f) his future task is described	1.14–17	1.32–33
4) An objection by the person	1.18	1.34
5) A sign is given	1.19–20	1.36

The common pattern helps highlight important differences between the two: John will be *great in the eyes of the Lord* and will have the task of a *forerunner*; Jesus *will be great and will be called Son of God* and *his reign shall never end*. John *will be filled with the Holy Spirit* from *his very birth*; Jesus' conception is due to *the Holy Spirit coming upon* Mary. Zechariah's failure to believe results in him being dumb until his restored gift of speech establishes the truth of the angel's message (1.63–4); Mary responds in obedient compliance, and the sign given her is Elizabeth's pregnancy!

However, this bias towards Jesus is not yet in view as we read the message given to Zechariah. Instead John is marked as having a uniquely significant role in his own right. No longer evident in Greek, in Hebrew his name would have meant 'God is gracious' and may also have carried an allusion to Zechariah's *prayer* in v.13; his abstinence from *wine and strong drink* would be a sign of his dedication to God (cf. Num. 6.3) and would recall Samson's special calling (Judg. 13.5–7); as forerunner of God he fulfils the prophecy of Mal. 3.1, while Mal. 4.5–6 spoke of the coming of the prophet Elijah 'before the great and terrible day of the Lord' who would 'reconcile parents to their children and children to their parents'. How John fulfils these Old Testament expectations will become clearer in ch.3 (see commentary and also 7.24–35), but already we see that he does not only belong to the world of the Old Testament: for Luke the coming of the Holy Spirit is very much a sign of God's new act of salvation (see v.35 below), and John will be filled with that Spirit *from birth*. Therefore he also anticipates and belongs to the future.

The epilogue to Zechariah's story only refers briefly to Elizabeth, his wife, although she will become the central figure in later scenes. The story assumes, and assumes on her behalf, that to be childless is a *disgrace* felt by the woman alone, a common theme in the Old Testament (Gen. 30.1; I Sam. 1.5–11; cf. Isa. 54.1). Elizabeth *lived in seclusion for five months* not out of shame at her pregnancy, but because in Luke's telling of the story her condition must be a secret in order to be the sign given five months later to Mary.

Both Matthew and Luke associate Jesus' infancy with *Nazareth*, although Matthew only has the family settle there after Jesus' birth (Matt. 2.23). For Luke there may be a contrast between Judaea where the annunciation to the aged Zechariah takes place in the Temple, and *Galilee* where the annunciation to the young girl Mary takes place in a small *town* – by our standards little more than a hamlet. Luke sets some store by the fact that it was *Joseph*, to whom Mary was betrothed, who was of Davidic descent; he does not seem to see any problem in thus claiming for Jesus Davidic descent, appropriate for the Messiah in popular belief, while also presenting him as born without a human father's intervention (see 3.23–38 and commentary).

That Mary was *betrothed* would mean that her relationship with Joseph was already a legally binding one, but that she had not yet had sexual relations with him; she could therefore be described as a *virgin* and not just as *'a girl'* as in the REB's translation (v.27). Later, in response to the angel's promise of a child, she protests, *'How is this to be, since I do not know a man'*; the REB's *'I am still a virgin'* conveys the sexual meaning of 'know' but wrongly puts the emphasis on her physical state. If we were reading this only to recreate the original scene we might wonder at such a response; as a betrothed woman could she not assume that before long she would have intercourse with Joseph and might conceive very quickly? There is nothing in Luke to support imaginative reconstructions of his advanced age, any agreed plan to postpone consummation, or her intention to remain virgin. But Luke has his readers in mind as he recounts the scene, following, as we have seen, a familiar pattern, perhaps particularly also the story of Hannah (I Sam. 1). For them Mary's objection makes it crystal clear that this child is not born by normal human means but by a supernatural, divine act.

This divine act does not mean that God or the Holy Spirit provide a substitute for the male principle in conception – unlike Graeco-Roman stories which told of women impregnated by a male deity and bearing a special child. *Power (of the Most High)* is associated with the *Holy Spirit* in Luke (4.14; Acts 1.8; 10.38), and is a special mark of Jesus' ministry and of the life of the early church (Luke 4.36; 5.17 [see commentary]; Acts 4.7 6.8). It will already be at work in Mary as the first stage in God's new initiative. This is why, and not because God is physically involved as father, the *child . . . will be called Son of God*.

Mary has no prior qualifications for this destiny; whereas the gift of a child to Elizabeth was in part a response to Zechariah's prayer (v.13), for Mary it is the unlooked for act of God. The greeting as *most favoured one* is an affirmation of God's choice of her and does not mean that, by divine favour or her own virtue, she already has been marked as different from other women. As the story progresses Mary's response (v.38) becomes a model of obedient acceptance of God's will, in contrast to Zechariah's unbelief: her words *'I am the Lord's servant'* are those any believer must say (17.7–10). It is all too easy to draw from here a picture of Mary who passively submits, and to use it to exalt such passive submission as a virtue. Luke does little to answer this charge, but presumably even for his story her acceptance was necessary for God's action, as Elizabeth's blessing (v.45) will suggest, and her song in vv.46–55 does something to redress the balance. Later, perhaps more positively we may recognize that she did indeed hear the word of God and do it (8.19–21 and commentary).

The focus of the story is not Mary but the child to be born. The name to be given him, *Jesus*, is not interpreted (as in Matt. 1.21) although 'salvation' is the implicit theme of what follows. First (32–33), he *will be called*, recognized as, *Son of the Most High*, heir to the promises and hopes of a descendent of David (e.g. Ps. 2.7; 89.3–4; II Sam 7.11–16) which by now had crystallized into a firm but still fluid expectation of a 'messiah' to come. He will also be recognized as *holy*, set apart, and as *Son of God* (35). This could mean nothing more than God's chosen Messiah as in 32–33, for there is now evidence that the messiah could be called 'Son of God' in Jewish thought without implying he had supernatural origin or divine nature. Yet, as we have seen, more is probably intended; the title 'Son of God' had for the early Christians a meaning which went beyond that of messiah; it is a designation made possibly by the extraordinary creative power of the spirit, in Rom. 1.3–4 active in the resurrection, here in his conception. Luke would not think in terms of divine nature, nor, again, does 'Son of God' mean that God fills the generative role of father; but Luke does want to affirm that that unique role and status Christians claimed for Jesus was not one he acquired but was his from birth by God's initiative in human affairs.

The **'virgin birth'**, that Jesus was conceived without the involvement of a human father while Mary was still a virgin, is assumed by both Matthew and Luke. Each tells a story to express this, stories which both differ from each other significantly and have significant points in common. How widespread this belief was among the early Christians, and how early we can trace knowledge of it are questions we cannot now answer. For Matthew the prophecy of Isa. 7.14, taken as referring to a virgin (which in the original it need not), plays a significant role (Matt.1.23), but there is no hint that this passage has influenced Luke's account. Neither is it likely from what has been argued above that Luke thought that if Jesus was the Son of God he must have been born without a human father. Yet this does not mean that we can trace the story confidently back before Luke – and there is nothing to support the theory that Mary was his confidante; instead we have seen how he has shaped the story to express a number of convictions and to introduce some significant themes. Yet, important as that belief has been in Christian faith, some readers find that it also produces problems. Mary can become a submissive figure, a model to be imposed upon on others of passive acceptance of the impositions, and worse, of whatever is declared God's will, or of those with power. If Luke contains the seeds which can lead to such a view, he also, as we shall see, contains the seeds which may subvert it. For some the stories also express a very ambivalent attitude to human sexuality and to the role of women. On the one hand, the assumption that childlessness is not just a sadness for some but a disgrace to be born by the woman is one we cannot affirm as Luke seems to. On the other, to exclude Jesus from the natural cycle of intercourse, conception and birth can seem to devalue that cycle as unworthy of God, and also to separate Jesus from normal human experience. All this would be foreign not just to the biblical conviction that God created and blessed human relationships in their physicality (Gen. 1.26–28), but also to Luke's intention. This is to express through story form a conviction that in Jesus God was acting in a new creative way, yet also in continuity with the past, not by avoiding human involvement, but through the lives and the bodies of men and women who were faithful. We may even go a step further: for the unmarried Mary, becoming pregnant would not be seen as the sign of blessing that it would for Elizabeth, but as disgrace; yet it was her child who would be recognized as holy. However, Luke ignores this social dimension (ctr. Matt.1.19) and all its ambiguities.

The visit of the two women
1.39–56

Although Elizabeth appeared only in the epilogue to Zechariah's story, she now comes to the fore as the mother of John. Although we have been told that Elizabeth and Mary are related, the visit Mary makes to her cousin's house has no domestic purpose; for Luke it ensures that although Elizabeth is older, and her son will be born first, even before the birth of the children both of them acknowledge the precedence of Mary, who has received *God's blessing among women*, and that of her son. Yet there is harmony between these two women, and not the jealousy the once barren Sarah felt for Hagar. Just as Mary knows by angelic revelation of Elizabeth's pregnancy, so Elizabeth recognizes Mary's by divine inspiration, which Luke characteristically expresses as being *filled with the Holy Spirit: the loud voice* is the sign of the inspired. Even before their birth Esau and Jacob's struggling in the womb anticipated their future relationship (Gen.25.22–23), but the unborn John *leapt for joy* in the presence of the one Elizabeth, like later Christians, confesses as *my Lord*.

Elizabeth acknowledges that Mary, we might say contrary to all social judgments, was the recipient of God's blessing, and that her faith in God's word is a sign of her sharing in God's salvation: the bland *'happy'* is the word translated *blessed* in 6.20; Mary responds not directly to Elizabeth but in a hymn of praise which has come to be known from the Latin of the first word as 'the Magnificat'. (Although, as the REB footnote indicates, some manuscripts of the early Latin version ascribe the hymn to Elizabeth, it seems certain that Mary is the speaker).

This is the first of three such **hymns in Luke's infancy narratives**, the others being Zechariah's hymn in 1.68–79 ('the Benedictus') and that of Simeon in 2.29–32 ('the Nunc Dimittis'). They are similar in that each could be removed from the text without effecting the sequence and the story, and in that each fits only loosely in its setting with few clear allusions to the 'historical event' to which they are a response. They are rich in the imagery and language of the Old Testament, although without clear quotations; in fact it has often been argued, without certain proof, that they are a translation of earlier Hebrew versions. Each is a response to what God has done, and not will do, in a decisive act of salvation; yet they also look back to God's promises in the past, especially to Abraham, which are now being fulfilled. As we shall see, some of the themes also reflect the convictions of early Christian preaching. It has been suggested that they may have been hymns from the early Christian communities of Jews who saw their Christian faith in complete continuity with the faith of their forbears who had put their trust in those promises and whose piety we find in the psalms and in other similar literature. If so, Luke has used them to express his conviction that Jesus' birth did indeed fulfil those promises, and, despite later conflicts with Jewish leaders, was recognized by those in Israel who were faithful to God. As his Gospel progresses, and later in Acts, he will have to struggle with the question why all Israel did not recognize Jesus.

Like many of the psalms, Mary's song of praise moves from the celebration of what God has done for her as an individual to what God has done for all *those who fear him*. God, who as *Saviour* may allude to the meaning of the name of Jesus, is praised as the one who rescues the oppressed; the imagery of his *might* (*of his arm*) and covenant faithfulness, and particularly his help of the oppressed recall the Exodus accounts (Ex. 6.6–8), and the psalms (Ps. 89.2,10; 102.12, 17; 118.15–18 etc.). In many of the psalms those whom God helps are the humble or poor, in Hebrew the *'anawim'*; they are those who put their trust in God, while the arrogant who oppress others and spurn God will be put to shame (e.g. Ps. 34.6–10, 18–22; 37.10–11; 69.32–36; 74.18–21 etc.). It seems that the idea of God as deliverer of the oppressed people from Egypt led to the conviction that God particularly favoured the poor and oppressed within the people, even when their oppressors were their fellow countrymen and women.

The belief we find elsewhere in the Bible that prosperity is a sign of God's favour has to be balanced by this conviction of God's siding with the poor. Yet the poor are not only the materially poor, they are those who trust God and do not rely on their own resources. This is the spirit which breathes through Mary's song. So when she describes herself as *lowly* in v.48 she does not mean spiritual humility, nor her insignificance as a woman, nor the shame of her unmarried pregnancy, although all these are part of the picture; she is counting herself among the *lowly* of v.52 and of the psalms. It is not surprising that the Magnificat has come to mean so much where Christians have rediscovered the truth that God is on the side of the poor, and has become a central text in liberation theology. Its convictions cannot be spiritualized, neither can the vision of justice when the *hungry are filled with good things* be postponed to some distant future hope; for this hymn God has already acted so, even if experience awaits the fulfilment. Contemporary readers must decide what it means to live as those who believe in such a God, and although Luke does not make the connection explicit, the use of wealth becomes an important theme in his Gospel.

However, the last two verses are a reminder that this understanding of God is based on Israel's experience and not on general convictions. At this moment, for Luke, what God is doing testifies to an enduring faithfulness to what God has done before for Israel as the chosen *servant* (cf. Isa. 41.8), and to the promises to Abraham (cf. Gen. 17.1–8), and perhaps to David (cf. II Sam. 22.51).

The birth of John and Zechariah's hymn
1.57–80

In the account of John's birth and naming all the emphasis rests on how the promises of Gabriel are being fulfilled – as the reader more than the participants realizes. There is an echo of how Abraham *named* Isaac and *circumcised him on the eighth day* (Gen. 21.3–4): the latter was the norm for every Jewish male (Gen. 17.12) and signalled the child's belonging to God's covenant people. We do not know when naming normally took place but here it is being given a significant and public setting: the theme of how others hear of what God has done (cf. v.65) is one Luke continues to trace. Probably we should assume that Elizabeth insisted that *he is to be called John,* contrary to the practice of naming after the father, or frequently grandfather, by divine revelation and not because Zechariah had forewarned her; thus his confirmation of this is indeed seen as a cause for *wonder* (rather than REB's *astonishment*), and naturally leads to *awe,* which is a response to God's action, when Zechariah recovers his speech. That unusual events surrounding a birth pointed to the future significance of the child was a common theme in belief and literature of the time. Although the words which follow, that *the hand* (or 'the power') *of the Lord was upon* (or with) *him* (cf. Acts 11.21), could continue the musings of *all who heard,* they are probably a comment by Luke to prepare for v. 80 and the events of chapter 3.

At this point Luke includes the second of his hymns (cf. above). It has been prompted by Zechariah's *praising God* in v.64, but Luke characteristically again sees *the holy spirit* at work; prophecy, for Luke, also belongs to the time of God fulfilling the promises, particularly in the life of the church (cf. Acts 2.17–18), and Zechariah the priest now anticipates that experience. Right from the opening *'Praise to the Lord'* (cf. Ps. 41.14; 72.18–19) it recalls the language of the Old Testament, but this time there is an explicit appeal to *the holy prophets* who had also spoken of that deliverance: this too was a common theme in early Christian preaching and an important one for Luke (cf. 24.25–27).

Like the Magnificat, this act of praise celebrates God's deliverance of God's people, Israel, in faithfulness to the covenant and in fulfilment of the promises in the past: again deliverance is from oppression, but it also has a goal, *that we might worship him,* something that was also the purpose of the Exodus deliverance (cf. Josh. 24.11–15).

However, although the Benedictus also looks back to the oath sworn *to our father Abraham* (cf.Micah 7.20), the primary emphasis is on the hope of a *deliverer from the house of . . . David* which was rooted in the promises of II Sam. 7 (cf. vv.16,26). In this way Zechariah recalls for the reader the promise of Gabriel to Mary concerning her child who would be given 'the throne of David his father' (v.32), and gives first place to Jesus, whom the reader knows has already been conceived. What then is the role of the baby John? Since only verses 76–77 address him, it is possible that the original early Christian hymn, if such it was, did not include these verses: Luke may have added them to fit the scene and to continue his theme of the relationship between Jesus and John. That John would be *forerunner of the Lord* had already been prophesied in 1.17 and, as there, there is a reference to Mal. 3.1 which also says this figure would *prepare his ways*; the theme of repentance had been hinted at in 1.17, and now it becomes clear, *for forgiveness of their sins*. Each of these themes will be repeated in 3.3–4 as John starts his ministry and were already part of Christian tradition (Mark 1.2–4); Luke shows how all this was part of God's plan from the beginning.

Yet the climax of the hymn returns to the greater deliverer to come; the imagery of *salvation*, of light in *darkness*, is again that of the psalms (107.10,14) and of the prophets (Isa. 9.2; 60.1–3), while the final note of *peace* anticipates the song of the angels at the birth of Jesus in 2.14. Having done that, the account returns to where it left off in v.66; just like Samson and Samuel, also children of divine promise, (Judg. 13.24–25; I Sam. 2.21), John grows up in preparation for his future task; it is *in the wilderness* (cf. 3.2 and commentary) that we shall next meet him.

The birth of Jesus
2.1–20

While Jesus' birth is related as briefly (2.7) as that of John (1.57), the events surrounding it are far more impressive. The story starts with *the whole world* – the REB adds *Roman* to indicate that only the Roman Empire could be involved, but Luke is more interested in the universal setting which will eventually become the setting of the Christian Gospel, an interest repeated at 3.1–2. There could, perhaps, hardly be a sharper contrast than that between the universal power of *the Emperor Augustus* – the title 'Augustus' had now become a name – and the baby placed in the only space available or appropriate, a manger or stall (see below). Yet before the story is over angels will proclaim his birth as saviour, just as the birthday of the Emperor was celebrated as a source of salvation, and they will praise God encompassing both highest heaven and earth.

The appeal of the story to the imagination has ensured its retelling ever since in word, drama and art. How much this is due to Luke's literary skill, how much to the traditions which came to him is difficult to tell. That Jesus was born in Bethlehem when Joseph and Mary were living together but had not yet had sexual relations is common to both Matthew and Luke; but the census and the journey from Nazareth it necessitates, the circumstances surrounding Jesus' birth, and the coming of the shepherds are found only in Luke. Moreover, there are a number of historical problems, particularly concerning the census, which have been widely discussed. It may be important to separate these, and the question how far Luke's account can contain genuine historical reminiscences, from the more important question of why he tells the story as he does.

The **census** which is the occasion for Jesus' birth in Luke has been much debated. The most natural reading of Luke's description of it as *the first registration of its kind* and as *when Quirinius was governor of Syria* is to refer it to the census which Quirinius supervised in 6 CE when Judaea came under direct Roman rule after Herod the Great's son, Archelaus (4 BCE–6 CE), had been deposed. The Jewish historian, Josephus, gives an account of this census because it prompted a revolt under a certain Judas who saw compliance as submission to slavery; Josephus implies that the attitude of Judas and his followers, who formed a new party or 'fourth philosophy', played some part in the final revolt and defeat of the Jews in 66–70 CE (Josephus, *Antiquities* 18.1–10; cf. Acts 5.37). This was not a world-wide census as Luke implies – there was not such a thing – but it could be seen as part of Augustus' more extensive policy of assessing the resources within all the provinces. It has also been objected that Roman censuses did not require return to the ancestral home, and that as an inhabitant of Nazareth which did not come under direct Roman jurisdiction at this time Joseph need not have been involved. A solution to this has been offered by suggesting that Joseph may have wanted to safeguard his claim to family property at Bethlehem, although this is, of course, supplying information that Luke does not mention, and Joseph later returns to Nazareth.

Whether Mary, as a woman, needed to make the journey has also been disputed, although Luke needs her to be there! More serious is the difficulty of having Jesus born in 6 CE following the events of ch.1 which are set in the reign of Herod the Great who died in 4 BCE: that his son Archelaus was intended there is unlikely, and Matthew agrees with the dating to Herod the Great (Matt. 2.1). An attempt to overcome this problem has been made by translating 'this registration was . . . before (instead of *first*) Quirinius was governor of Syria': thus the reference is to an otherwise unrecorded census, presumably while Herod was still alive, which Luke is dating by reference to the later, notorious one. This is ingenious, but we may wonder whether the desire to preserve historicity is at the cost of discovering Luke's real intentions.

The stage narrows from the universal setting to the city of David, not here, as often, Jerusalem but Bethlehem; the story is told without reference to the events of ch.1 – we are only told that Mary was pregnant and yet only *betrothed* to, and therefore not in a full sexual relationship with, Joseph. Yet in the light of ch.1 the reminder that Joseph was of Davidic descent and that he has come to the city of David is heavy with meaning, although, unlike Matt. 2.6, Luke does not quote Micah 5.1. The circumstances of Jesus' birth are told without elaboration, unlike subsequent retellings. In fact *the inn* may not have been a public inn but merely a guest room or even lodgings – the same word is simply translated *room* at 22.11; *because there was no room* might mean that it was too crowded or that there was no 'fitting place' for a mother and new-born child, as indeed there may not have been in a single room shared by a number of people, perhaps both guests and family. The *manger* could equally well be a 'stall'. This is the only element in the story to which Luke draws particular attention (cf. vv.12, 16): although countless interpreters have used it to underline the poverty of Jesus' birth, for Luke its unusualness allows it to become part of his theme of prophecy, sign, and fulfilment. Some have tried to see a parallel between Jesus being bound in *swaddling clothes* at his birth, and his binding again at death (23.53), but for Luke the former is the natural care of a mother for her child.

The scene then switches to the fields outside Bethlehem and to the shepherds. Like Zechariah and Mary before them (p.3), they too are visited by an angel, react with terror, are told not to fear, and are given the message of the birth of a child with a special task, and they too are given a sign which will confirm that message. The angel's message may recall Isa. 9.6, 'For a child has been born to us . . . wide will be the dominion and boundless the peace bestowed on David's throne and on his kingdom'; yet for Luke's readers it may also have evoked the celebrations of Augustus' birthday which welcomed him as a saviour and saw him as bringing in a longed-for age of peace: a celebratory inscription of the time describes Augustus as 'A Saviour for us and our descendants, he will make wars to cease . . .' If Luke sets Jesus' birth on the stage of universal politics, in the Gospel and more so in Acts he will also seek to explore the relationship between the Christian Gospel and the holders of political power.

The song of the angels is echoed by the praises of the disciples when Jesus enters Jerusalem in Luke 19.38 (p.154); neither that event, nor the birth of a baby, might seem obvious occasions of *glory* and *peace*. *Glory* is the honour due to God, the acknowledgment of who and what God is such as Isaiah experienced (Isa 6.3); *peace* in the biblical tradition is not just absence of conflict but implies wholeness in relations between people and God, among one another, and between all the created order. Here the promise is *to all in whom he delights*; this is probably the right way to take it rather than the familiar 'on earth peace, goodwill toward men' of the Authorized Version: this is not yet a promise of universal serenity. At his baptism in 3.22 Jesus also will be declared the one in whom God delights, and throughout these chapters it is those who are open to God who experience God's favour or delight and God's salvation. Why shepherds should be among such is only partly clear; later Jewish texts describe shepherds as outcasts but there is nothing to suggest that this attitude was already around in Jesus' time, and elsewhere the Gospels describe Jesus as a shepherd without implying this meant anything disreputable. Perhaps the shepherds recall David, himself a shepherd, and naturally belong to a story set in Bethlehem; at the same time they continue the theme of Luke's story that all those involved in Jesus' birth are ordinary men and women, far removed from circles of religious or political power.

The sign promised to the shepherds is confirmed, so confirming also the angel's declaration that this baby is *the Messiah, the Lord*. What Mary had been told in private, and Elizabeth learnt by divine revelation, is now made known to *all who heard*. As in 1.66 Luke introduces this audience to show how the message of the Gospel spreads, causing wonder and astonishment (cf. 4.32, 36), while those whose experience it was praise God (cf. 1.64). This time, however, there is a contrast with Mary who remembers and dwells on it all: as for Jacob (Gen. 37.11) and Daniel (Dan. 7.28), there is a further meaning which will only become clear later and which those who respond immediately do not see.

The naming and presentation of Jesus
2.21–40

Whereas it was John's circumcision and naming in the home which provided the opportunity for his role to be revealed, in Jesus' case these events are swiftly summarized, except for a reminder that once more the angel's promise is being fulfilled in *the name given* him. Instead the story returns to where it began, to the Temple in Jerusalem and to fulfilment of *the law of the Lord*. The offerings of v.24 are those required of a poor woman following the forty days of her *purification* after the birth of a male child (Lev. 12.1–8), and it is these which would necessitate a visit to the Temple. Entirely separate was the 'redemption' of the firstborn son: according to Ex. 13.2, 11–15 the firstborn male offspring of living creatures was considered to belong to God and so to be sacrificed unless 'redeemed', as were human sons. That this also involved a visit to the Temple does not normally seem to be assumed, and Luke may be thinking of how Samuel's parents took him *to present him to the Lord* in I Sam. 2.24. We have already heard other echoes of the story of Hannah and the child given to her, Samuel; now, just as his parents were met by Eli, so too Jesus and his parents are met by the aged Simeon.

Simeon is described in similar terms to Zechariah and Elizabeth (1.6). Like them, and like Anna in 2.36–37, he belongs to the humble devout who put their trust in God. Both he and she are awaiting with urgent expectation God's coming *restoration of Israel*, and assume that it will start from Jerusalem. *Restoration* is the same as 'comfort' in Isa. 40.1; 52.9; 66.12.13; 'comfort' should not be spiritualized, but neither should 'restoration', nor the *liberation of Jerusalem* in 2.38, be seen as purely political. There was a wide spectrum of belief about God's hoped-for salvation of the people, and the *Lord's Messiah* could be seen as bringing the freedom from political domination as well as the establishment of God's reign of faithfulness, justice and peace. As we have seen through these chapters, Jesus birth is in the context of and fulfils such hopes; but the Gospel as a whole will have to answer how that fulfilment is worked out.

Although the setting is one of Temple and Law, both Simeon and Anna are prophetic figures; again Luke sees the activity of *the Holy Spirit* as a hallmark of Jesus' birth. Now Simeon, independently of the angel's predictions of Jesus' future role to Mary and to the shepherds, recognizes in Jesus the fulfilment of his hopes, while his parents, despite those earlier events, respond in wonder (cf. 2.18; 1.65 and commentary).

Simeon's praise, the Nunc Dimittis, is the third, and the briefest, of the infancy hymns, and the one which fits its context best: the opening words can only refer to Simeon's release in death. The allusions to the scriptures are even clearer, particularly to Isaiah (cf. Isa. 52.9–10; 49.6). These allusions introduce new aspects of how Jesus fulfils Israel's hopes; the *deliverance* or 'salvation' is not only for *your people Israel*, but is also *a light that will bring revelation to the Gentiles*. Although the phrase, and the Isaiah passages, could instead refer to the exposure of the Gentiles to judgment, this positive meaning suits Luke's wider interests. His two-volume work, and particularly the second volume, Acts, will trace the progress of that revelation; yet, written out of an experience when many in Israel did not believe in Jesus as that deliverance, it also wrestles with the question how Jesus is also 'glory to your people Israel'. Despite the negative note on which Acts ends (28.24–28), here the *glory* for Israel still forms the final climax.

Simeon's words to *Mary his mother* anticipate the problem and ignore any place for the Gentiles; Jesus *is destined for the falling and rising of many in Israel*: the REB reverses the image and reorders the elements in this prophecy. The idea is probably not, however, that the falling will be followed by rising, but that there will be division: some among Israel will fall, others rise. The emphasis seems to be on 'falling' for he will be *a sign that is rejected*, in contrast to the signs we have met so far in this story. The language and imagery again recalls Isaiah, this time the sign of Isa. 7.11–14 and the stone which causes many to stumble in Isa. 8.14–15, a passage that Luke returns to in 20.17–18 where again the theme is one of rejection (see commentary and Ps. 118.22). The sword will even cut through Mary herself: the meaning of this prophecy is disputed but in the context there is no reference to her grief at Jesus' death, and in Luke's Gospel she is not present at the cross; rather, even Mary will experience the cutting division that Jesus will cause – no one is spared in a process which will expose even *secret thoughts* to judgment, a process Luke illustrates in 5.21–22. Perhaps for the first time in these chapters, the picture of the faithful of Israel open to God's salvation has been over-shadowed by the theme of conflict which will shape so much of Luke's story.

It is characteristic of Luke to match a male with a female figure, and he does so here. Anna joins the brief list of prophetesses in Israel's history (cf. Judg. 4.4, Deborah), but perhaps anticipates the women of the early church who, like the daughters of Philip, had that gift (Acts 21.9). Her virtuous and long widowhood, which could be *eighty-four years* long rather than *'to the age of eighty-four'*, also reflects an ideal matched best in Israel's history by Judith (Judith 8.4–8; 16.21–24). Yet it equally echoes the requirements of Christian widows in I Tim. 5.5; just as the hymns may reflect early Christian praise, and a life in the Temple and in prayer reflects Luke's picture of early Christian life (Acts 2.42, 46), so Luke may be describing his ideal figures in ways that would make them a model for subsequent Christian believers as well as reaffirming the continuity between the church and the faithful of Israel. Thus she too adds her testimony to Jesus as the fulfilment of Israel's hopes.

The prophetic gifts of Simeon and Anna do not for Luke contradict Jesus' and his parents' obedience to *everything prescribed in the law of the Lord*. These initial events have now fully prepared us for Jesus' future ministry. It is enough that, like John the Baptist (1.80) and like Samuel (I Sam. 2.21), Jesus continues as a child to bear all the marks of his special destiny.

Jesus in the Temple
2.41–52

Although with the last scene in the Temple and the return to Nazareth the infancy narratives seem complete, Luke does add a further story. Later tradition was to fill the general silence about Jesus' childhood with stories demonstrating his divine powers even then. It was a common theme in the ancient world that the future exploits of a hero had been anticipated in his youth, and Luke's story fulfils this role. With no other parallels in the New Testament we cannot tell from where he has drawn this account. It continues the picture of Jesus and his family as faithful to the Temple and to the Jewish requirement that every male, if able, travel to Jerusalem *for the Passover festival*. Although by the age of twelve Jesus was near-ing the age of adult responsibility under the law at least by later reckoning, there was in his time no formal recognition of this – no 'bar-mitzvah'. Like the *three days* that it takes for his parents to find him, twelve is a common number in stories and should not be used to fill out precise details. For Luke the story illustrates the wisdom of v.40; yet we should note that Jesus is listening, questioning and answering in response to *the teachers* who gathered in the Temple: he is not, as he will later do in the Temple, teaching (them) (19.47; 20.1).

His mother takes the lead as she does throughout these narratives. However, her question, the neutral references to *his parents*, and their subsequent inability to *understand what he meant* apparently betray no knowledge of the story of the annunciation of his virginal conception or of all the intimations of divine calling already given. Was this story originally told without knowledge of those earlier accounts? Yet there is also an unmistakeable contrast between his mother's *'your father'* and his answering *'my Father'*. Luke sees the story as confirming and developing what it meant for Jesus 'to be called Son of God' (1.35).

In fact it is Jesus himself who confirms this even before his baptism, which, as we have seen, in some Christian traditions marked the (public) beginning of his sonship. The *'I was bound to'* also anticipates the necessity that will mark Jesus' ministry, his suffering and his death in fulfilment of scripture and of God's will (4.43; 9.22; 13.33; 17.25; 22.37; 24.7, 26,44). *'In my Father's house'* could be translated 'about my Father's business' or even 'among the household of my Father'; Luke may be intentionally imprecise, but a reference to the Temple would suit the important place it has held in the infancy narratives, and continues to hold for Luke as the place where Jesus teaches (19.47) and where the earliest Christians meet both at the end of the Gospel (24.53) and at the beginning of the story of the church (Acts 2.46). The story ends by returning Jesus to his childhood dependence on his parents, albeit with the continuing marks of his future destiny (cf. 2.40), and with his mother again dwelling on events of a yet-to-be-revealed significance (cf. 2.19). For Luke, this, like all the stories of the 'coming of Christ', is not a sentimental tale to delight his readers; it prepares them for what is to come, and for those who know the events yet to be told it is full of premonition, but also of perplexity, for the faithfulness and the harmony with Law and Temple will not be sustained.

John the Baptist and Jesus
3.1–38

The ministry of John
3.1–20

Luke now makes a new start to his narrative with John the Baptist. There is no reference back to the first two chapters nor to everything we have learnt about the destinies of John and of Jesus from them. It is as if the readers, unlike the participants in the events, have been given a vital clue to understanding what follows, but at times we may wonder whether the story could be, and perhaps once was, told without those earlier narratives – as it is by Mark and by Acts 10.37.

Despite the heading in the REB, the first episode is about John alone, with only a hint of Jesus for the aware (see vv.4, 16–17). The careful relationship between the two which Luke has spelt out in the infancy narratives is here much more bluntly portrayed. Jesus is not introduced until John's story is almost completed with his incarceration in prison (v.20); only after that is Jesus' baptism described, with John's presence and participation all but ignored (see v.21 and commentary). It would be easy from a quick reading to assume that the two men never met (see also 7.18–23); later Jesus will say, 'The law and the prophets were until John: since then, the good news of the kingdom of God is proclaimed . . .' (16.16). The 'baptism proclaimed by John' certainly marked the beginning of the good news of Jesus (Acts 10.37), but John also belongs to 'the old order', and it is never quite clear on which side of the divide Luke wants to place him.

Luke's introduction in part places John alongside 'the prophets' of 16.16, as promised in 1.76. As to the prophets of old, particularly Jeremiah, *the word of God* came to John at a point carefully dated by the reigning powers of the time (Jer. 1.1–3; also Isa. 6.1; Ezek. 1.1–3). The experience of those predecessors will lead us to expect that these worldly powers do not provide just a convenient means of dating but also the opposition the prophet will meet, although this will come chiefly from *Herod* Antipas, son of Herod the Great and *tetrach of Galilee* from 4 BCE to 39 CE. We shall meet him again in an ambiguous relationship to Jesus in 9.7–9, 13.31, and finally together with *Pontius Pilate*, the Roman *governor* or prefect of *Judaea* from 26 to 36 CE, in the trial of Jesus (23.6–12). Herod the Great's kingdom had been divided between his sons after his death in 4 BCE; Archelaus ruled over Judaea only until 6 CE when he was replaced by direct Roman rule (see above), while the third son, *Philip*, who does not feature again in the story, retained his control of *Ituraea and Trachonitis* and other areas to the east of the Jordan until his death in 34 CE. *Annas*, high-priest from 6–15 CE, and *Caiaphas*, high-priest from 18–36 CE, are not named in Luke's account of Jesus' trial (cf. Matt. 26.3, 57, and see Luke 22.54, 66), although they reappear in Acts 4.6; in naming them together when in fact it was Caiaphas who was high-priest, Luke may reflect popular confusion or discontent with the Roman deposition of Annas and substitution of a series of his family (cf. John 18.13–14, 24 for a similar confusion).

By including also the otherwise unknown *Lysanias* of the eastern kingdom of *Abilene*, and by starting with the Roman Emperor *Tiberius*, whose *fifteenth year* was about 28–29 CE, Luke is probably doing more than showing a continuity with the earlier prophets; he is, as he had done in 2.1–2, setting a universal stage for the events to follow, foreshadowing their eventual goal in the city of Rome itself (Acts 28.14). This interest in providing a historical context for Jesus (see also Acts 5.36–37) may reflect Luke's desire to show non-Jewish, and perhaps non-Christian, educated readers that this was 'no hole-and-corner business' (Acts 26.26) but one which could take its place alongside other accounts of historical worth.

Yet the overall mood is that of the Jewish world. The quotation of Isa. 40.3–5 shows that John is not just another prophet but heralds the fulfilment of past prophecies. Although in that passage it was originally the way which was to be prepared in the wilderness, Luke sets the crying voice there, following Mark 1.3 and also the Greek version of the scriptures. John's association with the wilderness has led to speculation as to whether he was connected with other Jewish movements located in the wilderness of Judaea, most notably the community at Qumran close to the shores of the Dead Sea and probably responsible for the texts known as the Dead Sea Scrolls. There is little to support such speculation, and more important was the traditional association of the wilderness with God's revelation ever since the Exodus traditions; that God's new salvation should have its roots there is entirely appropriate.

Similarly, attempts have been made to find other parallels for John's *baptism*; that this was in *token of repentance* is one possibility, but it is also possible that the baptism (literally *'of repentance'*) followed repentance as a token of God's forgiveness and cleansing. Certainly other Jewish groups, including that at Qumran, gave an important role to purification, yet for them this was a repeated necessity in response to defilement as defined by their understanding of God's law. The need for repentance is of course a familiar theme in the Old Testament, as too is reliance on God's forgiveness; washing can be a symbol of God's cleansing (Ezek. 36.25; Ps. 51.2) as well as of the renunciation of evil by people (Isa. 1.16). Yet in Luke's account John's baptism is different from these in that it has a 'last chance' element to it, and is in preparation for a coming and a judgment of absolute finality. The early Christians were convinced that this coming and judgment were realized in Jesus, and so the second line of the Isaiah quotation becomes a *straight path for him* instead of 'for your God'. John himself, in line with many others of his day, may have seen his calling as a preparation for God's intervention, and yet the details of this, and of other aspects of his ministry, can only partly be recovered. What we have here and throughout the New Testament is a Christian understanding of the relationship between John the Baptist and Jesus, who started his ministry in the context of John's ministry.

Luke, as we have seen, follows Mark in appealing to Isaiah 40, but his quotation is fuller: the 'filling' of *every ravine* and the 'levelling', or better, the 'humbling' of *every mountain and hill* recall the reversal of the Magnificat (1.51–3) which we shall meet regularly through the Gospel (6.21–26; 13.30; 18.9–14 etc); the addition of the final line, *and all flesh shall see God's deliverance* or 'salvation' anticipates, as does 2.32, the universal scope of the salvation to come through Jesus. In these ways Luke weaves through his telling of the story hints of its deeper significance.

Unlike Matthew and Mark, Luke does not describe John's dress and life-style; he seems more interested in the message and its effect than in the man. As one who *announced the good news* (v.18) John anticipated later Christian preachers, and his fate could be seen to presage theirs; his preaching certainly shares Lukan interests, such as the tax-collectors and the use of wealth, but it is also presented as only anticipatory of the one to come.

The account of John's preaching to the *crowds of people* is almost identical to that given by Matt. 3.7–10, and probably comes from a common source. In Matthew, however, it is addressed to Pharisees and Sadducees who came for baptism: both authors are already introducing their own special concerns. Although the Jewish leaders will play a very important role in Luke's story, he is particularly sensitive to the ordinary people; generally Luke paints them in neutral or vaguely positive colours, but the apparently unprovoked attack against them here may be to warn the readers against any complacency either for themselves or as they read the story to its final end when the people join with their leaders in calling for Jesus' death (23.4, 13). The condemnation is harsh, with images of judgment echoing the message of the prophets (Amos 5.18–20; Isa. 6.13; 10.33–4). Later Jesus affirms, perhaps contrary to popular attitudes, that the woman bent double and Zacchaeus the tax-collector were children of Abraham (13.16; 19.9) and equally deserving of God's saving action; here, John, with a play on the similar sounding words (in Hebrew), *'children'* and *'stones'*, reminds them that belonging to God's chosen ones guarantees no security unless lives match promises of repentance. God is faithful to past promises but cannot be held to ransom by them, neither can men and women determine where and how God will yet display mercy.

Luke alone explains just what *the fruit you bear* might mean in starkly simple and yet radical terms. As so often in popular stories there are three groups but they are representatives rather than the sole objects of the injunctions. It is easy to feel that this teaching has become so terse and direct that it expresses an ideal more than a practical reality. Yet it is earthed in the directions to the *tax-collectors* and to the *soldiers*, Jewish men in the service of Herod; Luke has chosen these groups to reflect his interest in the despised of society, and in the practical application of the Gospel in matters of wealth, as well, perhaps, as in the possibilities of the exercise of state power in accordance with God's will. The self-limitation he imposes on them would run counter to the prevailing ethos of the time just as much as does living only with what is necessary and sharing with the powerless.

Although during the first century there were several figures who adopted a 'messianic' role of a deliverer, Luke probably introduces the people's speculations whether *John was the Messiah* in order to recall the answer already given in the opening chapters. Now in v.16 John himself confirms his own inferiority in words which were a common part of early Christian tradition (Matt. 3.11; Mark 1.7–8; John 1.26–27), although Luke omits any suggestion that Jesus comes 'after him'. The Messiah was not popularly expected to offer a spirit 'baptism' or anointing, and the promise of a baptism *with the Holy Spirit* reflects a later Christian understanding; the additional *and with fire* together with the metaphor of *winnowing* which follows, both found only in Matthew and Luke, may suggest that the original emphasis was on the judgment and refining soon to be inaugurated and not on the continuing experience of the spirit within the life of the church. As the quotation of Joel 3.1–5 in Acts 2.17–21 indicates, the outpouring of the spirit was itself associated with the final days. Although Luke recounts the continuing experience of the church, and is sometimes seen as softening the earliest urgent expectation of the Christians, he does not soften John's message, nor the context within which he sets Jesus; instead he makes it very clear that it is this message which counts as announcing *the good news*.

With that Luke briefly completes the story of John; unlike Mark (6.17–29) who is followed by Matthew (14.3–12) he gives no account of John's confrontation with Herod when the latter married *his brother's wife Herodias*, neither does he describe Herod's eventual murder of John. The other two Gospels tell that story later to explain Herod's fears about the true identity of Jesus; Luke prefers to keep John and Jesus separate. John's story is now over and the task given him done; Jesus' can begin.

The proclamation of the Son of God
3.21–38

The heading in the REB, 'the ancestry of the Messiah', obscures the fact that in this section Jesus is shown to be 'Son of God', first and foremost when he is baptized, then with the support of his genealogy. Compared with Mark's account, Luke down-plays Jesus' actual baptism which is simply described as having taken place in the course of the general baptism *of all the people*. John the Baptist is not even mentioned although we are left to assume from the previous account that it was he who performed it. Although Luke does not tackle what was a problem for some early Christians – why Jesus needed to be baptized (see Matt. 3.13–15) – he does avoid any suggestion that Jesus was dependent on John. Perhaps more important, he moves the main moment of attention from the baptism to when Jesus *was praying*. Prayer in general is an important theme for

25

Luke, but he draws special attention to Jesus' practice of prayer, particularly at key moments (5.16; 6.12; 9.18; 11.1; 22.32); as on the Mount of Transfiguration and at Gethsemane, Jesus' prayer is answered by a divine revelation (9.28–29; 22.43). Thus Jesus both acts as a model for his disciples but also by his prayer enables others to experience God's revelation.

First, *heaven opened* as it had for Ezekiel (Ezek. 1.1), a symbolic way of signalling a moment of divine revelation when the secrets of the heavenly world became evident to the human observer, here not just Jesus but presumably *all the people*. Luke emphasizes that what happens is no spiritual or metaphorical idea but something with objective reality. Presumably this is the point of the assertion that the *Holy Spirit descended on him in bodily form like a dove*; in the original story it may have been the spirit's descent which was likened to a dove, as perhaps Mark 1.10 suggests, just as in Gen. 1.1 the spirit 'hovered' like a bird over the waters. There is nothing in the context or in contemporary literature to support the common suggestion that the dove represents gentleness or peace, and in the scenes to follow the spirit is a driving force. This indeed is, for Luke, the focal moment of the baptism, and one which initiates all that is to follow: it will be *full of the Holy Spirit* that Jesus will go into the wilderness to be tempted (4.1–2), and again that he will return to Galilee to commence his ministry (4.14).

Even within the infancy narratives the Holy Spirit marked God's new activity (1.15, 35, 67; 2.25–27); yet Jesus' possession of the Spirit does not simply align him with those who anticipated his coming. For with the descent of the Spirit there comes a voice, addressed to Jesus (unlike Matt. 3.17) but with no doubts as to its objective reality. The words echo those of Ps. 2.7, addressed by God to the king, and understood by Christians, and perhaps already in Jewish hope, as to the Messiah, 'You are my son.' The additional 'beloved' may recall Gen. 22.2, for the relationship between Abraham and Isaac, the son he was ready to give up, became for the early Christians a model of God's offering of Jesus, the *beloved son*. Some manuscripts of Luke continue the quotation from Ps. 2.7, 'this day I have begotten you', but the REB may well be right in deciding that this was not what Luke wrote. Instead the affirmation 'in you I delight' evokes God's declaration concerning the servant (not son) in Isa. 42.1, 'in whom I delight', particularly as that verse continues 'I have put my spirit on him'. Although later Christian interpretation saw the so-called 'servant songs' of Isa. 42.1–7; 49.1–6; 50.4–9; 52.13–53.12 as a prophecy of

Jesus, the Gospels only cautiously point in this direction; even here the words only evoke and do not quote the Isaiah passage. Jesus, then, is God's son, not because of the baptism, for in Luke we have had the infancy narratives, but publicly so acknowledged as he begins to fulfil his task. The scriptural echoes emphasize that it is his task or role that matters, not some quasi-physical relationship of being between God and Jesus. Equipped with the spirit, Jesus is to fulfil a task that no one else could; he is more than servant – only 'son' can express the unity of will and intention, and the obedience which ensures God's *delight* (cf. 2.14).

Luke puts Jesus' genealogy here, unlike Matthew for whom it comes at the beginning of the Gospel, to reinforce what has just become clear through the narrative. Certainly some Jews kept careful records of their descent, particularly those of priestly family and, we might expect, those of royal descent. Yet it is more important that genealogies were used in narratives and histories in Jewish tradition in order to explain relationships between individuals or groups, and to make claims about authority and position. Luke's genealogy is different from that given by Matthew for precisely that reason, and to try to harmonize them is to misunderstand this; it is for the same reason that Luke sees no problem in tracing Jesus' genealogy through Joseph, although he was only his son *as people thought*.

Unlike Matthew and many Jewish genealogies, Luke starts with Jesus and works backwards; in this way he can reach as his climax *son of God*. This we have seen through the birth narratives, affirmed in the baptism and now reaffirmed; next it will form the foundation for the devil's temptation, 'If you are the son of God'. On the way, Jesus' line of descent also makes him a *son of David*, recalling the promise to Mary in 1.32–33; he is also a *son of Abraham*, fulfilling, as Zechariah said, the oath God swore 'to our father Abraham' (1.73; cf. 1.54–55). Yet, unlike Matthew, Luke reaches beyond Abraham to *Adam*, himself by virtue of his creation 'son of God', and representative of the whole human race who are encompassed by Luke's universal vision. Perhaps on the way we should also notice *Nathan, son of David*; in some Jewish tradition this Nathan was identified with Nathan the prophet during David's reign, and those who knew this tradition may have recognized Jesus as also the heir to the prophets. With such multiple authentication Jesus is now ready to *begin his work*.

The Temptation of Jesus
4.1–13

It is a theme common to the first three Gospels that Jesus' baptism was immediately followed by a period in the wilderness when he was 'tempted by the devil'. Luke and Matthew both fill out Mark's brief reference (Mark 1.12–13) with a detailed account falling into the characteristic three scenes; the closeness of their wording suggests a common source although the few differences point to their own interests in telling the story. Luke emphasizes, even more strongly than the other Gospels, that the temptation was not a sudden falling away of certainty, nor a sign of any inadequacy, but that Jesus was throughout both *full of the Holy Spirit* and *led by the spirit*. *Forty* is a common 'round' number in the biblical tradition, indicating a full period of time, and would recall the forty years spent by Israel in the wilderness when they too were tested by God, and tested God (see Ps.106); where they failed in trust and faithfulness Jesus remains true.

The wilderness of Judaea was the place for withdrawal from society by those like John the Baptist (1.80), and by other groups such as that associated with the Dead Sea Scrolls; some of these, including John (7.33), practised fasting or an ascetic way of life. Fasting was also seen as a preparation for divine revelation and as an accompaniment to prayer (Luke 2.37; Acts 13.2). For many readers the wilderness would have both negative and positive associations; negative because it was bleak and threatening to life, the home of wild beasts (Mark 1.13) and far from civilization; positive because it was in the wilderness that Israel's covenant with God was forged, and where a new beginning might be made (Isa. 40.3; Hos. 2.14). In all these ways it is appropriate that Jesus should thus 'begin his work' (3.23).

Although Luke assumes that Jesus was *tempted by the devil* throughout the forty days, he recounts only three final temptations, each of which take up the affirmation of Jesus' unique role, '*If you are the Son of God*'. Some have seen in the three temptations the attrac-

tion of the forbidden tree in the Garden in Gen. 3.6, 'good to eat . . .
pleasing to the eye . . . and desirable for knowledge'; others have
compared Israel's failings over the manna, the golden calf, and their
disbelief in God's promises in Ps. 106.14–15, 19–20, 24–25. The
parallels are attractive but not certain, and the tradition of the three
temptations was probably already fixed when it came to Luke. He
does nothing to interpret what was at stake, although interpreters
have debated whether, for example in the first, Jesus is being enticed
to use his power to meet his own needs, to meet the material needs
of the world, or to become a sort of wonder-worker for its own sake.
For Luke it is more important that Jesus meets the challenge to his
sonship by obedience to God and by appealing to scripture as an
expression of that obedience: Deut. 8.3, which he quotes in v.4, continues 'they live on every word that comes from the mouth of the
Lord'. This is the mark of true sonship and is perhaps an example for
Jesus' followers.

The second temptation, the third in Matthew's version, again
challenges Jesus' total allegiance to God; beyond this Luke does not
give any hint what form *doing homage* to the devil might take. That *all
this dominion . . . and the glory* has been given to the devil to give *to
anyone I choose* comes only in Luke and he does nothing to contradict
the assertion; however, contradiction may be implied by placing the
words on the devil's lips for elsewhere in his Gospel Luke does not
see worldly and state power as inherently evil or of the devil. Again
Jesus need only reply by quoting scripture, Deut. 6.13.

Luke's order means that the temptations reach their climax at the
Temple in Jerusalem, which has already played such a central role in
his story. This time scripture itself becomes the grounds for testing;
Ps.91.11–12 promises God's protection to any faithful Israelite and
not just to the son of God. Such ultimate confidence in God does not
deny the suffering that the faithful may experience along the way,
and which, as for Jesus, is the cost of true obedience. So Jesus quotes
scripture again, Deut. 6.16: true faith in God does not seek to
manipulate or force God's hand, for to do so is to fail in trust and in
recognition of God's lordship. Yet the words also form a fitting
climax: Jesus will not put *God to the test*, but the devil is rebuked for
in tempting Jesus he is putting *the Lord* his *God to the test*; gradually
words in the Old Testament spoken to or of God as 'Lord' were
applied by the early Christians to Jesus.

With this Luke alone says that the devil departed *biding his*, or
better *'for a' time*. That time will certainly have come to an end by

22.3 when 'Satan entered Judas', the 'hour when darkness reigns' (22.53). This does not mean that Jesus' ministry is entirely free of the presence of Satan as some interpreters have claimed: Jesus' ministry is his 'times of trial' (22.28); but for Luke the end of the temptations anticipates and prepares the readers for Jesus' death as the renewed activity of the devil.

The story of the **temptation of Jesus** reflects popular Jewish beliefs of the time. In the Old Testament the belief in God's total sovereignty means that there is no independent evil force; where Satan appears it is as a subordinate to God permitted by God to accuse humankind (Job 1–2; Zech. 3.1–10; I Chron. 21.1). In the two centuries preceding the birth of Jesus there had developed a sharper belief in evil as an active force in opposition to God, represented too by its own supreme power and/or by a number of lesser evil beings. Such beliefs may have been influenced by Persian thought which had a dualistic opposition between the forces of good and those of evil; they may also have been encouraged by the Jews' experience of living as an often oppressed minority under powerful nations which denied and sometimes persecuted their faith in the one God. Yet among the Jews such ideas never developed so far as to question the ultimate sovereignty and final victory of God who represents truth, justice and faithfulness. In a world of such beliefs it would be natural to see Jesus, the true representative of God, as in conflict with the devil, the representative of evil; that conflict reaches its peak in the death of Jesus, in which, as we have seen, Luke sees the devil as actively at work, but for the early Christians it was an inevitable characteristic of all Jesus' ministry. Yet in putting this conviction in story form, earlier stories of humankind's and of Israel's failure to remain faithful to God have added their influence, expressing the faith that Jesus reversed that pattern of failure; perhaps too, the Graeco-Roman tradition of the hero over-coming the obstacles and distractions to his quest and so being qualified to continue, has also played its part. For Luke, as we have seen, this is, then, no psychological attack of self-doubt, or panic after an emotional high, but the first steps of one 'full of the Holy Spirit'.

Jesus in Galilee
4.14–9.50

The sermon in Nazareth

4.14–30

In complete continuity, still *armed with the power of the spirit*, Jesus begins his ministry in Galilee where he was brought up. However, whereas Mark introduces us to a Jesus who preaches the gospel, declares the moment of fulfilment is come and demands repentance (Mark 1.14–15), Luke presents us with a Jesus who quickly wins fame and praise as he does nothing more than *teach in their synagogues*. In fact this brief summary is only a backdrop to introduce Jesus' sermon in Nazareth.

In Mark's account Jesus does not come to his home town until 6.1–6 when his ministry of miracles, parables, and the gathering of disciples is well established. Luke brings the event to the fore, and gives all attention to Jesus' words and the response they win. The scene becomes programmatic, setting the pattern for the whole course of events to follow in the Gospel and perhaps into Acts, and guiding the reader into an understanding of their significance: here we encounter the path of Jesus' ministry and the intention of God through it, compressed into a single occasion. It is a dramatic and evocative story and Luke has written it in such a way as to draw the reader into the experience.

Although we know little about synagogue practice in the first century, Luke's story fits later developments; the prophetic reading may not yet have been determined by a lectionary scheme but chosen by the reader, a task any adult male could fulfil. Acts too has similar accounts of a visitor, Paul, being invited to speak after the readings of the Law and prophets and taking the opportunity to preach the Gospel (Acts 13.14–41; 17.2–4), but this may be because Luke wants to show a continuity between the experience of Jesus and his followers, rather than because such invitations were common practice. As Luke describes each action – *he came . . . went . . . stood up . . . was handed . . . opened . . . and found* – he builds up our expectation until we hear the dramatic words of the reading from Isaiah, *The spirit of the Lord is upon me*; as the actions are reversed in v.20 we too wait for his own equally momentous words, *Today in your hearing this text has come true*.

The quotation comes from the Greek version of Isa. 61.1–2, and has been modified by Christian interests. Jesus in the synagogue would not have omitted a line, 'to bind up the broken hearted', or added another, *to let the broken victims go free*, which comes from Isa. 58.6; stopping short of saying he was also *to proclaim* 'a day of the vengeance of our God' (Isa. 61.2) also reflects Luke's desire to emphasize the promise of salvation. For the reader the anointing by God and possession of *the spirit of the Lord* identifies the speaker of the passage as Jesus whose baptism has not long ago been narrated; the prophecy now unfolds his task: the one in whom God delighted (3.21) is *to proclaim the year of the Lord's favour* or delight.

The passage in Isa. 61 which describes such a year as a year of release recalls the provisions of the jubilee year in Lev. 25: a sabbath of all sabbaths following every period of 7×7 years was to be a year of liberation for the soil, for debtors, for the disenfranchised, and for slaves, a year when all reverted to original freedom or ownership of the land. Whether or not such legislation was often put into practice it acknowledged that all possessions were held in trust from God and that all were equally dependent on God's liberating action; no system of oppression by some of others could become perpetuated as an enduring aspect of society or economy. This is no spiritual optimism which ignores social or political realities; it is a message of reversal: *release for prisoners and recovery of sight for the blind*. Luke too understood the passage to refer not just to spiritual *release* or forgiveness, but to physical release, as when the blind are healed and those held captive by disease or 'unclean spirits' set free; for him *the poor* are not just the spiritually dependent but those who lack the necessary physical resources (see 6.20–26). The ministry of Jesus, and of those who share it, must be *good news* for them.

Jesus' affirmation that '*Today . . . this text has come true*' must come as a shock. The original passage was not a prophecy waiting to be fulfilled; it was an expression of the vocation of the original prophet. Jesus claims it for himself and for the present. At times it will seem that even in the preaching of Jesus the promise it contains can only belong to the future: *the year of the Lord's favour* is yet to dawn and the promise that the hungry 'will be satisfied' (6.21) belongs to the coming kingdom. Yet it is central to Luke's Gospel, and to all the traditions of Jesus' preaching, that Jesus did not just point to something yet to happen; alongside the 'not yet' there was also a 'now', an 'already' or a *Today*, and in Jesus' ministry and preaching God's kingdom was already experienced. The conclusion must be that where poverty and oppresssion are not challenged God's kingdom is neither proclaimed nor experienced.

The sudden reversal from their response of *general approval* to the murderous attack which will close the account is surprising and not easy to follow. Unlike Mark 6.3, their knowledge of him as *Joseph's son* probably warms that approval. It is Jesus who challenges it by offering them the prospect of the prophet whose ministry is offered not *in his own country* – *town* in v.23 in the REB is the same as *country* in v.24 – but to outsiders. On one level this anticipates the miracles which Jesus will perform not in his own town but in Capernaum in the following section (4.31–41); yet the examples Jesus gives, Elijah's help for the *widow at Sarepta* in I Kings 17 and Elisha's healing of *Naaman the Syrian* in II Kings 5, point beyond this. Jesus too can be seen as a prophet, and in ch.7 he too will heal a foreigner, the centurion's servant, and give life to a widow's only child (7.1–10, 11–17); the former of these anticipates the offer and the acceptance of God's salvation to and by those who did not belong to Israel. The 'favour' of the prophet – the word translated *recognized* by the REB in v.24 is the same as *favour* in v.19 – and of his message will not be found in Israel. On this level the sterility of the Nazareth ministry and its fertility in Capernaum anticipates the path the Christian gospel will take through Acts from the Jews to the Gentiles until at the end of his account Luke has Paul say, 'Therefore take note that this salvation of God has been sent to the Gentiles; the Gentiles will listen' (Acts 28.28). The murderous rejection Jesus experiences not only aligns him with earlier prophets and fulfils v.24, but also anticipates the rejection Christian missionaries will also experience (Acts 7.59; 14.19).

For Luke that movement of the gospel is not a matter of chance but forseen already by Jesus at the very beginning of his ministry and even anticipated within the Old Testament. This is part of Luke's solution to one of the perplexities the early Christians faced, why the Jewish people to whom Jesus had been sent had largely failed to respond to him as God's promised one; he did not look for historical answers or for an understanding of Jewish attitudes or beliefs but only for reasons within the overall purpose of God as understood from a Christian perspective. Yet he does not make rejection by the people of Nazareth (= Israel) precede and provoke the move to the Gentiles as regularly happens in Acts (Acts 18.6; 19.9), neither does he, like Mark 6.5, conclude with Jesus' refusal to perform miracles there. We are left asking, perhaps uncomfortably, whether it is Jesus rather than their unbelief who has denied them the experience of salvation, and whether that is indeed the end of the story or whether there is hope for Nazareth/ Israel beyond the offer to the Gentiles. The uncertainty is partly a result of the way Luke has compressed the story to use it as an anticipation and 'programme' for the future and partly because even in his own time those questions could not easily be answered.

Miracles in Capernaum
4.31–44

Despite what has just been recounted, Jesus continues within a non-controversial Jewish setting, on the sabbath attending and teaching in the synagogue, now at Capernaum on the north side of the Sea of Galilee. So far Luke has given priority to Jesus as teacher whose *authority* wins his audience's amazement, although he has given few hints as to the nature of that teaching. Only now will he present that *authority and power* as also expressed in Jesus' healing powers; but even here the emphasis is not on Jesus as a wonder-worker but as one who speaks, whose word is effective and powerful (v.36).

Given that Jesus had rejected the devil's offer of an alternative *'authority'* (= *dominion* in the REB) in 4.6, it is appropriate that his first demonstration of his authority should be through a man who within the understanding of the day was *possessed by a demon, an unclean spirit*. Whatever explanations we might look for within our understanding of illness or mental states, their assumptions about such possession are essential for reading the story. The first three Gospels, but not John, see exorcism as a particular mark of Jesus' healing ministry; it is the best illustration not just of 'release for prisoners' but of Jesus' victorious conflict against the forces of the devil (see 11.20). Whereas ordinary people remain perplexed by Jesus' identity, those with unclean spirts recognize him as God's agent, *the Holy One of God*, determined *to destroy* all they – *us* in v.34 – represent. Similarly, in the summary in v.41 the demons proclaim him as *Son of God*. It is a consistent theme in Mark, and continued in Luke as in

Matthew, that Jesus silences such acclamations which Luke explains as recognition that *he was the Messiah* or Christ. Although the reader knows this to be true, such recognition will only unfold slowly and among those who believe; it cannot be anticipated – in fact Jesus does not seem to have been widely acclaimed as in any way messianic during his lifetime – and perhaps Luke would feel it was inappropriate when driven by fear and hostility. The intensity of the hostility is marked by the violence with which the demon leaves the man, although that it was *without doing him any injury* testifies to Jesus' gift of wholeness as well as of release.

Although *Simon's mother-in-law* has a more conventional *high fever* Jesus also *rebuked* it and *it left her*: all disease can be seen as manifestations of the forces of evil, and Jesus' healing ministry is not only 'to let broken victims go free', but is part of his defeat of those forces; both in turn are part of what it means for him to 'announce' the good news of the kingdom of God (v.43, using the same word as in 4.18). When modern debate about miracles starts from the necessity of faith it implies a different way of understanding what Jesus was doing from that in the Gospels.

This is the first we have heard of Peter – Luke has not followed Mark in first describing his call (Mark 1.16–18, 29–31) – so her healing is not even because of his discipleship. However, she responded *and attended to their needs*: the word is *'ministered'* and is related to the word 'servant' which came to have a more technical meaning, eventually 'deacon'; it is used again of the women in 8.3 and in 10.40 and of Jesus in 22.26–27 (see commentary on each of these). She offered them the appropriate hospitality, but she also anticipates those women who offer Jesus a wider ministry and share in a pattern of service set by Jesus himself.

The healings which follow, perhaps *at sunset* because by then sabbath was over, although as yet this has provoked no controversy (see 6.6–14), show that those two were but examples of Jesus' more general activity. This chapter has given us an overview of Jesus' ministry, his *announcing the good news*, which surprisingly even extends to *the synagogues of Judaea*, although for the rest of the Gospel Luke, like Mark, does not bring Jesus to Judaea until the closing stages of his ministry (see 9.51). Yet just as the chapter began with the leading by the spirit, so again there is a strong sense of Jesus being driven on to something more. Again he withdraws to a *'remote spot'* or *wilderness*, the same word as in 4.1 (cf. 5.16); he cannot be subject to the entreaties of the people, for what directs his path is *what I was sent to do*, which, as in 4.18, was 'to announce good news to the poor'.

The call of Simon
5.1–11

The incidents which follow give little sense of time or sequence, being introduced loosely by phrases such as *one day*; in fact Luke has drawn most of them from his reading of Mark, but, as we shall see, the way he has put them together reflects his interest in them. The first event, however, comes in Luke alone. In Mark Jesus called his first disciples as soon as he began his preaching of the kingdom and only then went on to heal the man in the synagogue and Simon's mother-in-law. In Luke Jesus has already established the pattern of his ministry, giving 'the good news of the kingdom' through word and act; only now does he begin to call men who follow him, and it is only after more healings and teaching which anticipate further that pattern and the division it will inspire that he choses twelve (6.12–16). Discipleship is a response not just to a 'charismatic Jesus' but to *this* Jesus with this ministry. So even here the account starts with Jesus teaching the crowds who have come *to listen to the word of God* by the *lake Gennesaret*, Luke's term for 'the sea of Galilee'.

In further contrast to Mark's account, *James and John, Zebedee's sons*, are added almost as an afterthought (v.10a) and Andrew has disappeared entirely, so that Simon is the real focus of interest. Partly this reflects the role that Simon was to play in the life of the church, which is perhaps why Luke already calls him *Simon Peter* in v.8 (omitted by REB), forgetting that that name has yet to be given (6.14). There is a similar story of a miraculous catch of fish in which Simon Peter plays a central role in John 21, there after the resurrection and explicitly looking forward to his task within the church. The relationship between the two accounts in the memory or story-telling of the early church is not clear, but they do seem to have something in common.

However, in Luke's account Simon has already been mentioned in passing when his mother-in-law was healed (4.38–39). His response to Jesus now is a response to miracle, both to that one and to the *huge* and, in day-time after a fruitless night, unexpected *catch of fish*. It is part of Luke's understanding of miracles that they do provoke amazement and praise (see 4.36; 5.26), not as if they were some superior magical show but because they point to the activity of God (see on 1.66). Such a dramatic and abundant miracle over nature is clearly not in response to human need – there is no suggestion that Simon and his partners faced bankruptcy or starvation after a single fruitless night. Luke would have had little time for modern rationalizing attempts to cope with the problem by suggesting Jesus could see or knew where shoals of fish were swimming in the dark deeper waters. He, and much of the biblical tradition, does not share the proper modern theological concern as to whether God does intervene to subvert the normal workings of nature. In their understanding of the world those endowed with divine power could act in this way. Here Jesus seems to perform this miracle mainly in order to display such divine power, and in recognition of this Simon *fell at Jesus' knees* and acknowledged himself to be a *sinner*. This is characteristic of an account of an epiphany or manifestation of God; Simon's sense of his own sinfulness is like that of Isaiah (Isa. 6.5) or like the fear of the shepherds (2.9); his *'lord'*, while it could be translated as 'sir' (as in the REB in v.12), acknowledges, at least for Christian readers, Jesus' true status; as in other epiphanies his fear is answered by Jesus' *'Do not be afraid'* and by his commission *'from now on you will be catching people'*. That image comes not, as the English might suggest, from fishing but from hunting, 'taking captive alive'; this should probably make us hesitate to see the huge catch which nearly overwhelms both nets and boats as an anticipation or parable of the future missionary activity of these disciples, as it may be in John 21. Jesus does not call them to follow him – the commission preempts this – but this is what they, including James and John, do, leaving *everything*.

When Simon declares himself a *sinner* he also introduces a theme which will become increasingly important as the story proceeds. Jesus will be criticized for associating with 'sinners' and will claim his mission is to call 'sinners to repentance' (5.29–32). We shall see then that it is very difficult to decide quite who was intended by this label 'sinners', particularly in the ministry of Jesus; at times they may seem to be the rejected or 'outcasts' of society, but Simon would not be included among such. In his case, as we have just seen, the term denotes his sense of his own unworthiness in the presence of Jesus; but it also initiates what becomes almost a stereotyped pattern for Luke by which those who respond to Jesus are 'the sinners' who recognize their need, while the authorities, often 'the Pharisees', who will be introduced in 5.17, fail to do so (see pp. 41 f., 44 f.); between the two are the anonymous crowds who come and listen or are healed. This simple contrastive scheme creates a clear story-line, but the reality would have been more complex and variegated.

Healing and conflict
5.12–26

Before developing this theme Luke describes a further miracle, found also in Mark (1.40–45), which now introduces the themes of Jesus' relationship with what was *laid down by Moses* and with those who administered it. It is often rightly emphasized that *leprosy*, which was not restricted to what we so name but included a number of skin diseases, would have made the sufferer a social outcast, driven to live away from normal human habitation. In fact Luke draws no attention to this and it was *in a certain town* that Jesus was met by a leper who made deep obeisance before him, called him *'lord'* (REB, *'Sir'*, see on v.8) and, for the first time in a miracle account, expressed the faith that Jesus was able to *make* him *clean*.

Within the biblical tradition, and there are parallels in other cultures, such skin diseases were not seen merely as a medical condition but as a source of impurity or pollution. Although patterns of purity and impurity often seem alien in the modern Western world, they are fundamental to the biblical tradition, where they are seen as ordained by God who requires that 'you are to keep yourselves holy, because I am holy' (Lev. 11.45); what is impure or unclean is to be kept separate from what is holy, and because some impurities can be communicated contact with them must be restricted or excluded. For reasons now lost to us, skin lesions and fungal growths on clothing or in houses were together seen as a serious source of impurity requiring detailed provision for their diagnosis and treatment (Lev. 13–14); as a matter of impurity, it was the task of the priest to diagnose its presence and its disappearance, and the declaration of a return to a condition of purity was to be accompanied by an appropriate sacrifice. Both the man's request and Jesus' reply, *'I will; be clean'*, take this understanding for granted, as too does Jesus' instruction that the man fulfil the requirements *laid down by Moses*.

However, if Jesus remains obedient to the law of Moses, there may be a hint of tension with or challenge to it. That Jesus *touched him* may be less of such a challenge than is sometimes assumed; in fact Lev. 13–14 says little about how such skin diseases may convey impurity by contact, and there were ways of dealing with communicated impurity: avoidance may have been as much socially or instinctually inspired, and, unlike Mark (1.41), Luke does not speak of Jesus' compassion. Yet in saying, *'Be clean'*, Jesus could be seeing as pre-empting, although not replacing, the priest's declaration. More of a problem are the final words of his instruction, translated by the REB *'that will certify the cure'*. While this is a possible translation, the words, literally *'for a testimony to them'*, could mean that in fulfilling what was required the man would at the same time be publicly demonstrating what Jesus had already done, perhaps apart from the law or priestly system.

This may seem at odds with Jesus' command that the man should not *tell anybody*. Luke seems to have taken this over from Mark where Jesus' regular demands for secrecy play a significant part in his story. Although in Mark the man disobeys the order, Luke prefers not to have such disobedience in one who had been healed; instead Jesus' request only underlines his irrepressible fame as *talk about him spread even wider*. With this Luke is able to draw back from the specific miracle to see it as but a moment within Jesus' continuing ministry which includes both teaching – *crowds kept gathering to hear him* – and healing – *and to be cured*. Yet it was for Luke also an essential part of Jesus' ministry that he would regularly withdraw to desert places and pray (cf. 4.42), something that may have indicated his relationship with God as well as setting a pattern for his followers.

The next incident follows on naturally, much more so than in Mark (2.1–12) and Matthew (9.1–8). Jesus is again both *teaching* and exhibits *the power of the Lord . . . to heal*; here 'the Lord' is God while 'power' reminds us of the activity of the spirit (4.14) and of the authority Jesus has already shown (4.36), for authority will be the theme of what follows. This time, although *the crowd* will block the way to Jesus (v.19), it is *Pharisees and teachers of the law* of whom we are most aware. The footnote of the REB is more accurate than the printed text, it is they who *have come from every village of Galilee and of Judaea and from Jerusalem*. The REB is understandably uncomfortable with what seems rather an exaggeration both at this early stage in the ministry and because it is questionable whether there were so many Pharisees, living everywhere, as this suggests. However, just as Luke has painted a picture of Jesus' ministry as being far more comprehensive than his detailed incidents suggest, so now he wants to paint the gathering opposition as equally comprehensive.

We are left to assume that they are crowded into a house, for when some men wish to bring a man, bedridden with paralysis, to Jesus they are forced to climb up the outside stairs on to the flat roof of the single storey building and presumably break through it: Luke envisages a hellenistic house with *tiling* rather than the Palestinian mud roof of Mark's account, but does not consider the labour and mess involved! For the first time in his Gospel Luke speaks of *faith*, that of the men, and, it is often assumed, of the one they bring, although he remains passive through all that happens until v.25. Yet, unexpectedly to the reader as well as to those present, Jesus does not heal him but declares *'Your sins are forgiven you.'* Certainly, in the ancient world sickness was sometimes seen as punishment for sin (cf. John 9.1), but we should not conclude that Jesus was simply adopting their own perceptions, nor even that he recognized that it was real or imagined guilt which had paralysed the man, something to which there are even modern parallels. Luke, like the other evangelists, is not concerned with such 'behind-the-scenes' explanations; in fact the man does not exhibit any cure until Jesus later tells him to *stand up, take your bed, and go home,* and then his response will be the one Luke sees as appropriate to a miracle, he goes, *praising God* (vv.24–25).

Instead, however we understand the events behind the story, as told by Luke it drives towards the remarkable challenge implicit in Jesus' words and his response to their shock. Technically Jesus' statement need not qualify as 'blasphemy', even when not narrowly defined; Jesus does not say that he is forgiving the man's sins; the passive *'are forgiven you'* means that God, who *alone can forgive sins*, has forgiven them, and that Jesus can declare what God has done. This might challenge the authority of those normally authorized to declare such forgiveness, the priests, and pre-empt the normal processes of sacrifice as well as of penitence, thus going a step beyond what we have seen in the healing of the leper – although as a prophet Nathan was able to declare God's response to David's penitence at the murder of Uriah and seizure of Bathsheba (II Sam. 12.13–14). Yet for Luke those present are right in seeing that the most important question must be *'Who is this?'* (not in Matthew or Mark). As yet the answer is veiled; Jesus' counter question simply silences them. They cannot reply that it *is easier to say, 'Your sins are forgiven you'*, for Jesus has said this, and will proceed to the 'more difficult' which will demonstrate the validity of his words; neither can they say that it is easier to *say, 'Stand up and walk'*, for then Jesus would have already said the more difficult. In its unanswerability Jesus' question suggests that not even his miracles can be thoughtlessly dismissed.

Yet when he goes on to speak the creative word of healing it is not to demonstrate that 'God has forgiven' or that 'I can forgive', but that *the Son of Man has the authority* (= REB *the right*), *on earth to forgive sins*. This is the first time that Luke has used this enigmatic title, and he gives no hint as to how it could be taken by those present. For Luke it shows that Jesus' authority, which we have already met in his teaching and healing (4.32, 36), extends also on earth to the forgiveness of sins; but it is authority he holds as 'Son of Man', a title which for Luke's readers would recall the one 'like a Son of Man (human being)' given sovereignty and power in Dan. 7.13–14, but which through the gospel would also speak of suffering as well as vindication (see further below). Yet it is not an authority which usurps that of God; the story started by reminding us that Jesus healed only by *the power of the Lord* (v.17); it closes with not only the man, but *all* – although Luke surely does not include *the scribes and Pharisees* – *praising God*. More than this, they are *filled with awe*, or fear, as before a manifestation of divine power, and, although *'beyond belief'* is but a conventional response to a miracle, their emphatic *today* recalls Jesus' words of the fulfilment of God's promises in his sermon at Nazareth (4.21).

The **Pharisees** were a group of mainly lay men which had come into existence at least a hundred years before the birth of Jesus. Different accounts present them in different ways and a clear picture is difficult. It appears that they were committed to interpreting the Law of Moses in ways which would make it relevant to daily life, often applying to their social dealings provisions regarding purity which originally referred to the Temple. In this they appealed to inherited traditions of interpretation. They are often presented as opposed to the other main grouping, the Sadducees, who purportedly maintained a more literalist reading of the Law and are sometimes associated with the priestly classes. The Gospels say little about the Sadducees, except for their well-known rejection of the relatively recent belief in some form of existence after death (Luke 20.27–38); instead the Pharisees appear as much more dominant and ubiquitous than seems probable in the life-time of Jesus, an impression that is confirmed by the way that in Matthew, Luke and John they are even more dominant than in the earlier Mark. In the telling of the story of Jesus the Pharisees have become main carriers of opposition to Jesus through his ministry, although not during his trial, where they do not appear at all in Luke. This increasingly high profile may reflect the experiences of the early Christians in strained relations with Jews in local synagogues and their leadership, who in some ways were the heirs of the Pharisees. Yet it also follows a purely literary development by which an originally complex picture gets increasingly simplified into 'those for' and 'those against'. For Luke the Pharisees are most frequently 'those against', although there are significant exceptions. However, this means that there is a strong element of stereotyping if not of caricature, and Luke's picture should not be taken as a straight historical description as has unfortunately too often happened. Often associated with the Pharisees are the scribes; quite whom the Gospels understood by these is not certain. If they refer to the local village scribes who would have had a variety of roles reflecting their literacy and knowledge of the Law, they need not always have been associates of the Pharisees; for the evangelists they may have also represented the 'authorities' whose 'power base' would have been Jerusalem but who typified the move from Temple to Law as a focus of authority within first century Judaism: again they have become a stereotyped fixture of the story so obscuring the original picture.

The **Son of Man** is both the most enigmatic 'title' in the Gospel tradition and yet the only one found – almost exclusively – on the lips of Jesus. As such it is found in Mark, in material common to Matthew and Luke, and in material peculiar to Matthew, to Luke, or to John. This does not mean that we can trace all occurrences back to Jesus and draw from them a picture of how Jesus understood himself as 'Son of Man'. Even within our sources, 'Son of Man' sometimes becomes 'I' or 'him' = 'Jesus' in a parallel passage (compare Luke 6.22 with Matt. 5.11; Luke 9.22 = Mark 8.31 with Matt 16.21), while at other times it is introduced in one source and not in the parallels (compare Matt. 16.28 with Mark 9.1 and Luke 9.27). Moreover, the background of the term, whether it is properly called a 'title', and what it would have meant in the time of Jesus, are all hotly contested. It is often pointed out that uses of the title fall roughly into three categories, those that refer to the future coming or glory of the Son of Man (e.g. Luke 17.30; 21.27), those that refer to the suffering he must endure (e.g. Luke 9.22; 24.7), and those that refer to Jesus' present experience (e.g. Luke 7.34; 9.58), among which we might include the present example (5.24). In fact there are links between these: Luke 17.24 (but not the parallel in Matt. 24.27) which speaks of the future 'day' of the Son of Man, says that first he must suffer; in 9.26 and 12.8–9 there is a connection between attitudes to 'me' now and future response by the Son of Man. As already pointed out, Dan. 7.13 would provide a natural background for the first category, but would not so easily explain the second – although that vision is a promise of vindication for the Jews after the suffering they were then experiencing – and even less the last. There is also little evidence that already in the time of Jesus the title was part of popular expectation, denoting a heavenly figure to come, and it is only later that the Son of Man becomes clearly a heavenly 'messianic' figure (e.g. I Enoch). Some have queried whether Jesus did see himself as coming again, particularly as it is not obvious how this would relate to his preaching of the kingdom, present or coming. Could the early church have applied Dan. 7.13 to Jesus and adapted the tradition of his sayings accordingly? More recently interpretation has started from the third category of sayings which fit a convention in Aramaic by which a speaker could refer to himself indirectly as 'son of man'. If Jesus did so refer to himself, at a later stage the church may have seen a connection with the figure of Daniel as just suggested and may have modified his teaching to make it more explicit.

However this problem is to be resolved, Luke will have known all three categories of sayings from his sources. For him the term is virtually a title and clearly refers to Jesus; it binds together the ambiguities of his present ministry, the suffering he must face, and the future vindication in which the faithful will share. That future vindication is anticipated by the authority he already holds on earth, shown particularly in declaring God's forgiveness of sins. Yet for readers of the Gospel it would be important that the first part of the Gospel speaks only enigmatically of that authority, and more forcefully of the rejection he and his followers must experience (see 6.22; 9.22, 58); it is in that context that there comes the challenge to a discipleship which is not ashamed of Jesus, and only then is the promise of vindication and reversal given (9.26; 12.8–9).

Tax-collectors and sinners, and the newness of Jesus
5.27–39

Luke ties the next scene closely to the story we have just had, for it continues the opposition of *the Pharisees*, this time provoked by Jesus' association with *tax-collectors and sinners*; this is a theme which will continue throughout the central section of the Gospel until Jesus once again eats with a tax-collector, Zacchaeus, in 19.1–10. *Levi* is a model of discipleship, for like the fishermen he leaves *everything* and follows Jesus in response to Jesus' call *'Follow me'*. Yet he is not one of the twelve apostles who will be named in 6.14–16; Mark (2.14) had called him 'son of Alphaeus' which allowed for the possibility of confusion with James the son of Alphaeus, one of the twelve; Matthew (9.9) renamed him Matthew whom he then included among the twelve. Luke keeps 'Levi' and omits his father's name. In Luke 5.1–11 Jesus has not called the fishermen, future apostles, to follow him, although this is what they did, but he will call others to follow him (9.57–62; 18.22), and all those who follow must learn what the cost will be (9.23–24).

Levi's response – in Luke only – is to hold a *big* feast for Jesus *in his house* to which *a large party of tax-collectors and others* were invited. This combines two characteristic themes of Luke's: he regularly portrays Jesus as a guest at meals which become the opportunity for teaching (7.36; 10.38; 11.37; 14.1, 7, 12, 15), something that may reflect the setting of Luke and his readers in cities of the Empire where both in practice and in literature meals were occasions for philosophical debate; but he also develops the charge against Jesus, already found in Mark, that he both associated and ate with *tax-collectors and sinners* (5.30; 7.34; 15.1–2; 19.6).

Why **tax-collectors** should be picked out in this way is not immediately clear; certainly in some later Jewish texts they are also presented as despised, but so are other groups who are not mentioned in the Gospels as associates of Jesus. Presumably working in Capernaum and collecting dues on goods passing through the city, Levi would be within the jurisdiction of Herod Antipas; therefore he would not be working for the Romans and would not be viewed as a traitor or 'quisling', nor would he have closer association with Gentiles, later seen as a source of impurity, than many others – although by the time the Gospels were written this may have been forgotten. The tax-system did allow for dishonesty, as John the Baptist's instruction that the tax-collectors should 'exact no more than the assessment' shows (3.13), but were all tax-collectors, and they alone, dishonest? **Sinners** are also an ambiguous group; they are hardly an occupation although to bracket them with 'tax-collectors' treats them as one. Within the biblical tradition of the Old Testament *sinners* are those who wilfully reject the way of God and oppose God's people or the faithful poor described earlier (p. 11). Yet it would be hard to conceive of a guest-list purely composed of such, although this may be why Luke prefers the general *'and others'* in v.29. It is sometimes suggested that in the eyes of the Pharisees the majority of the ordinary people, who by inclination or the realities of their daily lives were unable to follow the strict Pharisaic emphasis on purity, tithing or other aspects of the law, were 'sinners' to be avoided as sources of impurity (cf. John 7.49): if Jesus claimed knowledge and faithfulness to God's will why did he not also avoid them? Yet for the most part the Gospels do not see 'the sinners' as simply the ordinary people; they are treated as a recognizable group separate from the crowds but never further defined (but see also on 7.37). Just as 'the Pharisees' have become something of a caricature, lumped together as a single group, to represent the opposition to Jesus, so 'the tax-collectors and sinners' have also become a symbolic group, representing those whom Jesus has come 'to save' (19.10). The two groups stand over against each other in simple contrast, yet, as always, the historical reality would have been much more complex. The issue of Jesus' associating with 'tax-collectors and sinners' is so deeply rooted in the synoptic Gospel tradition, although it plays no part in the later preaching of the church or in John's Gospel, that it must go back to his ministry, but quite how we are to understand it has yet to be satisfactorily answered.

The complaint is made by *the Pharisees and their scribes* – an improbable scenario which the REB tries to improve – to *his disciples*, the first we have heard of these. Jesus is now joined by those who share his rejection and who rely on his support, and therefore it is he who gives the answer. He does not deny that those with whom he mixes are *the sick* and in need of a doctor; they are indeed *sinners*, a term that is now contrasted with those who are, and not just think they are, *virtuous* or righteous. In Luke Jesus' mission is not just *to call* them as in Matthew (9.13) and Mark (2.17) but *to call* them *to repentance*: Jesus' association with such might suggest that he accepted them as they were, and this may have been how it was in the earliest traditions, but for Luke there must be a response acknowledging and repudiating past ways (cf. 13.3, 5; 15.7, 10; 19.1–10).

Jesus' disciples again become the butt of criticism in the next scene; continuing the theme of the last, they *eat and drink* while *John's disciples fast*. For all the positive things that have been said in Luke about John the Baptist he belongs to the past; *fasting* in Judaism was particularly associated with times of penitence, although John followed an ascetic life-style in the wilderness which would have encompassed fasting. In Luke 2.37 Anna had similarly spent her time in 'fasting and prayer', so for Luke this practice was not in itself wrong but belonged to the time of expectation and not of fulfilment. However, a more negative note is added by associating John's disciples with *the disciples of the Pharisees*: the Pharisees would not have had identifiable disciples but in introducing them Luke continues the opposition between Jesus and the Pharisees, now each with their own group of supporters; John the Baptist is on the wrong side of the divide. Jesus' answer is at first a mini-parable, likening his presence to the presence of *the bridegroom* at the wedding which makes it a time for rejoicing; it is perhaps more than a parable, for a wedding banquet was a common symbol of the coming of God's kingdom. Yet it then becomes an allegory: *the time . . . when the bridegroom will be taken away from them* refers to no ordinary wedding but to Jesus' departure, probably his death. That Jesus would have anticipated his death so early in his ministry may be uncertain; the parable may have been extended in the light of later events, for its main emphasis is not as a prophecy but on the significance of the present moment.

The further mini-parables repeat the theme although they are not very clear and Luke has modified the Markan version (2.36–39). Now the stress is on the incompatability of old and new: using the new to patch the old will render both valueless; new wine as it continues to ferment will split the fully stretched old wineskins and again both will be ruined. For all his emphasis on continuity with what God has already done, Luke knows that Jesus' message will not be able to remain within the confines of Jewish experience; but does he also mean that left to itself the old retains its value? The final saying may imply that: of course those familiar with the old will reject the untried and unfamiliar taste of the new; or is there irony here – just what are they missing!

Sabbath controversies
   6.1–11

These two incidents are again drawn from Mark's account (2.23–3.6), and move the growing conflict into a new area. Again it is Jesus' *disciples* who provoke criticism: that the *Pharisees*, even if here only *some*, should have been on the watch even on a sabbath walk *through the cornfields* belongs to the dramatic polarization of the conflict as it is described by the evangelists. In *plucking the ears of corn* and *rubbing them in their hands*, itself ordinarily permissable (Deut. 23.25), the disciples were in effect harvesting and thus breaking the prohibition of work on the sabbath (Ex. 20.9–10; Deut. 5.12–13). Later interpretation had elaborated the ambiguous 'work' in order to provide guidance in observance of the Law; Jesus does not criticize that elaboration, neither does he ridicule applying it to such casual behaviour. Instead he appeals to the story of how David himself had broken the prescriptions of the Law by eating *the sacred bread* which was reserved for *the priests* (I Sam. 21.1–6; Lev. 24.5–9). The point does not seem to be that the Law could be over-ridden in matters of life and death, for even if *David . . . and his men . . . were hungry*, this hardly applied to Jesus' disciples; neither is it making a point about sabbath observance, for it is not said that the earlier event took place on the sabbath, and Luke omits the verse where Mark has Jesus say 'the sabbath was made for man' (Mark 2.27). Instead it is a point about Jesus: if David could take such sovereign action and include 'his men' in it, then how much more could Jesus as the promised 'son of David'? Yet it is not as 'son of David' that Jesus claims that authority; instead we have the second '*son of man*' saying (cf. p.42f.): as son of man he is *lord*, more powerful than the REB's '*master*', *of the sabbath*. This need not mean that the sabbath and its provisions are done away with; it means that he acts with sovereign authority in relation to it.

The second sabbath controversy focusses even more on Jesus, and on this occasion his disciples do not appear. Jesus has not rejected sabbath observance; indeed he attends the synagogue and teaches there on the sabbath. The *man . . . whose right hand was withered* seems little more than a pawn in the tension that follows; that Luke adds to Mark's account *right* shows how easily stories become embellished. The dominant characters in the scene are Jesus and *the scribes and Pharisees*; even before anything happens they are hostile, on the look out for some charge to bring against him. That Jesus should be able to *heal him* apparently causes no surprise or anxiety; the issue is whether he will do so *on the sabbath* and thus again infringe the prohibition against work. Jesus sees it in the same terms; he calls the man out only after he knew their *'calculations'* – the word is that used by Simeon in 2.35 and perhaps has a negative tone. He then presents a challenge which puts the issue in starkly antithetical terms: of course they could not answer that it was not *permitted . . . to do good on the sabbath . . .* or *to save life*. The option of saying that it could wait until the next day since the man was hardly likely to die in the interim, is not given them; the only alternative Jesus offers is one they cannot affirm, *to do evil . . . or to destroy* life. This may seem as if Jesus is avoiding the question of the meaning of the sabbath and the command not to work on it, but the more fundamental question must be whether on any day, and how much more on the day which is 'holy' and dedicated 'to the LORD God' (Ex. 20.8, 10), the opportunity to do good can be passed by.

The miracle follows without reference to either the man's or the other onlookers' response; it has served only to establish Jesus' point. But for his opponents it only increases their total inability to share his understanding and their determination to *'do* something' to Jesus. Surprisingly this ominous note is not as dark as that which climaxes Mark's telling of the story where the Pharisees and Herodians, absent in Luke, plot to kill Jesus (Mark 3.6). For all their antagonism Luke knows that the Pharisees are not part of the story of Jesus' death; but he does not soften the negative aura which now surrounds them. For a while they disappear from the scene but the opposition they have introduced into the story of Jesus' ministry remains.

This explanation of the stories has emphasized an element of artificiality in the way they are staged; this is due to the frequent retelling of the stories in the life of the early church and to their use to make a point. That sabbath observance and interpretation of the Law were causes of conflict during Jesus' ministry is certain, but there may have been considerably more variety in practice and more debate among the Jews than we would now suppose from the stories, and even the Gospels do not say that it was this which led to Jesus' death. However, although the earliest Christians probably did continue to observe the sabbath and other aspects of the Jewish Law, whether they should continue to do so was a very real cause of concern, and the stories appeal to the example and words of Jesus to justify the practice which the early Christians eventually adopted. As

Luke tells the stories he is also interested in how they raise the question about Jesus' identity and hint at an answer; they prepare the readers for the conflict which will result in Jesus' death and suggest that there was an unbreachable gulf in understanding between Jesus and his opponents, a gulf that Luke and his readers were well aware of by their own time.

Jesus and his disciples
6.12–49

The opposition between Jesus and the Pharisees has already made us aware of the disciples who are drawn into it. As yet these disciples have no identity and for the most part we are left uncertain whether they have come of their own will or, like Levi, called by Jesus. This ambiguity about their identity will continue, and Luke will make it clear that to be a disciple is the beginning and not the end of a journey. Now he distinguishes between these disciples, who disappear from the scene, and the *twelve* whom Jesus *chose from among them* and whom he *named apostles*. The solemnity of this choice is underlined by being preceded by Jesus' withdrawal and night-long prayer: the choice is not his but God's. As yet they are given no task, in contrast to Mark 3.13–15 where they are 'to be with him . . . to preach . . . and to cast out demons', but in 'naming' *them apostles*, which means 'ones sent', he was designating them his emissaries. For Luke who has a second volume, although they are sent out in 9.1–8, 10 (see commentary) they really come into their own after Jesus' departure; yet even there their task as missionaries is limited and they appear more as leaders of the early church (Acts 2.42–3; 4.33; 6.6; 15.2,3,6 etc.). The importance of 'twelve' is shown when their number has to be made up after the death of Judas by someone who was ear- and eye-witness both to Jesus' ministry and to his resurrection (Acts 1.15–26), although when James is killed (Acts 12.1–2) there are no further replacements. As such they recall the twelve tribes of Israel, just as the *hill-country* to which Jesus withdraws should probably be translated *'mountain'* and recalls Mt Sinai where Israel was constituted: however Luke does not make much of this (except in 22.30) and does not develop the idea that Jesus is inaugurating a 'new Israel'. There is some variation in names when the lists in the three Gospels are compared – John (6.70–71) knows 'the twelve' but does not name them all – but this may be less surprising than the degree of consistency when we consider how little we, and probably Luke, know about them. For Luke the most notable ones will be *Simon* to whom we are now told, but without interpretation, that Jesus *gave the name Peter*, who heads the list *and Judas Iscariot* who comes at its end.

However, for the moment the twelve are forgotten as attention again focusses on Jesus and on the crowds from every region whom he attracts and who have come both to be taught and *to be cured*. As in 4.41 it is those *who were troubled with unclean spirits* who are singled out and we are left to envisage the other *diseases* which will be listed in 7.22. Again, as in 5.17 (see commentary), Jesus heals by *power* but here there is an almost magical feel to the way that it *went out from him* in response to the crowd *trying to touch him*. These regular vignettes of Jesus' miraculous powers frame his teaching and perhaps for Luke and his readers give it added authority; the conflicts which have been just described may cast a shadow but for Luke Jesus is a charismatic figure of enormous and obvious appeal.

All this forms only a backcloth, for Jesus' teaching is for *his disciples*; that broader group among whom Luke's readers would perhaps see themselves included. Some of what follows is familiar from Matthew's more famous 'sermon on the mount' (Matt. 5–7), hence the common title 'sermon on the plain' (cf. v.17), but each evangelist has selected and used the material to suit his own emphasis. Both start with 'beatitudes', a form common in Hellenistic and Jewish (Ps. 1.1; 34.8) tradition, not simply stating that certain people are fortunate, or encouraging such behaviour, but declaring what through God's action *is* (v.20) and *will be* (v.21); *the kingdom of God* is not just a promise for the future but is already breaking into the present. Yet who is to experience those blessings? For Luke the 'beatitudes' are not general teaching as in Matt. 5.3–12, but are addressed to his disciples, *you*; they are not 'poor in spirit' as in Matt. 5.3, but the literally *poor* (= REB *who are in need*), who *go hungry, who weep*. These are those without economic means or social value and status who in the Magnificat and in Jesus' reading from Isa. 61 at Nazareth are promised dramatic reversal. This socio-economic seriousness is even more sharply underlined by the contrastive woes, not found in Matthew and sitting uncomfortably in a sermon to disciples; did they include among themselves the *rich, well fed*, and *laughing*, who have little to look forward to, since they *have had*, technically *'been paid in full'*, the *consolation* (= REB *happiness* but see 2.25 for the same word)? Luke's concern for the use of wealth elsewhere in his Gospel suggests that it was a pressing issue, even if here the woes have a primarily rhetorical force, although with good prophetic precedents (Isa. 3.9–11; Jer. 17.5–8). Luke's church does not see itself as 'the church of the poor', for it awaits the reversal to come and does not campaign for it in the present, but the values it declares to be God's values may make that campaign inevitable.

It is, too, the community and not society who are addressed; the climax is reached in the hatred *you* experience. Luke's language of ostracism and slander probably reflects the experience of his own church, as it did that of others (I Peter 4.14); in his case they were probably excluded not just by *people* but by their Jewish neighbours, who alone could be seen as the heirs of those who rejected *the prophets* (cf. Acts 7.52), or of those who *spoke well* of *the false prophets* (cf. Jer. 5.21). Such rejection is *because of the Son of Man* (see pp.42f.); it will be the natural outcome of the authority Jesus has demonstrated and the conflict it has provoked, but therein too lies their total confidence in ultimate (*on that day*) vindication.

Luke sees no contradiction between uttering such woes and the command to *love, do good to, bless,* and even *pray for* those who bear such hostility in word and action. Whereas Matthew contrasts love of enemies with the supposed injunctions of the law (5.43–44) – prompting long debates as to whether Jesus' teaching was unique – for Luke they need neither justification nor antithesis, and stand at the head of all that follows. The language, as frequently in the biblical tradition, works by opposites, *love* versus *hate, bless* versus *curse,* and to fail to do one is to do the other. The examples which follow show, almost by exaggeration and absurdity, the seriousness of the command: even the thief is to be left in peace and offered yet more. Does the exaggeration mean the examples are not to be taken seriously? Luke will show Jesus as one who followed this pattern of non-retaliation (22.49–51, 63–65), and debate over its viability and validity has raged since (see pp.183f.). What Jesus here proposes is not a submissive passivity, but a seizing of the initiative to break the cycle of violence. Response to abuse, which is how *enemies* are defined, is not a legal question but a moral and a personal one.

This becomes clearer in what follows. The 'golden rule' of v.31 has various parallels in ancient literature in both its positive and its negative forms, but its application in vv.32–36 goes beyond its obvious meaning. To love where love is expected in response is natural but on its own inadequate: Luke here seems to use *sinners* in a conventionally dismissive way (cf. p.44f.). In Luke's world to *do good* implied benefactions in the expectation of return at least in the form

51

of honour. What is demanded instead is a radical self-giving which cannot expect to be reciprocated. There can be no natural, legal, or logical justification of such an attitude, despite the promise of a future *rich reward*, and so Luke can only appeal to the example of God. The age-old theological problem, how can a good and just God be *kind to the ungrateful and the wicked* is ignored, neither here is there any whisper of a final judgment against them; instead God's indiscriminate goodness is a model for those who would be his *sons* (and daughters).

That God is rich in compassion is fundamental to the OT (Ex. 34.6); whereas Leviticus had called for holiness (Lev. 19.2), and Matthew for perfection (Matt. 5.48), in likeness to God, for Luke the divine norm is to be *compassionate*. This means – v.36 should be taken with vv.37–38 – *not to judge*, or *condemn*, but to *pardon* and *give* in abundance. Again there is no reflection on the certainty that God will judge, nor on the circumstances in which judgment is necessary. These are not maxims to be applied generally without discrimination; they explore what it means to say *love your enemies*, and, in a world where reciprocity was the norm which bound some together and separated others, explore an alternative model of relationships.

The teaching which follows appears less coherent, and is made up of independent items of teaching, some found in different places in Matthew, linked more by association of words and ideas than by logical progression. The familiar 'parable' of the *blind* leading the blind perhaps argues the necessity for disciples to become teachers who can *guide* others. The following contrast between *pupil* and *teacher* probably is not intended to emphasize that Jesus as teacher cannot be surpassed; rather the *fully trained* disciple does become as *his teacher* – the REB's *can but reach* is too grudging. However, the hyperbolic *plank in your own* eye may either caution those who claim to have reached the teacher's level, or, better, repeat the injunction to avoid judgment in v.37. In ancient thought the *eye* was the mirror of the person; what *you look at* or pay attention to is the relationship you create, here with the *brother* who is a fellow disciple. Originally the *hypocrite* was the actor who wore a mask to represent the role assumed; in the NT it becomes a term of invective against conscious dissembling, most infamously in Matthew's polemic against the Pharisees (Matt. 6.16; 23.13–33; not in Luke). Here it is directed not against 'outsiders' but against a disciple, although the failure condemned seems to be more one of a lack of self-knowledge and humility than conscious deception. Therefore Jesus summons the disciples both to acceptance of responsibility and to due self-knowledge.

A similarity in sound between *speck* and *fruit* in Greek probably leads to the next 'parable', which seems little more than a proverbial truism; to be '*the good man*' (= REB *good people*) was an ideal in Greek ethical thought. Here, however, the focus is not the general point that outward deeds are a measure and product of that which is within, but the climax of the final words. The *heart* is the centre of human identity and intention in ancient thought, and here language is the best expression of the character within. The language which really counts is that of a disciple to the teacher, which acknowledges Jesus as *lord*; even so, such words on their own mean little. The final parable, final also in Matthew's sermon but with important differences (Matt. 7.24–27), offers a model of good discipleship; whereas Matthew speaks of prudence, and of rock instead of sand, for Luke it is the *foundations* which matter. The foundations are there in Jesus' teaching; the one who would be secure in discipleship and avoid final failure is the one who *comes . . . and hears . . . and acts.*

Miracles and their testimony to Jesus
7.1–17

The unexpected comment that Jesus' words had been spoken to *the people* (ctr. 6.20) prepares for the next public phase of Jesus' ministry. Once again Luke brackets teaching with healing, and it is appropriate that the next miracle should take place in *Capernaum* which has already been the scene of Jesus' healing powers (4.23; 31–43). The healing which follows is the only one to be found in the material which is shared by Matthew (8.5–13) and Luke but absent from Mark ('Q'), and it seems to have been told as much for what Jesus said concerning the centurion as for the healing of his servant. There is probably another version of the same tradition in John 4.46–53 where the son, not simply *highly valued servant*, of a man in royal service is healed, again at a distance.

Although during the rule of Herod Antipas this man would not have been a Roman *centurion*, we should assume that he was a non-Jew in Herod's military service. In this way he anticipates Cornelius, who in Acts 10 marks the spread of the gospel beyond the boundaries of Judaism. Thus, like the devout Cornelius, this man too is strongly supportive of the Jews, to the extent of having *built* for them *a synagogue*, or perhaps, considering the expense involved, having contributed towards it: this would not be the probably fourth-century edifice whose remains are now often visited in Capernaum, neither can we know that, as is often claimed, it lies beneath it. Both his standing in their eyes and his deference towards Jesus are shown in his advocates being *Jewish elders*, presumably not members of the Jerusalem council as usually implied by the term, but leaders of the local community. They confirm without any sense of impropriety that he *deserves* or is worthy of Jesus' help; it is the centurion himself who denies his own fitness.

In the light of the account of Peter and Cornelius it is often assumed that he recognized the difficulty that Jesus as a Jew would face in entering the home of a Gentile where he would be bound to come into contact with impurity (Acts 10.28). In fact neither the elders nor the man himself give any hint of this problem. Luke may have expected his readers to assume it, particularly since, when compared with Matthew's version, he unmistakeably highlights the parallels with the Cornelius episode; he may have wanted in this case to show the offer of the gospel to Gentiles not as a matter of observation of the Law but as the gracious and indiscriminating response to those who had faith and recognized their unworthiness (cf. 5.8). Again anticipating future converts the centurion never actually meets Jesus, but he does recognize the '*authority*' Jesus bears: the REB's '*under orders*' hides the use of this important term (cf. on 5.24). In fact it is not the authority he and presumably Jesus are 'under' which is the point of the comparison, but the consequent power of their *word*.

The climax of the story comes not in the healing, which Luke narrates almost as an afterthought and without any word by Jesus, but in Jesus' response to the *faith* the man has just demonstrated. Whereas Matthew sees the incident as a pointer to the precedence of many 'from east and west' over 'the heirs of the kingdom' (Matt. 8.11–12), for Luke Jesus' exclamation is on *such faith* wherever it is to be found.

As if to show that the *not even in Israel* does not mean that Jesus will not heal there, the presumably wealthy, male foreigner is followed by an impoverished female Israelite, a typical Lukan pairing which also introduces, since this story is unique to Luke, a typical Lukan interest in the poor and in women. Perhaps we should also recall Jesus' own comparison in 4.26–27, although Luke does not make the link. If the centurion recalls the foreign Naaman, the widow of Sidon certainly is evoked by the widow of Nain, even though the former was not an Israelite, as was emphasized in 4.26. As in I Kings 17.10, Jesus met the widow by *the gate of the town*, here Nain, at least a day's journey from Capernaum; the widow's *only son*, and only source of support, has died (cf. I Kings 17.17): through another pairing, Luke will emphasize that the wealthy Jairus also had an only daughter who dies (8.42). Jesus heals the boy, not by physical contact and prayer to God (as in I Kings 17.20–22), but simply by his authoritative command which could be translated either *'get up'* or *'be raised'*. Finally Jesus *restored* or 'gave' *him to this mother*, the same words as used of Elijah in I Kings 17.23. No wonder that the response is not just *awe* and praise of God, as characteristic for Luke (1.65; 5.26), but recognition that *'a great prophet has risen among us'*. Although in the first century it was often assumed that the age of prophecy was over, there were individuals who could only be interpreted in prophetic terms; but miracles were not the major characteristics of prophets, and it is likely that Luke has shaped the story to evoke that of Elijah as a backcloth to the next incident. Yet if *God has shown his care for his people*, this would be the dawning of God's longed-for intervention: the word is that used in 1.68. So, we are led to ask, was their response the right one?

Some of Luke's readers may have read the story in a different light; similar stories are told of other figures in the ancient world who held quasi-divine powers, most notably of Apollonius of Tyana, a wandering teacher towards the end of the first century. The vivid touches of the funeral procession, the accompanying *townspeople*, and Jesus' decisive action as he first *laid his hand on the bier*, can also be found in such stories. There is no initial faith here and Jesus acts out of compassion (cf. again 8.52), while the response is one of amazement. Yet once again, readers could too easily underestimate who Jesus was; Luke drops a hint when for the first time in his narrative he simply refers to Jesus as *the Lord* (v.13).

Again Jesus' fame spreads dramatically (cf. 4.37; 5.15), although the reference to *Judaea* rather than Galilee is surprising; Luke's precise knowledge of the geography may have been poor, or by 'Judaea' he may mean 'the Jewish people'. Yet his intention is clear: increasingly Jesus' identity and the purpose of his mission are being profiled. How are people to respond?

Jesus and John the Baptist
7.18–35

Once again the story returns to John the Baptist as a foil for under-standing Jesus. In Matthew's parallel account (Matt. 11.2–19), John is in prison, and although not mentioned by Luke this explains why he could only communicate with Jesus through *his disciples* (cf. 5.33). His question is repeated twice for emphasis, '*Are you the one who is to come?*' The epithet is almost used as a title, although it is not certainly known as such from contemporary Jewish writings. However, Mal. 3.1 speaks of the messenger to come who is further identified in 4.5 with Elijah, and in John 6.14 the people identify Jesus as 'the prophet who is to come into the world'. Yet although this meaning would follow on naturally from the previous miracle, we should probably envisage John as wondering whether Jesus was indeed the promised Messiah. Whether he spoke from dawning conviction or growing doubt is not clear; as we have seen, in Luke's account John's initial encounter with Jesus (3.15–22) gave no hint of his reaction.

Jesus does not answer their question but acts and then gives them the task of being witnesses to *what they have seen and heard*: since there were *two* of them they would be valid witnesses (Deut. 19.15). His words recall Isa. 35.5–7 and 29.18–19; that *the dead are raised*, not promised in Isaiah, points back to the widow's son, but the true climax is the offer of *good news to the poor*. This was the theme of Jesus' programmatic reading from Isa. 61.1 at Nazareth (4.18–19), and shows both that we are to understand the healings in this frame-work and that they point to the identity of the one who performs them. It does not seem to have been part of traditional hope that the Messiah would perform miracles, although recovery from all ills was part of God's promised age of salvation. The question, 'Who is Jesus?' is not to be answered by labels and categories of status but by his relationship to God's salvation and what God is doing through him. That is why some may find him *an obstacle to faith*, but why not to do so is to be *'blessed'* (cf. 6.20).

Yet if Jesus was something of an enigma to John, so was John to the early Christians, and Jesus' words reflect that dilemma. In the language of exaggeration he assumes and affirms popular assessment of John as *a prophet*; *a reed* would be a commonplace in *the wilderness*, a luxuriously dressed individual would belong else-where. Yet John was to be understood not just in prophetic terms but as the promised *herald* of God's coming: in this appeal to *scripture* the forerunner spoken of in Mal. 3.1 is combined with the 'angel' (the same word in Greek) promised in Ex. 23.20; the 'before me' (= God) of Mal. 3.1 has become *'ahead of you'* as in Ex. 23.20. Although not originally so intended, Christians would have thought of these words as addressed to God's Messiah, Jesus. Implicitly, but not explicitly, John the Baptist is being identified with Elijah to come, no longer as God's forerunner as in Jewish hope, but as the one who prepares for Jesus.

John can in no way be under-valued: the REB's *no one has been greater* implies a temporal limitation, with John belonging to the past; a better translation would be *'there is no one greater'*, and the contrast is between those *in the kingdom* and those *born* of women. Some interpreters have taken *the least*, literally 'the lesser', as a reference to Jesus, temporally later than John, but as the one who brings in the kingdom, greater than he. More probably the contrast is intended only to stress the unsurpassed nature of the kingdom as the new thing now being brought in; John's relation to it, whether he remains outside, is still unclear (see 16.16).

Certainly no denigration of John is intended, as Luke shows in an editorial comment on the response of the hearers. He characteristically sets in opposition *the tax-collectors*, here included among the ordinary *people*, and *the Pharisees*, to whom he adds *lawyers*, a term which for his Graeco-Roman readers would explain something of the status and interests of 'the scribes' and those who shared the Pharisees' outlook (cf. 10.25; 14.3). The first group, by submitting to John's baptism, had shown they *acknowledged* God's *just demand* and claim (rather than the REB's *goodness*); the latter, in rejecting his baptism, had, unwittingly, set themselves against *God's purpose*.

Jesus continues exploring the relationship between John the Baptist and himself through a popular simile, although its exact meaning is not clear. We may either envisage two groups of *children*, one playing weddings, the other funerals, neither willing to join with the other; or else it is one group, trying first one game, then the other, but never able to satisfy their peers. Yet in general terms the application is clear: John and Jesus appeared totally different, the one an ascetic, the other not; the people were either like the watching children, never satisfied, or like the players, always wanting something different. Jesus' proverbial mixing with tax-collectors (see note on 5.27–39) would not itself make him a *glutton and drunkard*, but the charge has an ominous echo within the biblical tradition (Deut.

21.20; Prov. 4.17). *Son of man* here seems only a way of saying 'I', perhaps the original force of the epithet (see pp.42f.).

The final saying is equally enigmatic; it is verbally linked to what precedes by the *children* and by *proved right*, the verb translated 'acknowledged the goodness of' in v.29. *Wisdom* – REB adds an explanatory but unnecessary '*God's*' – is used in the OT almost as a feminine personification of God's plan and intention, which can be set alongside God as mentor and guide (cf. Prov. 8–9); the idea had developed further in the period before the time of Jesus: 'She is but one, yet can do all things . . . age after age she enters into holy souls, and makes them friends of God' (Wisd. 7.27, cf. 7.22–8.18). Her children are either John and Jesus, or perhaps more probably those who respond, who, as in v.23, find no obstacle: despite the contrariness of the majority, the unbelief and rejection, there are those who show themselves to be children of wisdom and prove the rightness of God's purposes.

The Pharisee and the woman
7.36–50

Luke may have included this story here to illustrate the contrasting responses of 'a sinner' and of a Pharisee. It is found only in Luke but bears many resemblances to the anointing of Jesus' head at Bethany during the last week of his life in Matt. 26.6–13 and Mark 14.3–9, and in John 12.1–8 of Jesus' feet. While in those accounts the anointing is in anticipation of Jesus' death, here it is in response to Jesus as the one who offers forgiveness. Whether there were two incidents, or two traditions and Luke, having included this alternative, omitted the later anointing which he would have known from Mark, or whether Luke deliberately modified the Markan anointing, which did not fit his understanding of Jesus' death, in order to make a more telling point here, cannot easily be decided. In their present form and place within the Gospels the stories have to be treated as separate ones, following the intention of the evangelists, and details of one should not be used to elaborate the others as has often happened.

For Luke the scene is set in Galilee with Jesus *reclining at a banquet* (= REB *took his place at table*). Such occasions provide a favourite Lukan setting for Jesus' teaching (11.37–52; 14), reflecting the Graeco-Roman tradition of a 'symposium', a shared meal whose purpose was discussion and debate of significant issues. Nothing suggests that the Pharisees who acted as hosts had devious motives, or that Jesus was any less willing to accept their hospitality than that of 'tax-collectors and sinners' (cf. 5.29–32). The woman is simply described as one of that group, *a sinner*; despite the ambiguity of the term (see pp.42f.), it has often but unnecessarily been assumed that she was a prostitute, or *living an immoral life* (REB). She is not named and should not be identified with the Mary of the Johannine story (John 12.3) nor with Mary Magdalene. Her dramatic and costly action, for *myrrh* was an expensive perfume, is given no interpretation; her *weeping* could be a sign either of penitence or of deep joy and devotion. There is nothing here of the 'messianic anointing' of the Matthean and Markan versions, but the focus on Jesus' *feet* is one of a number of details Luke's Gospel shares with John.

Whereas in the other accounts the complaint comes from among Jesus' disciples and is provoked by the waste involved, here it is the *host*, pointedly identified again as *the Pharisee*, who decries Jesus' willingness to allow such a woman, *a sinner* (not the REB's *bad character*), to touch him. The Pharisee assumes that if Jesus was a prophet, the theme which has bound together the chapter, he would have recognized her hidden character: she was not, then, 'a painted prostitute' even if the unloosing of her hair was as unconventional as is often assumed. The picture is implied, and again it belongs to the tendency to caricature the attitude of the Pharisees, that any physical contact with 'outsiders and rejects' was anathema.

Jesus does know what is hidden, for he knows both his host's silent musings and the woman's true intentions. The parable he tells is a simple one and reflects the cruel realities of contemporary life where men were easily trapped into increasing cycles of debt (cf. Matt. 18.23–35); *a silver piece* or 'denarius' would be a day's wage. As in many parables which work by combining the familiar with the impossible, the action takes an unthinkable turn: no money-lender could afford to cancel debts of those unable to pay.

The woman's actions are those of one released from the greatest burden; at each stage what she has done carries a double contrast with her host, now identified as *Simon* (cf. Simon the leper in Mark 14.3). She herself, and not a servant, washed his *feet* not with water but with her own *tears*; she kissed not once but repeatedly not his cheek but his *feet*; she *anointed* not his *head* but his *feet*, and not with regular *oil* but with *myrrh*. If Simon had omitted these conventional niceties then his hospitality would have been a contemptuous pretence, something never hinted by the opening of the story. The purpose is not to expose that pretence, nor to admit that he was only a little debtor, but to demonstrate by familiar hyperbole the magnitude of the woman's offering, and so presumably of her love; besides that, Simon's hospitality fades into insignificance.

Jesus now turns to the woman, who in the characteristic ambivalence of Luke's attitude to women has remained the passive object of the men's conversation and must remain anonymous. The REB follows most interpreters in explaining that *her great love* just shown is proof of a forgiveness she had already experienced, and which Jesus now publicly proclaims; the NIV's *'her many sins have been forgiven – for she loved much'* captures the ambiguity of the Greek which could make Jesus mean, contrary to the parable and the last words of v.47, that the forgiveness Jesus goes on to declare is a response to her love. The final declaration and dismissal fits the scene less comfortably than it does that of the woman with a haemorrhage in 8.48, for where has this woman shown *faith* and how does it fit in the equation between love and forgiveness? Luke may have wanted a tidy end to the story and to have given Jesus the final and familiar word which would commend the story to his hearers.

Whether or not the story has been crafted by Luke, it is a vivid and dramatic enactment of the theme of the Gospel: the rejected outsider becomes the model of the one who is accepted, while the host whose invitation proves his acceptability is cursorily dismissed; the man who bears the honour of offering hospitality is shamed, while the woman who is marked by shame is given a place of highest honour. If the banquet and its philosophical debates were familiar to Luke's readers, its reversal of all conventional standards would be startling.

The women around Jesus
8.1–3

For Luke Jesus' early ministry was one of almost continual travelling through Galilee (cf. 4.43–44); everything he has done, by word and miracle, has been *proclaiming the good news* (cf. 4.18). The result has been opposition, but also the gathering of those who join him, the *Twelve*, whose choosing we heard of in 6.13–16, and now *a number of women*. In Mark's Gospel we first hear of these women at the cross (Mark 15.40–41), but Luke alone announces their presence during Jesus' ministry itself. The names of these women differ among the Gospels (cf. also Mark 16.1; Matt. 27.56), suggesting that the tradition of their presence was stronger than that of their identities; the constant figure is *Mary of Magdala* (cf. also John 19.25; 20.1), who in all the Gospels is a primary witness of the empty tomb, yet even in her case the later traditions of the early church, including Acts, are silent. Some would argue that this silence reflects the early church's unease regarding the position of women, in contrast to Jesus' readiness to include them among his close followers. It is also often argued that Jesus' attitude contrasted sharply with the disregard or even contempt accorded women in contemporary society; in fact this is a misrepresentation, and while later male-authored 'religious' texts – in the early church just as much as in Judaism – can be dismissive of the role and potential of women, there is evidence that in the time of Jesus women could and did act with considerable independence; Jesus' attitude was probably less revolutionary than is often assumed. Women with *their own resources* had greater opportunities for independence, and these are the type of women Luke introduces here: *Susanna* is not otherwise known; *Chuza* is an Aramean name and clearly held a position of some influence, which would have given his wife, *Joanna* (cf. 24.10), standing; *Mary* is identified by her place of origin and not by any male relative. Yet Luke's attitude to these women is also qualified: unlike the Twelve who had been chosen, all these are defined by their need for healing particularly from *evil spirits*; Mary, who was to have such a significant role later, had been particularly badly afflicted – *seven* is a number of completeness – but speculation on the nature of that affliction is pointless and she should not be identified, as she so often has been, with the woman of the preceding story. Moreover, while the Twelve were *with him*, the women have the task of 'providing' *for them*; *provided* could be translated *'ministered'*, and should not be seen as fulfilling domestic chores, but for Luke the ministry of women is one of service to Jesus and his male apostles!

Parables of obedience to the word
8.4–21

The theme of discipleship continues now through Jesus' teaching. The 'parable of the sower' is well-known from Mark 4, but whereas there it is a prime example of Jesus' extensive and regular teaching 'by parables' (Mark 4.2), in Luke Jesus gives this specific message *in a parable* (see further on 8.9–10). In his telling, the parable is more succinct, lacking some of the Markan detail, so that the emphasis falls more sharply on the *seed*, while the final climax is muted with only a *hundredfold* yield (ctr. Mark 4.8). The details of the parable no doubt would have been familiar to Jesus' rural audience; the story would make good sense if sowing preceded ploughing so that the nature of the underlying ground was unknown, although there is some disagreement whether this was first-century Palestinian practice.

That Jesus taught by **parables** is fundamental to the synoptic picture, although less so in John; yet there has been considerable debate as to why he did so and how his parables were originally intended to be understood. Here Jesus goes on to give the parable an allegorical understanding, where each detail points beyond itself; generally this does not happen, and it seems unlikely that Jesus' parables were all intended allegorically, although later church writers soon began supplying allegorical interpretations to other parables, as preachers have done ever since. That all parables have a single straightforward message, being little more than illustrations, equally fails to explain the key role they play in the traditions of Jesus' teaching. Recent study of the parables has focussed on the way they 'work' or the effect they have; indebted to language and imagery which already carries symbolic meanings from the past (e.g. the OT) they explore truths or provoke reflection in ways which cannot be reproduced by non-metaphorical or logical language. An important element is often surprise or contrast; here the contrast between the magnitude of harvest and the insignificance or precariousness of sowing would be a natural one, especially as the harvest was a common image of the inbreaking of God's final age (cf. Mark 4.26–29; Matt. 13.24–30, neither in Luke). Yet, at least as told in the Gospels, this is not the only focus of 'the sower' and our attention is drawn more to the sowing and to the detailed different fortunes of the seed. Already in the early church it seems that Jesus' parables were becoming enigmatic. In retelling, the details could be refined to fit the teller's understanding of their meaning; as we have seen, a tendency to allegorize developed, and could be attributed to Jesus. The way each of the evangelists uses the parables differs. Yet the parables also became a means of reflecting on the way that Jesus, for all his public teaching, was met by rejection. Mark does this in 4.10–12 where he virtually implies that parables divide Jesus' hearers into an inner circle and 'those outside' whose failure to understand is predetermined.

Luke takes over from Mark this interpretation of Jesus' parabolic teaching, but he makes it specific to *what this parable meant*. If discipleship has particular demands, it also has particular privileges, chief among which must be insight into *the secrets of the kingdom of God*. *Secrets* or *mysteries* refers to the divine purpose which is only revealed to a few (cf. Dan. 2.18–19, 47; I Cor. 2.1,7); those who do not take the path of discipleship remain without that understanding. That the intention is *so that* they may remain in the dark may seem not only to make Jesus', or any, preaching counter-productive, but also to give Jesus, and so God, the responsibility for people's failure to come to faith. Luke has taken this from Mark 4.12, who, as we have seen, was reflecting on the results of Jesus' preaching and perhaps reassuring his readers in the midst of their own experience of being a minority. Behind Mark lies Isa. 6.9–10, where Isaiah's preaching is given a similarly devastating purpose, perhaps again from hindsight. Luke's allusion to the Isaiah passage is more succinct but he retains the difficult *so that they may* (ctr. Matt. 13.13). It has been suggested that in the Greek of the day 'so that' could be understood as 'with the result that', not purpose but actual consequence; this is unlikely. Luke is drawing from Mark, and trying to cope with some of the same dilemmas created by the growing obscurity of the original intention of Jesus' parables, and by the actual response to Jesus' ministry. He modifies Mark by omitting the final exclusion of the possibility of forgiveness from Isa. 6.9–10, but the passage and the dilemma is one he will return to (Acts 28.25–28).

Jesus immediately goes on to explain *what the parable means*, although it is less clear than in Mark whether the explanation is only intended for the disciples. Again Luke stresses more than does Mark the seed as *the word of God*. It is a parable both of the fortunes of the preaching and of the experience of those who hear: *the devil*, *time of testing*, and *cares and wealth* are all potential obstacles to the reception which will lead to salvation. The goal is not the certainty and richness of the reception in 'the good soil', as in Mark, but that those who hear 'the word' with *a good and honest heart . . . hold it fast . . . by perseverance*. Luke is addressing a situation where these were the challenges facing the church.

The parable which follows, although not so called, echoes that of Mark 4.21–25; another version is found in 11.33. The content is self-evident: an oil-lamp covered with *a basin* would be snuffed out, and *under the bed* it would give no light. Discipleship is not to be hidden but must result in making light visible to others, just as in the pre-

vious parable it must result in fruit. The certainty of exposure here
does not refer to final judgment but to the necessity of declaration.
Listening on its own means nothing; it is the manner of response that
is determinative and ensures its own fruitfulness.

Jesus' family now appear as models of such discipleship, although
Joseph has disappeared from the story, presumably having died.
This is very different from the Markan parallel where Jesus virtually
rejects his kin in order to establish a new set of relationships of
those who do the will of God (Mark 3.31–35). Luke has omitted the
incident where Jesus' relatives treat him as mad and in need of care
(Mark 3.20–21), and here omits Jesus' dismissive 'Who is my mother
and brothers?' and his appeal to his immediate hearers (Mark
3.33–4). For Luke, who has already shown Mary as quietly obedient
and responsive and who will later place Jesus' family among the
earliest believers (Acts 1.14), they too are not excluded from the
family of those who both *hear* and *act upon* the word of God, true
illustrations of the good soil.

Jesus' power over the forces of chaos
    8.22–39

Luke now makes another of his shifts, from the teacher to the
dramatic miracle-worker; yet there is also a continuity, for the
miracles which follow both ask '*Who can this be?*' who invites
discipleship, and point to what discipleship 'by perseverance' and
'in the time of testing' (4.13, 15) will mean. A *heavy squall* would not
be unusual on the Lake of Galilee, surrounded as it is by steep-sided
hills, and equally sudden calms are also well attested. For those who
find the 'nature miracles', where Jesus apparently subverts the
processes of nature which are part of God's creation, difficult, an
explanation which relies on known natural phenomena and on
coincidence may seem an attractive way of understanding the
stilling of the storm. Yet this is not how Luke understands the story;
in the ancient world storms did indeed represent a frightening and
uncontrollable threat to life, and, not surprisingly, feature in many
stories – those of Jonah and of Paul in Acts 27.8–44 could also be
joined by pagan parallels and by Jewish traditions where storms
were calmed by prayer or the intervention of a 'holy' person. Yet this
storm suggests that the answer to their characteristically Lukan *fear
and amazement* (cf. 7.16) and to their question '*Who can this be?*' goes
even further. Jesus *rebuked the wind* as he would rebuke a demonic

spirit (cf. Luke 9.42; Mark 4.39 makes this even more explicit); in the biblical tradition the violence of the sea pointed to the chaotic powers which could engulf people but over which God had won a certain victory (Ps. 89.9–10; 69.10–15); the only one who could *give his orders to the wind and the waves, and they obey him* would be God (Ps. 107.23–32). This means that the miracle becomes a parable of discipleship within the life of the Christian community: as in Ps. 107.28–30 'they cried to the LORD in their trouble, and he brought them out of their distress [. . . and] made the storm be still', so should the disciples learn to call upon the one they address as *Master*.

Luke understands the journey as having taken them to the east side of the lake of Galilee, although *the country of the Gerasenes* in fact is about thirty-three miles SE – hence the attempts by early scribes to provide a more suitable place-name (cf. REB footnote and Matt. 8.28). He considerably abbreviates Mark's vivid account of the miracle which follows (Mark 5.1–20), but the story remains rich in detail. Although the man was *from the town*, his nakedness, his home *among the tombs*, traditionally both unclean and the habitat of demonic spirits, his uncontrollability, and his utter subjection to the forces which drove him out *into the wilds* or wildernesses (cf. on 4.1), show him as one who is excluded from all civilization (*a house*) or normality. As in 4.34, 41 those *possessed by demons* recognize Jesus in a way not open to normal human insight, and know him as their arch-opponent; coming from a predominantly non-Jewish area this man adopts the pagan formula *Most High God*. The picture is not of a man seeking healing but of bitter conflict between Jesus and the forces of evil whom he has come to *torment* (cf. Rev. 14.10–11) or to *banish to the abyss*, the depths of the sea (cf. Ps. 107.26) but also of lasting torment (cf. Rev. 9.1,11). There may even be a sense that it is a hard-won conflict, for *Jesus was already ordering the unclean spirit* before he went on to ask his name. Knowledge of the name was believed to give power over the person concerned: just as this man/demon knew Jesus now Jesus must know his name; *legion*, technically a body of six thousand soldiers, indicated the irresistability of the forces as much as their numerical strength.

Fearing annihilation in *the abyss*, the demonic powers negotiate with Jesus to be allowed to find a new home in the near-by *herd of pigs*, a further indication of a non-Jewish area. There may be a certain irony in that although permitted to do so, they nonetheless end up in the depths of the sea. It is only now, and at first indirectly, that attention turns to the man; through the eyes of *the people* from the surrounding area we see him now restored to normality and therefore *clothed*. He also adopts the role of a would-be disciple, *sitting at Jesus' feet*, but although he wants to continue as such and *to go with him*, Jesus will not allow this. Perhaps here Luke recognizes that a non-Jewish mission was not part of Jesus' own ministry; yet as a model of the mission of the early church the man is instructed to make known *to his own home . . . what God has done*. It is not just psychological realism but Luke's awareness of the real nature of Jesus' authority which has the man declare *what Jesus had done*.

Interwoven with his response is that of *the whole population* of the district; they too are dependent on the testimony of *eyewitnesses*, and their response is again one of awe or *fear* (cf. 8.25; 7.16). Yet here such fear will not lead to faith; perhaps again because we are in a pagan environment the reaction is one of terror in face of the mysterious and powerful: such power is dangerous and better sent away. Thus they reinforce the sense that in this story we are not in a world of prophetic acts of power (cf. 7.11–17), but in one of supernatural forces and almost magical elements where to know a name is to control, where Jesus engages in a hard-won conflict, and where demons can inhabit and destroy a herd of pigs.

Jesus both accepts these assumptions and shows no concern either for the fate of the pigs or for the destruction of the livelihood of *the men in charge of them*. To suppose that only so could the man be convinced of and so experience his own healing is to introduce a psychological element foreign to the story. Moreover, in its early telling the story would also evoke for its hearers a number of other themes: a 'legion' would remind them of the oft-resented Roman presence which some would see as 'possession' and as polluting; the pigs would be seen in Jewish eyes as a symbol of the Gentiles and their destruction might be seen as the purification of the land and of the people; on another level charges or fears of demon possession sometimes reflect a society in conflict with itself. How far these and other associations have helped shape the story is now impossible to recover; certainly it reflects a world more familiar to its earliest than to its modern readers. For Luke it is a powerful manifestation of Jesus' authority and identity, and a telling parable of the responses this provokes.

Faith and healing
8.40–56

Although the miracles which follow are no less dramatic, there is a sharp sense of contrast when Jesus is forced out of pagan territory and returns, presumably to Galilee, to an expectant welcome. The 'sandwiching' of the stories of Jairus' daughter and the woman with haemorrhages, already characteristic of Mark's account (Mark 5.21–43), both heightens the sense of suspense and sets up a contrast between them. *Jairus* is *a man*, named, and a *ruler of the synagogue* (= REB *president*), a general term not further defined; Jesus will, as requested, go to his house where lies *his only daughter, who was about twelve years old* – mentioned here rather than later as in Mark – perhaps pre-pubescent. The *woman* remains nameless and without status; her *twelve years* have been ones of incessant bleeding, which, following Lev. 15.25–30, would keep her in a continual state of quasi-menstrual impurity. Her illness has impoverished her, although there is some textual uncertainty as to whether Luke, traditionally a doctor, admits *she had spent all she had on doctors* (REB footnote; NRSV text). She does not approach Jesus directly but can only hope that *the edge of his cloak*, perhaps the 'tassels' of an observant Jew (Deut. 22.12), would carry some of the residual power of its wearer, an almost magical idea also found in Acts 5.15; 19.11–12.

Her immediate cure confirms that hope, but Jesus too seems to subscribe to the idea of his power as something quantifiable which might be released and its loss felt. Such an idea is only partly in harmony with the Lukan emphasis that as healer and teacher Jesus was indeed equipped with a power which has its source in the Holy Spirit (cf. 4.14, 36; 5.17). Jesus' direct affirmation, the crowds' disclaimer, and Peter's explicit dismissal, all details sharpened by Luke, set the scene for the woman's confession; whereas in Mark 5.33 it is Jesus whom she addresses, in Luke she declares both her action and her immediate cure *before all the people*: her testimony becomes a model for others, similar to that of 'legion' in v.39. Jesus' almost formulaic response, where *healed* could also be translated 'saved', is not just retrospective, looking back to her determination to touch Jesus; it gives Jesus the last word of declaratory absolution, acknowledging that those who have experienced salvation must both make their response and are dependent on Jesus' word (cf. 7.50 where it fits less comfortably).

It is sometimes argued that Jesus would have incurred impurity by being touched by the woman in her state, and that by healing her he was freeing her from the impurity independently from any restrictions of the law, and thus allowing her full participation in both social and religious life. However, this does not seem to be part of any of the evangelists' understanding of the story: actual provisions for and attitudes to women in a state of menstrual impurity may have been less exclusionary than is often assumed, and, for whatever reasons, the issue is not one which early Christians seem to have debated in the way they did regulations dealing with food and table fellowship.

Like the 'only son' of the nameless widow (7.12), the *only daughter* (only in Luke) of Jairus now *is dead*. In fact the normal and highly expressive mourning had already begun. Again the theme is one of *faith* and the certainty of being *well* or 'saved'. Jesus' remark that *she is not dead: she is asleep* does not mean that their diagnosis was faulty and he percieved signs of life; 'sleep' can be a metaphor for death (cf. I Thess 5.10), but Jesus cannot simply be reminding them that all death can be viewed as but sleep. The assumption must be that she had really died but that Jesus was saying that in her case this death was but a sleep in a unique sense: his word *Get up* – Luke omits as too obscure Mark's aramaic formula – could also be translated 'rise'. Luke understands death as the departure of *her spirit* or breath, which now returns, and returns her to full health and vitality, and appetite!

It is surprising, both in view of the preceding miracles and of the public nature of her death, that this healing has a strong sense of secrecy. For the first time we meet an inner circle among Jesus' disciples, *Peter, John and James,* who alone, with the child's parents, are present. The story closes with a strict injunction not *to tell anyone what had happened*. This is a theme which Luke has taken over from Mark (5.43, ctr. Matt 9.26), where it is part of a more extensive 'secrecy motif'. Luke, however, has regularly described the awe Jesus' healing provokes, and the way word of it spreads, not least in the testimony of those healed. It is not clear why he has avoided this here and followed his Markan model. It may be to stress that Jesus' fame even so cannot be suppressed, or to create a pause before the next phase of the story.

Jesus and the Twelve
   9.1–6

Jesus' ministry in Galilee has been one of 'power and authority' (cf. 4.32,36 etc.); he has gathered around him disciples who must share his path, and he has chosen from among them *Twelve* (6.13–16). As yet these have had no specific task or purpose (ctr. Mark 3.14–15). Now they are given the *power and authority* he has displayed, particularly in the last two chapters, and are *sent* – which means as his agents – to continue his own task. So far *to proclaim the kingdom of God* (cf. 8.1; 4.43–44) has not meant 'to teach about' it or 'to announce its imminence' so much as by word and action to declare the hope and the demands it offers; *to heal* has been a particular manifestation of his power (5.17; 8.46), and those afflicted by *demons*, as then understood, have been powerful indications that his healing is part of the establishment of God's sovereign rule.

Why they are given this task is not explained. It has been suggested that in the context of Jesus' ministry it may have symbolized a dramatic appeal to the whole (= twelve tribes) of Israel who are represented in the Twelve (cf. note on 6.13), but Luke gives no certain hint of this; yet neither does this seem to be a 'dummy run' for or an anticipation of their future, post-resurrection, mission, for it comes at this specific moment as a bridge between Jesus' ministry so far and the question they must answer, 'who do you say that I am?' (v.20). The conditions they must fulfil are equally ambiguous: the demand that they *take nothing for the journey* is countermanded in 22.35–36, perhaps not just in the extreme circumstances of Jesus' death but in the conditions of danger and persecution which will thereafter be in force. Their surrender of any provisions would be rashness, and presumably expresses their total dependence on God and commitment to their task, but the prohibition of moving from lodgings to lodgings, perhaps in search of something more comfortable, could fit later Christian missions when this might be a real temptation. Shaking *the dust off* their *feet* would be severing any connection or association (cf. Acts 13.51); as a *warning* or 'witness' to those who reject them it implies that this was their last chance. Luke alone describes a further mission, of seventy-two, in 10.1–12 which breathes a similar air of urgency; the parallelism has sometimes been seen as an anticipation of the missions to Israel/'the Jews' and to the Gentiles, but although this would fit Luke's interests in Acts, he does little to signal it. The tradition of the sending out of the Twelve was one Luke found in his sources (Mark 6.6–13); he has made it into an introduction to a section of his Gospel which asks those who follow him what they think of him and how far they are prepared to follow.

'Who do you say that I am?'
9.7–27

The title that the REB gives to the whole of this section, 'Jesus and the Twelve', would indeed be appropriate, for it is their response to the question which will be climactic; for the same reason, as we have just seen, the preceding section could have been incorporated with this with its leading question. At this point in the narrative Mark 6.14–29 (cf. Matt 14.1–12) goes on to describe the death of John the Baptist at the hands of Herod Antipas. Luke, who has referred to John's imprisonment even before the start of Jesus' ministry (3.19–20), does not want attention diverted back to John, whose task is over. He therefore is only concerned with *Herod's* perplexity at *all that was happening*. Popular debate reflected the categories within which Jesus could be understood: *Elijah*, as we have seen, was to be the forerunner of God's final coming (Mal. 3.1; 4.5–6; cf. commentary on Luke 1.17; 7.26–27); *one of the prophets* might refer to the hope of a prophet like Moses (Deut. 18.15) or be a more general designation. These were the terms in which people had also responded to John the Baptist (cf. 7.26–27), and so they are represented as wondering whether *John had been raised from the dead*. Unless this means 'another John-type', such an idea would have been impossible for those at the time who knew that John and Jesus were contemporaries; Luke seems to be rejecting a tendency to see John and Jesus too much on a par (cf. also p.21). Thus, in sharp contrast to Mark 6.16, he has Herod decisively exclude that option: Herod, who will maintain his interest in Jesus (13.31; 23.8), now only voices the question '*Who is this?*'; the following incidents continue the debate.

The pattern of Jesus' thwarted search for privacy which marked the beginning of his ministry (4.42) is repeated when *the apostles*, i.e. 'those who had been sent', return. The geography of what follows is obscure: Luke has them retire to *Bethsaida* on the NNE edge of the Sea of Galilee, which he designates *a town*. Yet when the crowd joins them it is assumed to be *a remote*, or 'desert', *place* (v.12) where only the surrounding *villages and farms* will provide food and lodging. Again Luke is drawing from Mark, who names Bethsaida as their destination after 'the Feeding' in 6.45, and is more concerned for the pattern and the events than for geographical precision.

This miracle is the most deeply-rooted in the Jesus traditions, being found in the Johannine as well as in the synoptic traditions (Mark 6.30–44; Matt. 14.13–21; John 6.1–15), and also having a parallel 'Feeding of the Four Thousand' (Mark 8.1–10; Matt. 15.32–39), which Luke omits. Each of the evangelists draws their own significance from the miracle; in fact the miraculous element seems the least significant. There is no description of 'the multiplication' of the food available, it simply proves upon distribution to be sufficient; there is no response by the crowd or by the disciples as there so often is in Luke (ctr. John 6.14); the number of those fed, *five thousand men*, presumably with wives and children, is not given as a dramatic climax (so Mark 6.44), but merely to explain *all these people*, and prepares for their orderly seating. Jesus does not act out of compassion nor to meet desperate need, for the assumption is that the people would be able to meet those needs from the surrounding area. Jesus' retort to his disciples' request that he *send the people off*, *'Give them something to eat yourselves'* presumably is not intended to expose their inadequacy but merely sets the scene for what is to follow.

To focus on the miracle, with the attendant problems of Jesus' manipulation of the natural forces ordained by God, or to seek naturalistic explanations, such as the triumph of generosity over selfishness as the crowds share their hidden supplies, is to misunderstand the resonances this story held, both within the earliest Jesus traditions and in its retelling by the evangelists. Thus while Jesus' actions as *he looked up, said the blessing, broke*, and *gave* would be the normal actions of any meal – although the blessing would be directed to God and not the bread – early Christian readers would almost certainly be reminded of Jesus' actions at the Last Supper (22.19) and of their repetition in the eucharistic life of the church (cf. 24.30 and note). The meal would also recall not simply that God had fed the people in the wilderness, a theme only John develops, but the hope that God would again feed them in the age to come (cf. Isa. 25.6). The *twelve baskets* filled with scraps point again to the whole of Israel who have a share in that anticipated salvation. These two sets of evocations are not mutually exclusive, for Jesus' own symbolic meals with his disciples anticipate the kingdom (Luke 22.15–18). How far these themes can be traced behind the Gospel traditions into an event in the ministry of Jesus is impossible to answer, although

71

their strength implies some foundation. Not only Jesus' words had parabolic power; his actions too were a proclamation of the kingdom, and meals in which he participated, and perhaps initiated, were a central part of that proclamation.

Luke immediately follows this incident with Jesus' question to his disciples. This means that he omits the material we find in Mark 6.45–8.26, which begins and ends in Bethsaida. Whether a single reason explains this omission, assuming Luke knew of the section, is disputed. Its consequence is that Herod's own question, and Jesus' evocative feeding in the wilderness provide the prologue to the question *'Who do the people say that I am?'* As usual in Luke before any focal events, Jesus *had been praying alone*, cf. 3.21; 6.12. The question he asks about poplular ideas is only preliminary to the question directed to the disciples for we already know of these from vv. 7–8. *Peter*, for the first time the spokesman, gives an answer presumably on behalf of all the disciples: in contrast to Matt. 16.17–19 he is not singled out by it. His answer, *God's Messiah*, could also be translated as 'the Christ of God': in the context of Jesus' ministry the term would have to be 'Messiah', necessarily qualified as the one sent by and acting for God (cf. 2.26); for Luke and his readers the Greek equivalent 'Christ' was becoming at least an independent title and virtually a proper name in its own right – thus Mark 8.29 gives the unqualified answer 'You are the Christ/ Messiah', while Matthew 16.16 removes any ambiguity by adding 'the Son of God'.

What the reader has known from the beginning (1.32–33; 2.11), demons have acknowledged (4.41) and John the Baptist has pondered (7.19), has now been openly declared by his disciples. It is therefore at this moment that they are committed to secrecy because of what they have yet to understand: the REB by starting a new sentence in v.22 obscures the close connection whereby v.22 provides the reason for the injunction to silence in v.21. Jesus does not answer in terms of Messiah or Christ but of *Son of Man* (cf. pp.42 f.), as in the two subsequent prophecies of suffering to come (9.44; 18.31–33). In the context this cannot be merely an allusive self-reference, for there is a pointed contrast with Peter's 'Messiah' which Jesus does not use of himself. Yet the 'one like a son of man [human being]' of Dan. 7.13, although representing the people who had experienced oppression, is triumphant and vindicated, not *rejected*. There is limited evidence within Jewish thought of the time that the Messiah could be expected to suffer, and the 'son of man' was neither a suffering nor technically a 'messianic' figure. Thus the term and its use here cannot be interpreted by its external associations. Within Luke, 'the Son of Man' has exercised an authority which could be seen as in God's hands (5.24; 6.5), but it has been an authority which is rejected, and so suffering 'because of the Son of Man' (6.22) has become a possibility. Now there can be no acknowledgment of Jesus as Messiah without recognition of the rejection he as Son of Man *has* to face: this is not a prophecy of what will happen but an affirmation of what must be.

The elders, chief priests, and scribes represent the Jewish authorities without any clear awareness of their different functions; here they presumably are the cause of his great suffering and death – only in 18.32 is the role of 'the Gentiles' introduced. His raising *on the third day*, rather than Mark's (8.32) 'after three days', is the language of early Christian confession (cf. I Cor. 15.4; so also Matt. 16.21) and could mean 'shortly' (cf. Hos. 6.2) rather than any temporal precision. These details raise the questions not only whether Jesus anticipated his own death, which in the light of John the Baptist's fate is not improbable, and also did so in the detail here suggested, but also whether he foresaw his vindication in terms of being raised again: how far have the experience and faith of the early church shaped Jesus' words here? If Jesus did so speak, why did his disciples meet his death with such despair and his resurrection with such incredulity?

Mark answers this problem with Peter's protest and Jesus' rebuke (Mark 8.32–33); Luke omits this, perhaps out of kindness to the disciples but more because it enables him immediately to follow Jesus' words with the demand of discipleship now addressed *to everybody*. If confession of Jesus leads to discipleship, discipleship must lead to 'taking up the cross'. In the world of first-century Palestine where crucifixion was a regular and horrific Roman death penalty, to *take up one's cross* would have an immediate and fearsome potency – it was not a metaphor to be used lightly. For the early Christians it would have added meaning in the light of Jesus' own death, but v.22 has not suggested Jesus himself foresaw the manner of his death; again the saying may have been shaped by early Christian experience. *Renounce self* too need not be a metaphor of abstinence from pleasure: to renounce is '*to deny*', and if early Christians did not take the option of denying Jesus the consequence would sometimes be their own death, losing their life '*for my sake*'.

Yet Luke may also be applying these demands to the lives of those who did not face daily persecution, and he adds *day after day* (ctr.

Mark 8.34), so that this becomes an ever present possibility and attitude. *Winning the whole world* might be retaining the security that
silence or the refusal to confess would offer; it might point more
generally to a life which is lived with material gain and existence as
its only goal. Both result in self-destruction, not simply the present
denial of one's true potential and nature but the final destruction of
divine judgment. Only in this context can *the Son of Man* appear in
the glory given the figure of Dan. 7.13–14; that vindication lies
beyond the present suffering, but those who are not prepared to
make common cause with the suffering cannot share in the vindication.

Whereas in Daniel the 'Son of Man' comes to God and receives
glory, here the image seems to be of his coming from God as judge;
this is a Christian development of the theme and led to the idea of
'the second coming' and the future judgment then to be enacted. The
threefold glory, *his, of the Father,* and of *the holy angels,* may also be
developing an earlier idea into a more 'trinitarian' (although NB
'angels') direction (ctr. Mark 8.38). Luke does not explain the relationship between *me and my words* of whom one might be ashamed,
and *the son of man* who will reciprocate, perhaps reproducing an
ambiguity in Jesus' own language: for early Christians the balance
indicated identity.

This section forms a pivot in Mark's Gospel, on which Luke is
heavily dependent; whether it represented a similar turning point
in Jesus' ministry is much discussed. Its function is different in
Luke who still has a long way to go before the final week (Mark 11.1
= Luke 19.29), although as a climax to Jesus' Galilean ministry and to
the question of the identity and discipleship of Jesus it is no less
significant. It is clear that as the story has been retold in the life
of the early church and by the evangelists, it has been shaped by
their own experience and understanding. Luke is exploring how
Jesus is to be confessed and what such confession must mean in the
circumstances of those for whom he wrote. This does not mean, as
has been suggested, that by his 'day after day' he has lost the
urgency which believed that the ultimate test might come any
moment, either in persecution or in the final in-breaking of God's
kingdom, but there is perhaps a tension between the two. Thus the
final words are particularly ambiguous; what does it mean for some
within their life-time to *have seen the kingdom of God*? If Jesus spoke
those words then was he not wrong? Did Luke see the kingdom of
God in the life of the church, or was he reminding his readers that

the 'day after day' could only be sustained in the belief that fulfilment was imminent?

The glory of Jesus
9.28–36

A naive reading might suggest that 'the Transfiguration' which now
follows was a partial or anticipatory fulfilment of the promise of
v.27, but *about a week* would be a banal fulfilment of some not tasting
death, and Luke would not have thought that the kingdom of God
had now been properly seen. Yet what *Peter, John and James* see is not
to be explained purely as an isolated and supranatural event; it
continues the question, 'Who do you say that I am?' and offers a
further answer.

The timing is vague and so is the location; much later the *mountain*
was identified with Tabor, but in the original telling of the story a
mountain was primarily the traditional place for divine revelation or
encounter (Ex. 19.16–19; 34.2–9; I Kings 19.11–13). Again Jesus goes
to pray (cf. v.18 etc.), but what happens is not so much the effect of
his prayer as the decisive event which Jesus' prayer always heralds
in Luke. Luke does not, like Mark (9.2), describe what then occurs as
a metamorphosis or transfiguration, which might evoke pagan
mythology, but more prosaically as the changing of *the appearance of
his face*. Although Luke does not make the comparison explicit, this
may recall Moses, 'the skin of [whose] face was shining' after his
meeting with God on Mt Sinai (Ex. 34.29–35); his *dazzling white*
garments are the clothing of those who share the life of God's kingdom (Dan. 12.3; cf. Luke 24.4). *His glory* which they experience is not
just the brilliance of the scene but the way he is touched with the
divine presence: 'glory' in the OT is the expression of the inexpress-
able presence of God (Ex. 24.15–18; Ezek. 1.28; 43.2–5).

Moses and Elijah, in contrast to Mark 9.4 in chronological order,
share that glory as those who both had had such experiences in the
past and who can now point to the future. Luke does not suggest
that they represent the 'Law and the Prophets', and in fact Moses
could equally well be associated with prophecy; whereas Mark
announces their presence without comment on their role (Mark 9.4),
for Luke they both stand in solidarity with Jesus and allow attention
to focus on what he is now to do. 'His departure, the destiny' in the
REB represents a single noun, 'his Exodus'; while it can be a term
simply for 'death', within the Gospel story it probably combines

75

death, resurrection and final departure in one united act; it may too recall that other 'Exodus' and the deliverance it wrought through Moses. Yet the sense of destiny is strong in that he is *to fulfil* it; that sense has been there from the start (1.32–34; 3.34–35) and in the necessity which marks Jesus' ministry (4.43; 9.22), but with the focus now on its goal *in Jerusalem*, it will govern the next stage of the Gospel narrative (9.51).

Attention so far has focussed on Jesus, but now it turns to the three close disciples, *Peter, John, and James* who had accompanied Jesus. Psychologically, that they should have *been overcome by sleep* may seem strange; perhaps Luke is apologizing for Peter's rather bemused response, but he may also be stressing that this was a real experience, as he did when describing Moses and Elijah as *two men*, and not just a vision or hallucination. Peter's suggestion of building *three shelters* has prompted much speculation; that he wishes to prolong the experience is unlikely: why 'three' and why not also for the disciples as observers? The 'shelters' would be temporary accommodation and some have seen a connection with the Feast of Tabernacles when such 'booths' were used in commemoration of Israel's sojourning in the wilderness. There is also the idea that those who share God's kingdom also have a 'dwelling' there (Luke 16.9; Rev. 13.6). Yet perhaps the words have come to Luke from the earlier tradition, and he also did not really know what Peter was saying. Now the suggestion, with its attention on all three figures, serves to contrast what follows. A *cloud* too is part of the traditional 'scenery' of divine presence (Ex. 24.15–18; Ezek. 1.4; 10.3–4), although it is not clear whether the *they* who *entered* it are the three men or the disciples also, whose fear would be entirely appropriate.

The *voice* which now speaks turns all attention on Jesus alone; Moses and Elijah are not now rejected but they are ignored, for Jesus is given a status which no longer keeps him on a level with them, '*This is my Son*'. The words recall those spoken at the baptism (3.22 and see note, and Ps. 2.7), but whereas there they were addressed to Jesus here they are a declaration at least to the disciples; the further epithet, *my chosen*, recalls Isa. 42.1 there spoken not of 'the Son' but of 'the servant', although Moses is similarly described in Ps. 105.26. The epithet need not designate Jesus as Messiah, and the so-called 'servant passages' of Isaiah were not seen as messianic by Jews of the time, although they were by later Christians. The further exhortation, *listen to him*, evokes Deut. 18.15 spoken of 'the prophet like Moses', which was interpreted of an expected figure in some circles.

Thus the declaration does not appeal to a single expectation and say it is now fulfilled in Jesus; different images are being combined, whether or not for the first time, and are used to centre all attention on Jesus and provide yet another answer to Herod's initial question.

The origins of the 'Transfiguration story' are now lost to us, and there is little to be gained by discussing mystical, visionary or hallucinatory experiences, whether by Jesus or by his companions. It has been compared to the resurrection narratives, but it is too distinct merely to have been such a story misplaced or retrojected into Jesus' lifetime. For the evangelists it is inseparable from the confession of Jesus by his closest disciples and from his own teaching of the suffering he, and those who follow him, must face. It serves to lift the veil for a moment, ostensibly for the disciples although it leaves no lasting effect, but more importantly for the readers, who again are confirmed in their understanding of Jesus' true identity, but also reminded what this identity must entail. That is why for Luke Jesus' 'departure in Jerusalem' is not a temporary misfortune to be more than compensated for by glory, but lies at the heart of what his glory is about.

Discipleship and power
9.37-50

That Jesus is for ever shadowed by *large crowds* who demand his attention after periods away or teaching, and who seek healing, has become a regular part of Luke's picture. Here the healing is to be of a boy, whom Luke alone again identifies as an *only child* (cf. 7.12; 8.42), suffering from what we would probably identify as epilepsy but first-century people understood as seizure by an unclean spirit. The violent *convulsions* the boy suffers as he approaches Jesus probably are to be seen as the *demon*'s recognition of Jesus' identity and greater power (cf. 8.28). Jesus heals the boy and restored him to his father, as he did the young man of Nain to his mother (7.15), although Luke merely describes and does not remark on the way Jesus' healings were thus not just of the individual but of the family or society to which they belonged. Characteristically he closes the miracle story with the universal awe (cf. 5.26); *it is the greatness of God* that they marvel at, but the preceding stories have begun to explore the relation between God and the Jesus whose actions are described (cf. also 8.39).

The story is made distinctive because, in Jesus' absence, the man had first approached his *disciples*, who, despite the power given in 9.1, were unable to *drive out* the demon. Jesus' despairing cry of *an unbelieving and perverse generation* is the more powerful because the reader at least knows that there may not be much more time while he is with them. Yet was Jesus addressing the crowds who still sought such miracles regardless of who performed them, or the disciples whose failure is implicitly ascribed to their unbelief, or both together, who in their need and their incapacity underline the pathos of the brevity of Jesus' ministry? Luke leaves the answer unclear, particularly as he omits Mark's emphasis on faith and, more surprisingly, on the necessity of prayer (Mark 9.22–24, 28–29). Instead he uses the response of *general astonishment* as the setting for a further announcement of the 'handing over' of *the Son of Man* (cf. 9.22). The solemn introductory exhortation to *Listen*, the lack of any details, so that it is not 'how' or 'by whom' that matters but only *the power* (lit. 'the hands') *of men*, and the absence of any assurance of final vindication, help deepen the mood of urgency.

For those who wonder why Jesus' prophecies of his coming death still left his disciples so unprepared when it happened, their inability to *understand what he said* offers some solution, and, since Luke alone (ctr. Mark 9.32) says it *had been hidden from them*, some excuse. In 8.9–10 insight had been granted the disciples, and it was only the others who could have no understanding; now when it comes to Jesus' 'destiny' (cf. 9.30), they too are among the 'outsiders', and Jesus stands alone. Although discipleship has become and will continue as an important theme, it is always vulnerable and can never claim total confidence or superiority.

Two more disconnected incidents underline this. In the first their confidence leads them to vye for priority. Jesus, presented as one who need not even ask what was *going on in their minds*, responds through an acted parable. Children had no independent rights; they could not return a favour or offer honour or patronage. Jesus does not question this, neither is this incident really about children as such; it is about status not consisting in who or what the disciples are or can do, but only in how they reflect and represent Jesus himself. Even a child, without status, can be one who represents Jesus and is to be treated as such. In ancient thought a person's representative carried their honour and status; the respect or the dishonour accorded the representative was deemed as directed to the one who sent them: here Jesus' status is not his own but only that of one who represents God, but this means that the respect or dishonour accorded any through whom he is represented is ultimately given to God. In this light even the most insignificant is as *the greatest*.

The second incident has to be seen in the same setting, for in 11.23, in another context, the apparent opposite can be said. Here the disciples wish to restrict to themselves the right to represent Jesus. Exorcism was a practice in the time of Jesus (cf. Luke 11.19), and a particular name or power of proven efficacy might be evoked by practitioners (cf. Acts 19.13). Here Jesus prohibits any attempt to claim exclusive rights to his authority.

These two incidents are linked by the phrase *in my/your name* which is probably why they have been remembered and told together. In Luke's telling they form a suggestive conclusion to a section which has centred on discipleship, and on the question of Jesus' identity. Although Luke's account of a miracle-working Jesus, dogged by crowds who react with wonder and amazement, can sound triumphalist, such triumphalism, either for Jesus or for those who acknowledge his identity and seek to be disciples, is sternly qualified in the light of what lies ahead. Thus the scene is set for a new stage in Luke's story.

The Journey to Jerusalem
9.51–11.13

So far Jesus' ministry has been centred in Galilee and in broad outline has followed Mark's account. Now Luke introduces a new phase
as Jesus *set his face resolutely towards Jerusalem*. It is, however, only in
19.28 that he will finally reach the outskirts of the city. This central
section of Luke's narrative is often called 'the Travel account'. In
practice the sense of a journey only appears occasionally (9.51,53;
13.22,33;17.11;18.31;19.11), and it is not possible to reconstruct a
route or time-scale, neither of which may have been very clear to
Luke himself. Neither are the contents of the section a coherent or
connected sequence: various attempts have been made to find overall themes or patterns, usually of a literary rather than an ambula-
tory character, but none have won unreserved acceptance. The bulk
of the material, particularly until 18.14, is not found in Mark, and
Luke seems to have used this as an occasion for including material
he had separate access to, some of which is also found in Matthew.
Miracles play little role, and so from the earlier section it is teaching
on discipleship and a growing sense of conflict between Jesus
and 'the authorities' which provide the dominant themes; this is
inevitable in so far as the Gospel now directs our attention towards
Jerusalem, although, as we have seen, this is often subdued.

Commitment to the journey
9.51–62

Moses and Elijah had spoken of Jesus' 'departure' at Jerusalem
(9.31), but now Luke prepares for him to be *taken up*; the REB's
addition of '*to heaven*' might suggest that Luke saw the ascension as
the goal of Jesus' journey (cf. Acts 1.11, 22), and certainly the
language does recall those OT worthies who had not died but had
been taken directly up to heaven, Enoch, Elijah and, according to
later tradition, Moses (Gen. 5.24; II Kings 5.24; 2.11). However, in the

light of the earlier events, 'taking up' must encompass his death and resurrection also as part of a single act, and not, therefore as a disaster followed by its speedy resolution. Jesus is not the victim of circumstances or of power politics but retains the initiative.

The hostility between the Samaritans and the Jews was already of long-standing by the time of Jesus, although its true origins are now obscure; attacks in Samaria on Jewish pilgrims heading for Jerusalem were not unknown, and many would make a detour down the other side of the Jordan in order to avoid going through Samaria – although Luke by only having Jesus go *on to another village* may not have realized this would be necessary. For Luke the hostility with which Jesus is immediately met as soon as he *set his face resolutely towards Jerusalem* prefigures the gradually intensifying opposition he will face as his journey reaches its goal. It will not only be a mark of the Samaritans, who will also offer positive examples. James' and John's response, which some, but not Luke, have seen as appropriate to their nick-name 'sons of Thunder' (Mark 3.17), recalls the reaction of Elijah to those who opposed him (II Kings 1.9–12); Jesus rejects such a response, as later he will reject the use of the sword to defend him (22.52–3). Discipleship, or following along *the road* or *'way'* (cf. 24.32; Acts 9.2), demands a very different set of attitudes.

These demands are illustrated by three examples, the first two of which are also found in Matthew (8.19–22), but which Luke has carefully structured: in the first and third a man offers to follow and Jesus replies with a parable from nature, in the second Jesus calls someone and abruptly rejects his excuses. In each the emphasis is on the word of Jesus, and we know nothing of the individual, his background or his final response; nothing suggests that he was insincere in his discipleship, and the requests of the second and third were hardly unreasonable. The first is the barest and introduces a further use of *the Son of Man* (cf. pp.42 f.): this would be a good example of the phrase as an indirect way of self-reference, but even if this was its original force, after Luke's earlier uses of the phrase of the one who must face suffering (9.22) it gains added resonance; it is not just the travelling Jesus who has no home, for he will continue to receive hospitality, but as the one destined to suffer his only goal is fulfilment of that calling. If there is any covert reference to Herod 'that fox' (cf. 13.32), it is to one who holds political power and whom those who seek power must cultivate.

The second sought only to fulfil his filial duty; it is true that this might entail a delay of unknown length, but even so it is rooted in the contemporary recognition of a person's primary and total obligation to his or her parents, among which proper burial was essential. Jesus' reply sounds harsh; unless he is being deliberately dismissive of such obligations, improbable in such a society, he is saying 'let the spiritually dead bury the physically dead': the urgency of the kingdom must over-ride even family commitments (cf. 14.26). The third recalls Elisha called to follow Elijah (I Kings 19.19–21); to *say goodbye* would not just be a farewell but to seek a parental blessing and would be a necessary act of honour to parents, even by an adult. The point is not that the parent might refuse permission or blessing but again that natural commitments are subordinated to the demand to follow Jesus. For many of Luke's readers, settled in communities and homes, such stories would be as uncomfortable as to the modern reader – and there is an alternative tradition within the NT which reinforces familial obligations (Col. 3.18–22). In time of persecution or hardship they would come into their own, and Jesus' own ministry tested the allegiance of many to breaking point. In Luke's narrative context they intensify the seriousness of this journey to Jerusalem, even if it is a seriousness Luke does not maintain in what follows. Their uncompromising demand cannot be explained away and refuses any domestication of the call to discipleship.

The sending of the seventy-two
10.1–16

Luke's account of Jesus' journey to Jerusalem can be compared to Deuteronomy's narrative of the journey to the promised land. Just as Moses sent men ahead to seek peaceful passage or bring back reports (Deut. 2.16; 1.22–25), so too does Jesus (9.52). He now does so again, *in pairs* (cf. Num. 13.23) perhaps as a guarantee of their witness (Deut. 19.15). Their number, *seventy-two* has slightly better textual support than 'seventy', could recall Moses' choice of seventy elders to share his burden (Num. 11.16–17, 24–25), but this is not really the task of those whom Jesus appoints. Instead they may evoke the number of nations in the world according to Gen. 10.2–31; this would support the suggestion that their mission prefigures that to the Gentiles by the church, while that of the Twelve (9.1–6, see note) prefigures the mission to the Jews. However, here the seventy-two visit only *every town and place* Jesus would, i.e. within the borders of Israel. As with that earlier mission of the Twelve, it is debateable how far their sending prefigures that of the church: although the picture of *labourers to bring in the harvest* has become a missionary metaphor, it may originally have evoked ideas of eschatological judgment (cf. Luke 3.17; Matt. 13.30), and the prohibition of any provision for the journey or of the giving of casual *greetings* breathes a note of final urgency. However, as with the Twelve (9.4), their acceptance of both lodging and sustenance does fit the conditions of early Christian mission (I Cor. 9.3–38; II Cor. 11.7–9), as too does travel in pairs (Acts 15.36, 39–40; Rom. 16.3, 7, 12); the image which sees them as *lambs among wolves* also anticipates later hostilities.

Luke appears to have put together the story of the sending out of the seventy-two from his sources regarding the mission of the Twelve, for his account parallels Matt. 9.37–38; 10.9–16. He gives this group no name, not even 'disciples' (although cf. v.23), neither does Jesus bestow on them any special power (ctr. 9.1), and unlike the Twelve they do not appear again in his narrative or prefigure any group within the life of the early church. They prepare the way for Jesus and do what he does, *heal the sick* and proclaim the kingdom; now that proclamation has a specific content (see note on 9.2), *the kingdom of God has come upon you.* In Mark's Gospel this was Jesus' own message (Mark 1.15), but Luke had omitted it at that point in his narrative; the nuance of the verb, which has been much debated, is probably one of imminence (cf. NRSV 'come near') rather than presence, as implied by REB in v.11. Thus they intensify the sense of urgency which has begun to breathe through Luke's narrative; this is no casual journey, nor even a conventional pilgrimage to Jerusalem, but the determined and unrepeatable movement towards eschatological dénoument.

It is for this reason that not only are the messengers to *wipe off . . . the very dust* of an unreceptive town (cf.9.5), but Jesus adds a severe word of judgment. *Sodom* had been judged with proverbial severity (Gen. 19.24), yet its annihilation would seem far more bearable than the judgment prepared *on that day* – REB adds an interpretative of *judgment* – for such a town. The almost prophetic 'woe', *Alas for you*, (cf. Amos 6.1–7; Hab. 2.6–7), to the Galilean cities of *Chorazin* and *Bethsaida* is linked more by the common theme of impending judgment than by logical connection: it disrupts the address to the seventy-two and Matthew gives it another setting (Matt. 11.20–24). Despite the earlier narrative evidence to the contrary, it is assumed that these cities along with *Capernaum* had failed to respond to Jesus' healings: *Tyre and Sidon*, Gentile cities, had not had the opportunity, but although their wickedness was proverbial (Isa. 23; Ezek. 26–28) it is again assumed that they would have *repented, sitting in sackcloth and ashes* (cf. Nineveh in Jonah 3.5–9). 'Isaiah' had denounced the arrogance of the king of Babylon in the vivid imagery of Lucifer who was ejected from heaven for his pride (Isa. 14.12–15); now the same judgment is levelled not against the alien oppressor but against *Capernaum*, site of many of Jesus' miracles. By including this passage here, Luke anticipates the ultimate failure of Jesus' ministry in Galilee; he also gives a framework in which the mission of the seventy-two, and perhaps the mission of the church, is to be understood. The announcement of the kingdom of God is an invitation for people to acknowledge God's sovereignty; their refusal to do so is not a light matter: behind the messengers lies the authority of their commissioner, Jesus, and behind him that of *the One who sent* him, God (cf. on 9.48).

The eschatological vision
10.17–24

The eschatological framework is reinforced by Jesus' response to the messengers' *jubilant* return. Jesus' own exorcisms are clearly represented as a victorious encounter with the powers of evil (cf. 8.28); the success of the seventy-two over *demons* is to be understood in the same way for they achieved it not by their own power but through that of Jesus. Isa. 14.12 again provides the imagery of that victory, *Satan* falling *from heaven*; this means that Jesus may be invoking this OT symbolism rather than claiming a personal visionary experience. Satan is the *enemy* who has his own *power* (= REB *force*, cf. Luke 4.14, 36; 9.1), typically symbolized by *snakes and scorpions* such as threatened Israel in the wilderness (Deut. 8.15). The *authority* (= REB *power*) Jesus gives them is none other than the authority he holds and gives over evil forces (cf. 9.1); yet Jesus' own fate shows that the freedom from *harm* they are promised is not a guarantee of physical security and comfort, but the assurance that the forces of evil will not ultimately prove stronger. The idea of a heavenly citizen-list or 'book of the living' in which the names of the faithful are written even before they die and face judgment was a familiar one (Dan. 12.1; Ps. 69.28; Ex. 32.32); more important than manifestations of power or of the defeat of evil is the assurance of being among those who belong to God. In this passage the balance between an imminent judgment yet to be revealed and the present irreversible victory over evil is a fine one; imminence results in dire threat, victory already assured can open the door to a deterministic confidence.

Luke excludes any such self-congratulation by the seventy-two or by later believers by reminding them that God is the source of all insight and confidence. Jesus' profound spiritual exultation, unparalleled in the Gospel narrative, gives weight to the significance of the moment and to his words. He does not merely *thank* (REB) but *acknowledges with praise* God who in sovereign power delights – *choice* in v.21 is so translated at 2.14 (cf. 3.22) – to act in ways that counter human expectation. *Hiding* and *revealing* are in the biblical tradition, particularly in apocalyptic, the means by which God makes known his purpose according to the divine plan (Deut. 29.29; Dan. 3.28–30). The *learned and wise* are those who might expect divine insight (Dan. 2.21; Sir. 3.29), but instead it is those who can claim nothing for themselves, *the simple* or 'babes', who have experienced what God is doing: *these things* in context can only refer to all that their mission points to. This is a theme developed by Paul for whom it was best exemplified by the 'scandal' of the crucifixion (I Cor. 1.17 – 3.20).

For the first time in Luke Jesus addresses God as *Father* (cf. 11.2); much has been written about this appellation, sometimes claiming, wrongly, that it expresses a child-like intimacy unknown in contemporary Judaism. In fact the term comes more rarely on the lips of Jesus than is often assumed, and it is hazardous to use it to reconstruct Jesus' own self-awareness. Here it is followed by what has sometimes been called 'a thunderbolt from a Johannine heaven': Jesus' self-description as *the Son* who is at once both exclusively dependent on *the Father*, and yet can claim an almost reciprocal equality with him, has no parallel elsewhere in the Synoptics, but far closer ones in the Fourth Gospel (cf. John 10.15; 17.2). For some its presence here means that Jesus could sometimes have spoken as he does in John, for others it betrays an attempt by the early Christians to interpret Jesus' relationship with God, which John took much further by projecting it on to the mouth of Jesus himself. That relationship is explored not in terms of 'being' or essence but in terms of knowledge: the *everything* that is *entrusted* is in context probably not absolute or 'all power', but all that is to be revealed. Whereas Jesus' identity as Son might be a mystery to all but the Father, it could hardly be said that so far no one had known God, for the OT is founded on God's self-revelation to Israel and her responsive 'knowledge' in obedience; but now Jesus' ministry and proclamation are seen as the ultimate and unrepeatable call to respond, and so Jesus cannot merely be one who is sent by God (cf. 9.48; 10.16), but must have the unsurpassable authority to represent him.

The 'beatitude' (cf. 6.20; 7.23) to *his disciples* – it is not clear whether this includes the seventy-two since he is newly *alone* – reaffirms the present moment as the fulfilment of God's long-awaited promises. What they *see* and *hear* no longer refers only to the successful mission but to Jesus' ministry (cf. 7.22); Luke, living beyond that time, seeks both to reaffirm that in Jesus God's promises had been fulfilled, and yet to retain for himself and his church the urgent expectation of a final summons.

Love and the neighbour
10.25–37

That a *lawyer* (cf. 7.30) should want *to test* Jesus sounds an ominous note which contrasts with the preceding triumph: Mark (12.28–31) and Matthew (22.34–40) set a similar scene in the final week of Jesus' life. Whereas there the question concerns the commandments, here, as in 18.18, it is the conditions for *eternal life*, a concept not found earlier in Luke but which clearly indicates participation in God's promised salvation. Jesus assumes that the answer is to be found in scripture, in the 'Old Testament', for *the law* was given to give life (Deut. 8.1; 28.1–14). It is the lawyer, not Jesus as in Mark and Matthew, who implicitly summarizes the Law by combining two separate passages, Deut. 6.5 with its call to total love of God, which belongs to the foundational confession of Judaism, the *shema'* (Deut. 6.4–9), and Lev. 19.18 with its command to *love your neighbour as yourself.* Whether these two passages had been brought together earlier in Jewish thought is debated, and here they are treated as a single unit.

Although the significance of the lawyer's answer lies in his bringing together love of God and of neighbour, only the second is picked up, suggesting that the parable that follows was originally independent of the initial question. In its context the *neighbour* of Lev. 19.18 means the fellow Israelite who is not to be abused or taken advantage of; there is no implication that all others are to be hated, and there is little evidence of much debate about the application of the verse. Yet it is this that the lawyer asks, again with Luke suggesting his motives were less than friendly.

The familiarity of the parable, which comes only in Luke, means that it has lost some of its power to shock. It is also markedly devoid of explanation; knowledge of the different characters, the *priest*, the *Levite*, and the *Samaritan* is assumed. Although the dangers of the road *from Jerusalem down to Jericho* were probably well-known, the motives of the first two in going *past on the other side* are not explained: in particular it does not say, as commentators have been too quick to, that temple duties and hence the obligations of the Law were what kept them from obedience to the law of love. Rather, the priest and Levite are those who are extreme examples of the fellow Israelite, set up to contrast more sharply the archetypal outsider, the Samaritan (see 9.52 and note). Later, more allegorically minded, commentators found hints of the atonement and the sacraments in the details of the Samaritan's care for the injured man and, inevitably, Jesus embodied in 'the good Samaritan' himself. The details serve rather to give dramatic expression to the shape of the parable, the abrupt speed of those who ignore the man is followed by a slowing in pace as the hearer/observer is forced to acknowledge who in fact *was neighbour*. There is a subtle irony perhaps in the lawyer's failure even then to name him as 'the Samaritan' but only the more banal *the one who showed him kindness*. That answer implies only that to be a neighbour is to show kindness, and Jesus' response that he should *'Go and do as he did'*, reaffirms that point. Yet this hides the awkwardness of the parable in its context: the lawyer wants to know who is the neighbour whom he should love, and we expect the answer to be, 'Even a Samaritan if in need'; instead it is the victim who is in need and the Samaritan who 'loves', treating him as neighbour. We are reminded of the Samaritan leper who alone returns to give thanks for his healing (17.11–19), another Lukan 'special' which may hint at the future reception of the gospel by the Samaritans (Acts 8.4–25). This may confirm the suggestion above that the parable was originally independent; yet in its present context it does allow for a double shock not explicitly brought out by Luke: it is one thing to learn that the command to love encompasses anyone who is in need, even the outsider or enemy; it is far more disturbing to have to acknowledge that the enemy or outsider may be more quick to show love than those who are certainly fellow-'insiders'.

Martha and Mary
10.38–42

This story is again unique to Luke, although Martha and Mary are also known through John 11–12; there they are located in Bethany outside Jerusalem, but that can hardly be the *village* where they welcome Jesus here. The contrast between the active Martha and the 'contemplative' Mary readily appeals to the imagination, particularly as the description of Jesus as *the Lord* invites the reader to project their responses into the lives of later believers who so acknowledge Jesus. Yet what is the force of the contrast? Mary listened to *his word* (not *words* as in REB); Martha was *distracted* not *by her many tasks* as in the REB but *by much service* or *ministry (diakonia)*, and objected that she had been left on her own *to serve* or *minister* (cf. 4.39 and note), hardly negative concerns and significantly attributed to a woman. There is a not dissimilar tension in Luke's account of the early church when the 'twelve' decide to concentrate on 'the word' and appoint seven others to 'wait on tables' (Acts 6.1–6), but there both tasks are 'ministries' or 'service'.

Jesus' answer makes a contrast not between *anxious concern* (better than *fretting*) and quietude, but between *many things* and *one thing*, which alone *is necessary*. This does not mean that Jesus prefers a simpler meal, which could be implied by the alternative but probably secondary reading, 'only a few things' (see REB footnote). When Jesus says Mary *has chosen* 'the good portion', Martha's choice is not being excluded as is suggested by the REB's translation *the best*. Yet the story does imply that a whole-hearted commitment to Jesus and to 'the word' or the gospel has priority over all other things, even over ministry. It is significant that in John 12 it is again Mary whose total devotion to Jesus is defended by him as something she is to keep. Such total commitment continues the note of eschatological urgency which characterizes the earlier part of the chapter; its application in the continuing life of the church may already have been a problem in Luke's own time.

Teaching on prayer
11.1–13

Luke has made a point of presenting Jesus as one whose ministry is shaped by prayer (6.12; 9.18, 29). Now such prayer is to be the hallmark of those who follow him, although the sense both of the journey and of any connection with the preceding incidents is weak. Whereas in Matthew (6.5–13) Jesus offers his disciples this prayer as a model which avoids pretension and 'babbling', in Luke it distinguishes them from others such as the *disciples* whom *John taught* also to pray (cf. 5.33). The Lukan form of 'the Lord's Prayer' is much more succinct than the Matthean, which is both more Jewish and also more 'liturgical', as reflected by its use in subsequent Christian worship. Probably each evangelist inherited a different tradition, and any original setting and form in the ministry of Jesus are now lost to us.

Luke's direct and easily memorizable prayer consists of five petitions, two concerned with God, three with the disciples' needs. Perhaps more than Matthew, these needs are those of the present, in the *each day* of the third request, but the main goal of the prayer is to the future. God's *name* represents God's very self, but God's name only is, or will be, *hallowed* when God is recognized as 'the Holy One', when there is nothing and no one to detract from God being known for what God is: Ezek. 36.20–28 encapsulates this hope best. Only God can answer that prayer, which will also be the answer to the request *your kingdom come*. The hope and the appeal to God can be easily paralleled in Jewish prayers. Despite this it is often said that the opening address, *Father*, without Matthew's qualifying 'our', signals a radical departure from Jewish attitudes to God: Rom. 8.15 and Gal. 4.6 preserve the Aramaic 'Abba', the child's address to a father, as the treasured form in which Christians pray to God; in Mark 14.36 Jesus uses the same form, and it has often been stated that this betrays an intimacy unique to Jesus (cf. 10.21), but which he also opened to his disciples. However, suggestions that 'Abba' would best be translated as 'Daddy' are a modern sentimentalizing, while the term is addressed to God within Judaism. Luke's *Father* is not 'Abba' and although it may be unusually abrupt as an address to God in prayer, it is not 'uniquely Christian'; although the prayer was to become that, it, as much as any of Jesus' teaching, is as Jewish as was Jesus himself.

Some manuscripts expand the prayer to agree with Matthew while, perhaps with a greater claim to authenticity, others add a prayer for the coming of the Holy Spirit to cleanse; yet the original Lukan form is probably the briefest, following these appeals for the dawning of God's kingdom with what appears to be a far more mundane, if very necessary, request for *daily bread*. In fact, the word translated 'daily' is obscure, and has been variously understood as 'spiritual', as 'essential', as 'for today', or as 'for tomorrow'; the last translation might be taken literally or as a reference to the 'tomorrow' of God's kingdom, while 'essential' could refer either to material needs or carry a deeper allusion to the eucharist – as it was sometimes understood in the early church. Luke's *each day* suggests he understood the term to mean the bread of human sustenance, with 'for tomorrow' being perhaps slightly the most convincing derivation. There is an unmistakeable echo of the story of the giving of manna in the wilderness (Ex. 16), which itself became a symbol in Jewish hope of God's future meeting of all human need.

In the prayer for forgiveness Luke sees failure in personal relations as 'debts', hidden by the translation *who have done us wrong*; for Matthew the same is true of our wrongs before God, but Luke prefers the more general *sins*, perhaps out of consideration for his Greek readers for whom this biblical idea would be strange. While he does not imply that divine forgiveness is conditional upon human, the two are bound together: as those who offer this prayer *we* do – or can only! – *forgive* in the same understanding of God that inspires the request that God *forgive us*. Throughout these petitions there is the guiding theme that humankind is totally dependent on God's activity, both for the present and for the future manifestation of God's sovereignty. Only so can be understood the final request: within the biblical tradition God does *put* people *to the test*, but not as punishment, nor as a sign of their existing inadequacy – the story of manna is one such occasion (Ex. 16.4). The distinction between God causing and God permitting 'temptation', the more familiar translation, is for the most part a foreign one to the biblical tradition, despite the introduction to the story of Job; instead it is assumed that 'testing' has an inevitable place in the working out of God's purpose, both for individuals but also on a cosmic scale: a final 'test', or 'trial', is often expected to precede the coming of God's kingdom (cf. Rev. 3.9; II Peter 2.9, and perhaps Luke 8.13). Despite the opening petitions for that kingdom it may be this 'test' to which the disciples are to ask God not to '*bring*', better than 'put', them, for human weakness will not be able to stand firm.

Luke follows with a parable still on the theme of prayer which draws on daily experience. Hospitality to an unexpected guest at any hour of day or night would be a self-evident obligation; the *three loaves* would be rolls sufficient for a meal and, no doubt, would be repaid as soon as the daily baking were done. In message the story appears similar to that in 18.1–8: there the judge relents in face of the insistence of the widow, here perhaps we are intended to assume that the *friend* has refused to accept a rebuff and has forced acquiescence through his *persistence*. The word could also be translated *'shamelessness'* which might suggest instead that it was the transparency of the request and the churlishness of refusing it that was most persuasive. In either case we cannot press the parable as a model of God's character or motivation in responding to human requests. It serves rather as a vivid reinforcement of the assurance that prayer is both necessary and valid, for only if the prayer is made can it be answered. The assurance that it will be answered of course leaves untouched the dilemma of those who *knock* and receive no reply, but it would be wrong here to propose solutions to a problem that Luke does not acknowledge.

Instead Luke, like Matthew (7.7–11), follows the certainty of receiving with a series of examples which in fact stress what rather than that God gives in answer to prayer. The *snake* perhaps could be mistaken for a *fish*, or the curled up *scorpion* for an *egg*, but any normal parent – Luke instinctively sees a *father* and *his son* as the norm – would only give what was beneficial. Human parentage is not the measure of what it means to call God *Father*, but God cannot be less than what we recognize as what is normal or right. Yet Luke does not only see God as giving *good things* like the human father, as does Matthew; God gives *the Holy Spirit*. Although Luke sees the spirit as effective in Jesus' ministry, it is not a central part of Jesus' teaching, and here he may be thinking of the future experience of the church. *Heavenly* would be better translated *'from heaven'* and perhaps it is God who gives 'from heaven' this gift; whatever the other dilemmas of answered, or unanswered, prayer, for Luke the assurance of the gift of the *holy spirit* within the life of the church is the chief mark of their discipleship of Jesus and their sharing in his prayer.

Opposition and Questioning
11.14–13.21

One of the themes of the 'travel narrative' is the growth of opposition to Jesus: as some respond in faith and are led further into the meaning of discipleship, others challenge Jesus and begin to point the way towards his final rejection. Beyond this there is no strong sense of continuity through the material or of Jesus' physical journey.

The presence of the one who is greater
11.14–36

Again the material in this section hangs only loosely together although, except for the 'interruption' in vv.27–28, it broadly deals with two false responses to Jesus. The first reflects a potential, and probably real, difficulty felt by some, the significance of the exorcisms Jesus performed. Even John, who does not recount any exorcisms, retains the charge that Jesus was demon-possessed (John 8.52; 10.20), while Mark's account (Mark 3.23–30) probably is a separate tradition from that Luke gives. Here the healing of *a dumb man*, which is understood as an exorcism, evokes not only the customary astonishment (5.26; 7.16; 9.43) but also the charge that Jesus' control over *demons* testifies to his access to sovereign demonic power: *Beelzebul*, although not otherwise known in this context, appears to go back to a name of the Canaanite deity Baal, 'Baal' or 'Lord of the heights', but by the first century it had presumably entered the vocabulary of demonology. Jesus, whose own sovereignty is displayed by his knowledge of their thoughts gives a four-fold answer, ignoring the demand for *a sign from heaven* which anticipates the second section in vv.29–32.

What they are suggesting would in effect mean that the demonic world was deliberately engaged in a destructive civil war: *Satan* represents both the ultimate authority within and the totality of that world. Exorcism of demons by the prince of demons would be both self-defeating and presage a collapse of which there was no supporting evidence. The second reposte assumes the successful activity of other Jewish exorcists (cf. 9.49): were the objectors prepared to similarly dismiss their own practitioners or *people*? However, Jesus' activity is not on a par with theirs – and this is an assertion and not a demonstration – for he is manifesting the deliverance wrought by God: in Ex. 8.19 the plague of gnats is attributed to *the finger of God*, and elsewhere God saves by his right hand or his arm (Ex. 15.6; Ps. 77.15). Despite Luke's usual interest in the spirit he does not introduce it here as does Matthew (Matt. 12.28); his language of deliverance comes from the OT as he sees now the certainty of the ultimate deliverance. Even more than in 10.9 (see note), the *kingdom* is here not just anticipated but makes its presence felt; in the exorcisms God's sovereignty is unequivocally experienced, although Luke would not say that this left nothing more for the future.

The final argument takes the form of a parable: Satan was the *strong man* who held in thrall *his possessions*; but now what they are seeing is his routing by *someone stronger*, the same term which John the Baptist had used of Jesus as the one to come (3.16). Despite the earlier denial of any evidence of the collapse brought on by civil war, Satan's rule is here declared to be at an end.

The issue has been stated in bald alternatives, either Satan or Jesus as agent of God's deliverance. Despite the apparently contradictory saying in 9.50, in this context those who observe must decide where they stand; no neutrality is possible and not to join with Jesus is to oppose him and to counter all he does.

There follows a brief reflection on the meaning of exorcism for the beneficiary; it is not enough simply to be rid of the possessing power, for there remains the potential for a return to a yet more extreme state: *seven* is the number of completeness. The imagery of the *spirit* seeking a welcoming habitation assumes the ideas about the demonic, who normally inhabited *desert sands*, current at the time. Nothing is said explicitly as to how the danger is to be avoided, although it is usually assumed that the point is that an alternative 'owner' or indwelling power must be invited in. It is also too easy to give the passage a psychologizing message or to refer it to the power of sin; Luke does not do this, and it remains as an open warning, inviting reflection.

Only Luke recounts the incident which follows and which bears little obvious relation to the surrounding issues. It turns to the significance of Jesus' family, or here his mother, described in the vivid imagery of *the womb that carried you and the breasts which suckled you* (cf. 23.29; Gen. 49.25). Jesus does not necessarily deny his mother any place – the word translated by REB *No* is rather more equivocal; but more important than any physical bond with Jesus is response to him as the one who speaks *the word of God*. The same point was made in 8. 19–21 (see note), but here it recalls Elizabeth's blessing of Mary in 1.42, 45: it was Mary's belief in God's promise and not her physical bearing of Jesus which would ensure that 'all generations' would count her 'blessed' (1.48). The *word of God* was to encapsulate the whole Christian message (Acts 4.29, 31; I Cor. 14.36), and so, perhaps, for Luke it is not who Jesus is or relationship to him which matters, but commitment to the Christian proclamation.

The second false response, which also figures widely in the Gospel traditions (cf. John 2.18; Mark 8.11–12), is the demand for *a sign* (cf. v.16), a visible demonstration authenticating the claim to speak and act for God. Signs not only supported some of the prophets' messages (cf. Jer. 19), but were also associated with the deliverance from Egypt, although the people were castigated for their failure to respond to them (Ps. 78.32; Deut. 7.19). Jesus' response varies in the different traditions; here he offers only *the sign of Jonah* but gives no further elaboration. Matthew (12.40) understands this as a reference to the three-day incarceration in the whale as an anticipation of the burial and resurrection of Jesus, but Luke thinks only of Jonah as someone who preached *to the Ninevites*: he offered only his message and it was for them to respond or to ignore it. Jesus as *Son of Man* (see p.42 f.) is as ambiguous a figure as was Jonah. In fact *the men of Nineveh* did *repent at the preaching of Jonah*, and so they will act not just as a model for the present *generation* but as a source of reproof. Luke introduces a second such reproof, although he interposes her in her chronologically prior position: *the queen of the south* or of Sheba had made a long and arduous journey merely to respond to the famed *wisdom of Solomon* (I Kings 10.1–13). In the future judgment she and the Ninevites, both Gentiles who, however, responded, will be 'evidence for the prosecution' against those of Jesus' generation who refused to respond to him, who is *greater* than both Jonah and Solomon. The queen of Sheba's 'response' may seem a poor model, but her journey brings into the picture the kingship of Solomon, while Jonah represents prophecy: Jesus combines in himself both these identities, as well as the wisdom she came to hear (cf. 7.35).

The final sayings about light act as an awkward conclusion;

perhaps they reinforce the demand for a whole-hearted positive response. They also offer a warning, contrasting with the people who failed to see and respond. Luke has already given a similar saying about the need to display light (8.16); the additional sayings assume not just that the eye is used to perceive light but also that it acts as a channel for light to or from the body. There can be no half-measures or equivocacy in the response to Jesus, and the responsibility for choice lies with those who listen.

Conflict with the Pharisees and lawyers
11.37–54

The scene which follows is remarkable for its abrupt changes and lack of any real explanation of what is happening. The scene is again *a meal* to which Jesus is invited by a Pharisee, but again, as in 7.36–50, the mood swiftly changes from conviviality to aggression. The provocation appears minimal: *washing before the meal* would be to fulfil the requirements of purity, not cleanliness, and technically would only be necessary after incurring defilement for those who applied such concerns to their daily lives. Whether this included others besides the Pharisees is disputed, but Mark 7.1–8, a passage omitted by Luke, also records a dispute about it. Jesus responds with an uncompromising denunciation of *you Pharisees*, leading into three *woes*, which are matched by a further three *woes* against the *lawyers*, when one of them foolhardily objects to the charges which implicitly include them also. It is hard to avoid the feeling that the scene is stylized, and that Luke is using a favourite setting (see also ch.14) for this part of his teaching. Some of the material has a close parallel in Matt. 23 where it is set in the last week of Jesus' ministry and is addressed to the crowds and the disciples. The even stronger rhetoric of Matt. 23 is often explained as a reflection of the hostility between the Christians of Matthew's 'community' and their Jewish neighbours. As we shall see, although directly addressed to the Pharisees and lawyers, Luke's polemic shows little real awareness of the major concerns and characteristics of those groups; the passage both adds to the intensifying hostility and acts as a vehicle for the positive model Luke wants to express. It cannot be used to reconstruct the real Pharisees of Jesus' day, or even 'the worst of them' any more than the worst of any group.

Although the concern for adherence to the biblical laws of purity according to which vessels and utensils could acquire impurity

(Lev. 11.32–36) did lead to disputes as to how the outside effected the inside, such as are alluded to by Matt. 23.25–26, Luke makes a more moralizing move from *the outside of cup and plate*, rigorously cleaned, to the *inside* of the Pharisees, *full of greed and wickedness*. The charge is not substantiated: for Luke the counter-point is what matters. God created both *outside* and *inside* – here logic would prefer that these refer to the same thing – and presumably has the same demands of both. These demands are to be met by *charity* or alms-giving, an important concern for Luke (cf. 12.33) who regularly tackles issues of use of wealth; perhaps at this point *what is inside* is the contents of cup or plate which could be given, or a better translation might be *'what is within your means'*.

The next charge, the first of the woes, leads to a demand for *justice* and *love of God*, in the context probably as manifested in the attitude to others; against this is set their tithing of all manner of herbs, even though contemporary sources show that not *every garden herb*, including *rue*, was tithed. Tithing again is rooted in God's requirements (Deut. 14.22–29) and in acknowledgment that all that grows and that humans make use of comes as God's gift and blessing; Luke does not anull this obligation – *these you should have practised*. The two further woes offer no evidence and no alternative practice: they condemn the Pharisees for their love of status, and liken them to hidden sources of impurity, defiling people, or presumably leading them astray, unawares. It is hard to know whether Luke is simply repeating stock polemic for dramatic intensity, or has one eye to the potential dangers within his Christian community.

Purely on the level of the narrative, we may not be surprised at the aggrieved response of *one of the lawyers*: this group (cf. 7.30) matches 'the scribes' of Matthew's account (cf. also v.53), and presumably Luke understands them as a technically specialized group among or alongside the Pharisees. The first and third woes are again blanket charges without clear justification; if the lawyers were concerned with finer interpretation of the law, then the *intolerable burdens* might be the detailed prescriptions which would make daily life an impossible maze. Similarly their removal of *the key of knowledge* and exclusion of those who *were trying to go in* – Matthew's 'kingdom of heaven' (23.13) makes clearer sense – might expose the irony whereby the attempt to clarify the detail in practice excludes all but those who share the technical know-how and jargon. That process is a familiar one in many areas of life, but the picture that has often been drawn of the ordinary people of Jesus' day as weighed down by the joyless imposition of legalistic niceties through self-righteous religious leaders has no support from the Jewish sources. Again, Luke is adopting a denunciation which was already part of the tradition, and which, like all polemic, had already developed in intensity and detail; he may have had little sense of the real nature of the Pharisees and the lawyers, but, as we have repeatedly seen, they figured for him as the characteristic opposition to Jesus.

This becomes particularly clear in the second woe, that they *build monuments to the prophets* who had been put to death by the religious leaders of their day: within the biblical narratives Elijah and Jeremiah had come close to death, but the tradition of the prophets and other emissaries of God who were persecuted and killed became a standard one in the inter-testamental period, so that gruesome deaths were even invented for some of the earlier prophets. In and around the Jerusalem of Jesus' day the tombs of the prophets, whether or not authentic, had become places of pious reverence. Why to *provide the monuments* is seen as complicity in and not repudiation of the murders is not clear; the attempt to link the present leaders with their predecessors or *fathers* is more rhetorical than logical. Yet the importance of the theme is shown by its expansion in vv.49–51.

The *Wisdom of God* almost acquires a personal identity in Jewish thought after the exile (cf. 7.35), and was seen as active in Israel's history (cf. Sir. 24). The prophecy here attributed to her does not come in any known written source and may refer to an oracle circulating in Jewish or Christian circles; in Matt. 23.34–6 these words are spoken by Jesus whom Christian thought did see as the incarnation of Wisdom. The *prophets and messengers* sent by Wisdom might refer back to Israel's history, but since 'messengers' can also be translated 'apostles', and this combination is a Christian one (cf. Eph. 2.20; 3.5; Rev. 18.20), early Christian experience may also be included. *Abel*, although not a prophet, was the first murder victim (Gen. 4.8–10); *Zechariah* has been variously identified: the priest who denounced his contemporaries' apostasy and who was stoned by them 'in the court of the house of the Lord' in the time of Joash (II Chron. 24.20–22) would be the last 'biblical' murder if II Chronicles was the last book of the (Hebrew) Bible as then ordered; Matt. 23.35 (cf. Zech 1.1) thinks of the post-exilic 'writing' prophet of that name although nothing is known about his death; the Jewish historian, Josephus, describes the murder of a Zechariah during the Jewish revolt of 66–70 CE (*Jewish War* 4.335–44), which would bring the survey up to the present for Luke and his readers, perhaps still included among *this generation*. This is – and it works better in English than in Greek! – an A to Z of God's call and Israel's rejection which is now close to the point of no return; we hear the voice of the prophet who declares that God's judgment is imminent and that Israel's response has already sealed her fate. Jesus appeared as such a prophet, and his own death is not included in the indictment, as it would be by later preachers (Acts 7.52). A prophet who declared such an uncompromising message would be hoping for repentance, but for Luke the charge is probably a foretaste of the hostility which would result in Jesus' death, and he had less hope for any response.

Thus, although through this sharp denunciation it is Jesus who has taken the initiative, Luke leaves the scene with the, more traditionally named, *scribes* and *Pharisees* continuing to *assail* him: the images are of the hunt, with attacks and *snares*, and the mood thus created of impending danger should not be forgotten as the 'journey' slowly proceeds.

Challenge to fearless confession
12.1–12

The conflict with the religious leaders provides a stark background to the otherwise disparate collection of teaching which follows and which faces the hearers with the demands that discipleship makes in present loyalties and future judgment. The audience alternates between the disciples, who are those who have chosen a closer allegiance (2–12, 22–53), and the *crowd* who, although they respond in *many thousands* – an obvious exaggeration in Galilee – have yet to judge for themselves what is right (v.57; 13–21, 54–9). The opening warning against *the Pharisees* acts as a bridge from the preceding polemic, but the focus is now on the response of *his disciples. Leaven* is a natural metaphor for that which has a pervasive effect, good or ill, but as a type of sour dough it is particularly easily associated with corruption. In Mark 8.14, part of the section omitted by Luke, the similar warning against 'the leaven of the Pharisees . . . and of Herod', is left without any interpretation, while Matthew, who substitutes 'and of the Sadducees', interprets it as 'the teaching' (16.6, 11–12). In Luke it is *their hypocrisy*, in the light of New Testament usage probably their deliberate dissimulation (see 6.42). What has earned the charge is not stated, neither is it clear whether the disciples are to *be on* their *guard* against its effects or merely against imitating it; the negative example serves primarily as a backcloth to the exhortation to the disciples: they will not be able to keep hidden, presumably in the impending judgment, anything they *have said* or *whispered*.

Temptation to dissimulation might arise particularly under persecution, and so they are warned not to overestimate the threat posed by those who can only end their physical existence. God is the one who *has authority to cast into hell*, and a proper *fear* of God is the recognition of this. Such fear will lead to steadfastness under stress, but it should not become an abject terror, for this would be to misunderstand God's nature and concern. Therefore the disciples can also be told *not* to fear or *be afraid*, the same word in Greek. *Sparrows* were the cheapest form of meat for the poor, and yet it is fundamental to the biblical understanding of God as creator that all of creation, even such insignificant members, comes under God's care. Perhaps it is particularly as disciples and not just as members of the human race that Jesus can affirm their greater *worth*, known to God in each personal detail.

Yet this reassurance once again switches back to stern warning, for God's generous care should not be abused. To publicly *acknowledge* or *disown* Jesus might again be particularly pertinent under pressure or persecution, but need not be limited to such conditions, and the warning here would fit the experience of the early church in general. The choice made now earns its appropriate response in God's judgment, although when this takes place is not said; here *the angels of God*, one of Luke's special interests (cf. 15.10; 16.22), represent God's court, while *the Son of Man* (see p.42f.) appears as a heavenly prosecuting figure. This is one of those passages where there is a close relationship between Jesus in his ministry and the Son of Man, a heavenly figure, but not necessarily an identity; some have seen this as evidence that Jesus did not think of himself as the *Son of Man*, but, as in other Jewish eschatological texts, anticipated the latter's imminent judgment; others suggest that the term has come from such a background into the traditions of Jesus' own, less precise, expectations.

The warning which follows underlines the complexity of the issue. In the light of the awesome consequences of disowning Jesus, why should *a word against the Son of Man* be treated more leniently than slander against *the Holy Spirit*, who has not yet been mentioned in this discourse? The related but separate saying in Mark 3.28–29 contrasts the forgivable blasphemies that 'sons of men', probably people

generally, commit, and the unforgivable blasphemy against the Holy
Spirit. Various solutions to the problem have been offered, for
example that the slander (against the Son of Man) is the rejection of
Jesus in his human obscurity, or that made by unbelievers, while
that against the Holy Spirit is the wilful rejection of the risen Lord,
attested to by the Spirit, perhaps by those who have once believed.
The wider context in the Markan (and Matthaean, 12.25–37) forms is
the charge that Jesus works by demonic power, a slander against
God's action through the Spirit. However, it is difficult to think that
Luke understood the saying in any of these ways, given his different
context and the preceding use of 'Son of Man' for the heavenly
figure. It may be that he has joined sayings with a similar theme and
terminology without looking for a precise interpretation, wanting
only to underline the gravity of open confession.

Certainly the following word of encouragement seems to be
linked by setting – a 'prosecution' before Jewish (*synagogues*) or
Roman (*state*, literally 'powers and authorities') authorities – and
theme – the presence of *the Holy Spirit*. Fearless confession will be
possible, and so they are not to *worry* – the word will reappear in
v.22 – because of the Spirit's guidance. This is a theme which Luke
will pick up in his second volume; it seems that he has brought
together material from disparate sources – the parallels in Matthew
come in 10.26–33, 12.32, 10.19 – to prepare his readers for a discipleship which he will illustrate in his account of the early Christians
and which would continue to be part of their experience.

The pursuit of wealth and God's provision
12.13–34

The crowd, who have formed part of the silent backcloth, now
come to the fore as *someone* approaches Jesus as one would a *Teacher*,
experienced in interpreting the Law (cf. Deut. 21.15–17 on inheri-
tance), or a wise man who could be expected to *arbitrate* in family or
local dispute if, for example, a *brother* was refusing to realize and
divide the proceeds from *family property* held in common: we may
catch a glimpse here of how many of Jesus' contemporaries viewed
him during his lifetime before the faith of the early Christians read a
more exalted status into the stories. Jesus' reply recalls the retort
made to Moses in Ex. 2.14, but it would be reading in too much to
conclude that Jesus' is rejecting a Moses-type role. In the context of
his ministry and preaching such mediation would have detracted

from the proclamation of the urgency of the kingdom; here in Luke it becomes the occasion for a moralistic caution and a *parable*, which in practice is rather more an exemplary story.

The proper use of *possessions* is a major concern in Luke's Gospel and, despite all his sympathies for the impoverished and excluded of society, it is the attitudes and assumptions of the wealthy which form his starting point, perhaps suggesting that they constituted a significant element within his own community. For the poor, possessions of some kind are essential *for life*, and to tell them this is not so would be contemptuous of their situation; only those who have *more than enough* need to be told that 'life' as properly understood, the life of the kingdom, cannot be found in what one owns (cf. Ps. 49.16–20), and that the lust for more which is *greed* can only be destructive. The illustration only loosely fits the moral, for the *rich man* might seem only to be exercising a proper husbandry of his *produce*, ensuring its safe-keeping and his own security *for many years to come*. Within the biblical tradition all these are *good things* and to *eat, drink and enjoy yourself* is a proper response to God's blessings (Deut. 12.7; 33.13–16; Prov. 2.9–10; Eccles. 2.24–25). Unusually, *God* appears as a character within the 'parable' and exposes the failing in the man's calculations – the suddenness of death. There is perhaps nothing particularly novel or even 'Christian' about this grim comment on the transitoriness and unpredictability of life, or about the implication that it should lead to a careful reassessment of values. Yet because it is God who has uttered the judgment and addressed the man as *Fool*, the biblical dismissal of those who reject God's wisdom (Prov. 1.22–33), it reminds that a total preoccupation with material concerns may drive out all thought of God. Thus the final comment adds another thought: the man has piled up *treasure for himself* but remained *a pauper*, or better *had not been rich, towards God*. This had not been made explicit in the parable, and Luke may be trying to draw a further moral out of a fairly bland story, yet the point is a significant one: possessions do come from God but are held in stewardship, and are not to be used as a purely private matter; to be rich before God presumably comes from the proper use of wealth and other gifts in the service of others (cf. v.33). Thus the story starts with attention fixed firmly on the *rich man* and all his goods, it ends with God, and it is in the contrast that the message lies.

Attention again reverts to the *disciples* as those who are being shown what it means to live in obedient faith. The teaching which follows is found, with significant variations, in Matt. 6.25–33, 19–21 in the context of the 'Sermon on the Mount'. Here in Luke, in the climax of the parable (vv.20–21) and in the ensuing exhortation (vv.35–40), the context is the certainty but unexpected timing of God's final demand or judgment. To live in confidence in God's care is to live in confidence in the revelation of God's sovereignty.

The exhortation not *to worry about food . . . or clothes* would mean something different according to whether the hearers were the wealthy, the seriously poor, or the ordinary people in a society where the majority lived only a little above subsistence level; although Luke's community apparently included the wealthy it is perhaps the last group we should think of as represented among the disciples. *Life* here is not the same word as in v.15; sometimes translated as 'soul', it is combined with *body* to indicate the totality of human physical existence, and the realities of such existence are not being denigrated as they sometimes have been in ascetic forms of Christianity. However, the natural human concern for security is being relegated to a lower place. First there is an appeal to God's care for all creation, even *ravens*, unclean birds in Jewish law (Lev. 11.15); as in v.7 the disciples *are worth far more* than these. Secondly, superfluous worry can achieve very little: the Greek could also be translated 'add a cubit to your height', but this would not be *a very little thing*! Thirdly, God's provision in nature is far more extravagant than even human effort can achieve: there is almost a wantoness in the beauty with which insignificant field flowers are adorned, apparently to no purpose since their fate is to be fuel. Can God not be trusted to provide as abundantly for those with faith? Each of these arguments is given in vivid language drawn from a deep appreciation of nature, and carries force more from the colour of the imagery than from its underlying persuasiveness, at least for those for whom even survival is a precarious struggle. Experience shows that that struggle, when *the rest* – enough *to eat or drink* – does not *come . . . as well*, is not itself evidence of having *little faith*. In his society this would have been obvious to Jesus and to his followers, and his own life showed that a *mind* set on God's kingdom was not a guarantee of freedom from suffering.

Thus the passage is not a programme for the ordering of personal or social economy but is a statement of the absolute commitment demanded of disciples. It works by contrast: either/or. On the one hand are *the Gentiles* or *nations of the world* whose lives, it is assumed, are shaped by the pursuit of physical needs; on the other is the life of God's kingdom. Those who choose this are a *little flock* – the image looks beyond Jesus' immediate disciples to the church (cf. Acts 20.28–9); it is they, and not all humanity, who can look to God as their *Father*. They can set their minds on God's kingdom only because God has already been pleased (*chosen*: cf. 3.22; 2.14; 10.21 and notes) to *give* them *the kingdom*. This is a future hope which is grounded in an unalterable present assurance. Yet, even if the earlier examples cannot be taken as programmatic, they were not just hyperbolic rhetoric which can be ignored for all practical purposes. Perhaps now with an eye to a more wealthy audience Luke adds a blunt command which has no parallel in Matthew: the *possessions* which in v.15 are no source of life can only become so when given for others (*charity* in the REB sounds over-institutional). Again reverting to the teaching in the initial parable, although it was directed to a different audience, the *treasure* to be stored up is that which is held before God; it is both secure from the unpredictable disasters of human existence and the guarantee of that God-centredness which is the essence of readiness for God's kingdom.

The idea that charitable giving stores up treasure before God as a security for the day of reckoning is also found in Jewish sources, for example in Tobit 4.5–11, where it is part of a moralistic exhortation to a life which is upright in God's eyes; it need not mean that there is a real urgent expectation of imminent judgment, and in the earlier parable Luke has thought more of the judgment of death (v.20). One of the uncertainties in reading Luke's Gospel is to know how far the experience of the on-going life of the church, to which he gave real value in Acts, has qualified the urgent expectation which seems to be a mark of the earliest Christian preaching. Is the promise, or the fear, of the future largely a way of encouraging a new attitude to life in the present? How far was Luke, or his generation, able or concerned to sustain a vivid sense of the shortness of time.

Watchful and ready for God's kingdom
12.35–59

The teaching which follows, some of which has parallels in Matt. 24 where it forms part of a vivid eschatological discourse, reinforces the question just asked. How did Luke understand the command to *hold yourself in readiness*? He illustrates the need to do so by a series of comparisons which are part parable, part a mix of the reality with the picture language in which it must be described. In the first it is the unpredictability of the timing of the *master's return* which demands that his household always be in a position to respond to his coming; the imagery of 'return' and of his knocking belongs to the parable, although later such language became part of Christian hope (Rev. 3.20). When the master reverses roles, adopting that of a slave and waiting on them, the message has broken through the probabilities of the parable. In ordinary life such behaviour would be unthinkable, but such reversal lies at the heart of Jesus' teaching of the kingdom; to *wait on* is to *minister* (cf. 4.39; 8.3, where it is the special role of the women, and notes), and in Luke 22.27 Jesus claims this as the heart of his presence with them (cf. John 13.3–5). There may be a suggestion that the servants/Luke's readers are not to be discouraged if he seems delayed, coming even *in the middle of the night or before dawn*. In the second parable the focus is on the master's continual vigilance: although in real life, and perhaps for Jesus' original hearers, the unexpectedness of *the burglar's* coming is the problem, for Luke it seems to be the timing. Perhaps for a church working out the meaning of continuing discipleship through the years, the message that *the Son of Man will come* was not easily sustained; whether Luke envisioned further delay is not easy to determine, but he does seem to have felt that the dilution of that belief would have catastrophic consequences for the character of discipleship. Again *the Son of Man* belongs to the future, although it is his coming rather than his judgment which is described, and again it can be asked whether the church has made the original expectation of Jesus more precise (cf. 5.24; 12.8 and notes).

Peter's interjection here could be contrasting what is expected of disciples (*us*), with what is expected of the crowd, *everyone*. However, the following 'parable' of the *trusty* or *faithful, and sensible . . . steward* would fit the needs of the early church well if the steward represented those who hold office; although they might not *bully* their congregations or *eat and drink and get drunk*, abuse of their status was possible, and a real concern in the New Testament (I Tim. 3.1–10). The steward remains a *slave* (= REB *servant*, v.43), but has special responsibilities which may become either a blessing if well done, or ensure special judgment if abused: being *cut . . . in pieces* seems excessive in the framework of the parable and is perhaps a metaphor of final judgment *among the faithless* or *unfaithful,* and should perhaps be understood as 'cut off'. The message of imminent judgment, which was part of John's preaching and surely of Jesus', has now become not a threat to outsiders but a stern warning to the church not to sit back in somnolent self-congratulation: the assurance of the kingdom (v.32) demands greater, not less, preparedness, even if there is no certainty when or how it is to be tested.

Those who hold positions of leadership in the church are surely those who know their *master's wishes* and to whom *has been given much*; they at least will have much *expected* of them and carry a serious responsibility; yet who is the *one* who is still a servant but *did not know them*, and so neglected them out of ignorance? The description would not fit outsiders, but would it be fair to describe ordinary church members as not knowing their master's wishes? The point, however, seems less to excuse them, than to reinforce the responsibilities of the former; the seriousness of judgment is not a weapon to wield against others, but a harsh reminder to those who know that they have been *entrusted* with much.

Therefore the present is not without significance, nor merely a holding operation until the climactic moment. However, the urgent intensity which perhaps was a dilemma for Luke and the early church, was certainly a mark of Jesus' ministry and comes through with particular power in his 'declaration of intent' in vv.49–53. *Fire* is a metaphor of cleansing, but also of judgment; its association with *baptism* perhaps comes from John's preaching (cf. 3.16–17 and note) because 'baptism' is not otherwise a metaphor in Jewish or Greek thought. Being swamped with waters can express intense suffering in the Old Testament (cf. Ps. 69.1–2) but is not described as 'baptism'; however, the *baptism* Jesus knows he must *undergo* is surely an anticipation of the suffering ahead (cf. Mark 10.38–9). It is unclear from the Greek whether the words translated *and how I wish* mean it is not yet kindled, or the process is already begun; yet Jesus is seeing his ministry as one of judgment, a judgment in which his own destiny will be caught up. The message of Jesus' birth, 'peace to all' (2.14), is not being contradicted but given its proper context; then too Mary had been warned of the division he would cause which would even affect her (2.34–35). The proclamation of God's will and its accomplishment would cause division which would even strike through families and society; the imagery recalls Micah 7.5 when the turning of *daughter against mother . . . and daughter-in-law against mother-in-law* is a mark of society dominated by the godless, but it would also have been part of the experience of the early church when families often were split by their allegiance to Christ. Again, the demand of the kingdom is so absolute that the equivocation of compromise is not possible.

In the final section the crowds once again return to the fore.

Although up to now they have flocked to Jesus and responded to his miracles with awe, here more is expected of them. They should be able to see in all they have experienced the significance – *fateful* has too negative a note – of the present *hour* which points forward no less clearly than the unmistakeable, and it is assumed reliable, signals of coming storms or scorching heat. The condemnation *hypocrites*, rare in Luke (cf. 12.2 and note), implies their blindness is wilful. Finally Jesus returns to a theme similar to that first introduced by the crowd in v.13; why do they seek others to arbitrate for them? Would it not be better to *reach a settlement* with an opponent before the matter comes *to court*, than to risk being found the guilty partner and suffering severe penalties? This may seem a banal conclusion, which Luke has tagged on to a more or less appropriate setting. The similar teaching in Matt. 5.25–26 is part of Jesus' reinterpretation of the Law; here some have suggested that the *court* and *jail* point to the final judgment, and that the teaching has become a further exhortation to readiness and effective preparation for that judgment. Although this would help the passage fit its context, it is by no mean an obvious interpretation – for example it would be difficult to identify the *opponent* with Satan or Jesus; it may have to be accepted that in organizing the different traditions of Jesus' teaching that had come to him, often without any setting or context, Luke was sometimes forced to fit them in in the least inappropriate context!

Warning of coming judgment
13.1–9

The narrative moves to a new scene but the theme of judgment continues from the previous chapter. Some people saw disaster as punishment for, and therefore evidence of, sin, and it is part of the argument of the 'historical' and prophetic books of the Old Testament that Israel was punished for her disobedience by military defeat at the hands of foreign powers. Here Jesus refuses to draw the conclusion that those who had suffered in two recent incidents were necessarily either *greater sinners* or *more guilty* (lit. '*debtors*') than anyone else. Rather, their fate stands as a warning to everyone of the urgency of repentance. Neither of these incidents is known outside Luke although *Pilate* did act brutally and offend Jewish sensibilities on more than one occasion. To have *mixed* the blood of some worshippers *with their sacrifices*, if meant literally, would not only have been murder, even if 'judicial', but also would have desecrated the Temple where all sacrifice was performed. The occasion may have been Passover when men did perform their own sacrifice of the paschal lamb, and it is slightly odd that the historian of the period, Josephus, makes no mention of such an incident, but perhaps Luke's knowledge or sources were hazy or confused another event. If that incident was due to the malice of its perpetrator, the second was presumably accidental, the collapse of a *tower* at the water source of *Siloam* in *Jerusalem* – Siloam we know of from elsewhere but not its tower nor the latter's collapse. It has been suggested that the term *Galileans* refers to the revolutionaries who were opposed to Roman power, and that Jesus' warning implies the futility of their efforts; however, it is more likely that they were simply pilgrims from Galilee, like Jesus himself. Although in retrospect, perhaps even by Luke and his readers, Jesus' words could be seen as a grim prophecy fulfilled in the destruction of Jerusalem by the Romans in 70 CE, they point beyond that as an urgent call to repentance in the face of certain judgment.

The *parable* that follows, again peculiar to Luke, could equally be understood at more than one level. A *fig tree's* purpose, at least in its owner's eyes, is to bear *fruit*, and that which fails to deserves only to be *cut down* so that it wastes no more soil. If the fig tree is Israel, the reprieve and special attention for *one year* might refer to the opportunity afforded by Jesus' ministry, or by the preaching of the early church; however it is usually a vine to which Israel is likened (Isa. 5.1–7; Ps. 80.9–14), not a fig, and it would be wrong to turn the parable into an allegory, identifying both the owner and *the vinedresser*, for example as God and Jesus. However the destruction of Jerusalem in 70CE may have coloured people's reading of the parable in retrospect, its emphasis would also have reminded Luke's readers of the demand to be fruitful and of the urgency to respond – reprieve may only be apparent and temporary.

The liberation of the kingdom
13.10–21

For the last time in Luke we find Jesus *in one of the synagogues on the sabbath* and *teaching* there. The healing that Jesus there performs recalls the earlier one of the man with the withered hand (6.6–11), but introduces some important new themes. This, like its 'partner' in 14.1–6, is found only in Luke, and the two reflect his interest in male-female pairing (cf. 13.18–21; 15.4–10). Here her crippling spinal disease is attributed to possession by *a spirit*, and later Jesus will describe her as *bound by Satan*; the healing is both by word and touch (cf. 5.13), and, characteristically for Luke, the woman responds to her immediate healing by praising God (cf. 5.25–6; 7.16). For his part the *ruler* (= REB *president*) *of the synagogue* sees in what has happened a further infringement of the sabbath prohibition of work (Deut. 5.13; Ex. 20.9; see on Luke 6.6–11), but his complaint is directed not to Jesus as before but *to the congregation*: 'crowd' or 'people' would be a better translation, for by this time we have begun to see a growing separation between crowd and leaders, and between crowd and disciples (see ch.12). The woman's condition, being of *eighteen years* standing, was not life-threatening, but Jesus does not reply in terms of how this effects interpretation of the sabbath law (ctr. 14.1–6). The analogy of the daily loosing of an *ox* or *donkey* for water is only an approximate one; what Jesus has done is not just a regular act of giving access to true life, but is part of the defeat of Satan which belongs to Jesus' proclamation of the kingdom. *The sabbath*, as sign and symbol of God's creative power, is the supremely appropriate day on which that defeat should be effected and celebrated.

Yet there is something more: this woman is *a daughter of Abraham*. That God's salvation was for Abraham's children was celebrated in the infancy narratives (1.54–5, 72–3); they are the heirs of God's promises. Yet who are Abraham's children? John the Baptist had warned against claiming the epithet as a right and as a guarantee of divine favour (3.8), and later in this chapter Jesus will say that not all who expect to will share with Abraham in the kingdom (13.28). Whereas in some Jewish literature to be a daughter of Abraham was to be among the pious, in the best sense of the word (cf. IV Macc. 14.20; 15.28; 17.6), here the honoured epithet is given to a crippled woman, the victim of Satan and for long excluded from full participation in life. In the same way it will be the tax collector Zacchaeus whom Jesus will name a son of Abraham (19.9).

The earlier hint is confirmed in the conclusion: on the one hand are *all his opponents*, for the moment put to shame, on the other *the mass of the people* or 'all the crowd': they continue the theme of praise and support, at least for the present.

The two 'parables' Luke adds here, although he does not so name them (ctr. Matt. 13.31), are the only times in Luke that Jesus explicitly makes a comparison of *the kingdom of God*. Unlike Mark 4.31–2 and Matt. 13.32 Luke does not emphasize the smallness of the *mustard seed* nor the size of the tree; he is interested not so much in the contrast between the insignificant beginning and magnificent end, but in the certainty of its growth into *a tree*, which in its abundant provision may hint at the universality of the kingdom (cf. Dan. 4.12). In the same way, the *yeast* used by *a woman* – matching the man in his garden – can cause a very large amount of *flour* to rise. The woman *hid* (better than REB *mixed*) the leaven, just as much about Jesus' ministry appeared hidden (cf. 8.17), yet the all-encompassing power of the kingdom was guaranteed, and in the freeing of the woman from the power of Satan they were experiencing the out-working of God's kingdom.

The Continuation of the Journey
13.22–17.11

Since Jesus 'set his face' to Jerusalem in 9.51 there have been only occasional references to the journey he was making. The second stage of the journey begins with a reminder that his goal is *Jerusalem*, although we are not aware that he is much nearer than when he started, and in 17.11 he will still be in 'the borderlands of Samaria and Galilee'. Although the reminder adds weight to the challenges which will follow, this section too combines teaching for his disciples with more general teaching to the crowds and with growing hostility from the Pharisees.

Against complacency
13.22–30

In Acts 26.26 Paul will say to Agrippa, 'This thing was not done in a corner', and in his Gospel Luke wants to emphasize that Jesus made his appeal far and wide, *through towns and villages*, even if he had only limited evidence of actual events and their specific locations. Yet neither that broad appeal nor Jesus' concern for those whom society rejected, nor again the free gift of a tree from a seed, or of risen dough from leaven, should lead to complacency. Whether all, many, or only *a few were to be saved* was a question which exercised the minds of many: for example the community behind the Dead Sea Scrolls at times see themselves alone as the heirs of God's promises. Jesus' answer too is that entry into life demands *every effort* and cannot be counted upon.

Unlike the parallel in Matt. 7.13–14, there is not a contrast with the seductively pleasant 'wide path'; instead the *door* into God's celebration is too *narrow* to enter without forethought. Moreover, the time may come when it is too late to try entry. Here parable and application are combined: a *banquet* was a common image of sharing in God's sovereignty; those who are excluded have not only decided to

110

come too late, but also over-complacently rely on their past association with the *master of the house* whom now they name 'lord' – as elsewhere in Luke the ambiguous term is both *Sir* and an acknowledgment of the sovereignty of Jesus. These are perhaps Jesus' contemporaries who heard his teaching, and shared meals with him: yet this association, although so important in Luke, is inadequate on its own. Originally they may also have represented any within the life of the church who thought it was enough to be there, but who did not show the commitment and response demanded. Yet for Luke the warning points beyond these to the exclusion of those who counted on their right to be in the kingdom, and for whom association with *Abraham, Isaac, Jacob and all the prophets* was part of their certain hope. It is unclear whether Luke meant the exclusion only of the hostile leaders of the Jews or of all Israel, for he does not follow Matt. 8.11 in naming those who are thrown out as 'the sons, or heirs, of the kingdom'. The picture of the coming of the peoples from all the corners of the earth is drawn from the prophetic hope of the time when God's sovereignty would be recognized (Isa. 2.2–4; Micah 4.1–3); originally that hope, which was focussed on God's presence in Jerusalem, complemented and did not exclude God's own people. In Christian hands it became a prophecy of the coming of the Gentiles into the church, replacing the people of Israel. Luke plays his part in this development, but his language still lacks some precision; here he speaks not of Jews and Gentiles, but of *last* and *first*; in line with his love of the reversal of expected values, those who *now* are accorded least honour will find it heaped upon them.

Jerusalem
13.31–35

There is perhaps a fine irony that the claim of the latecomers that they experienced Jesus' ministry should be followed by a solemn declaration of the goal of that ministry; beyond this there is only minimal connection with the previous incident, and this passage chiefly serves to remind us of the shadow of Jerusalem. Although Luke has regularly portrayed the Pharisees in a negative light, it may be that their warning to Jesus here is a signal that some, like Gamaliel in Acts 5.34–39, were if not supportive at least fair-minded; yet such support is ambiguous, for Jesus assumes that they can report back to Herod, and although he does move on, it is not at their behest. We already know of Herod's imprisonment and self-confessed murder of John (3.19–20; 9.9), and in terms of the narrative we should not be surprised that he also *wants to kill* Jesus, although in terms of historical reconstruction it is not obvious why this should be so and none of the other Gospels refers to it. The *fox* was the proverbial representative of a number of characteristics, intelligence, cunning, weakness, and destructiveness, and if any should be isolated it is perhaps the latter which fits best in the Gospel context. Yet although the ominous clouds of opposition are gathering, Jesus remains in control of his own destiny, or rather goes only in fulfilment of God's purpose: the *must* in v.33 points to a divine necessity.

Yet Jesus' ministry is not just a preface to the future drama; the *today* when he drives out demons is the 'today' of God's salvation which he proclaimed at Nazareth (4.21; cf. 5.26; 19.5, 9). However, although for Luke that salvation was experienced in the present in Jesus' ministry, it also had a dynamic driving towards completion. The *tomorrow . . . and on the third day* is not a reference to the resurrection but to the inner coherence of this dynamic, and so is no different from the alternative image of Jesus being on his way *today and tomorrow and the next day*. Luke does little to interpret Jesus' death, but he does see it as part of the driving necessity that binds Jesus' ministry together, and not as a tragic mistake (cf. 12.49–50).

Jesus here aligns himself with the prophets of old, which is how many may have best understood him (cf. 7.11–17); the tradition that the prophets met their death at the hands not of outsiders, but of those they came to warn, was a developing one (Neh. 9.26), and where evidence was lacking new stories could be told (cf. 11.47). Thus *Jerusalem* stands for God's people who have experienced blessing and responded with disobedience; the historical fact of Jesus' death in Jerusalem is here seen as the ultimate sign of his rejection by those to whom he was sent.

Yet this does not result in denunciation but in anguished yearning. The return of scattered Israel to Jerusalem was part of prophetic hope (Isa. 60.4; Zech. 10.6–10), and Jesus here sees himself as one called to realize that hope as the agent of the maternal compassion of God. The lament is followed by a declaration of certain judgment; Jeremiah had condemned the people's reliance on the temple as a guarantee of divine protection (Jer. 7), and had prophesied God's abandonment of 'his house' (12.7): God's words in Jer. 22.5 'This house shall become a desolation' are now echoed by Jesus' *'your house shall be deserted'*, something obscured by the REB's more precise *Temple* and unnecessary addition of *by God*. Luke's readers would have seen this fulfilled in the Roman destruction of Jerusalem in 70CE, but if these words go back to Jesus the prophetic judgment would have been more important than uncertain prediction. This judgment is followed by a promise: they will yet respond in the words of the Hallel psalm used at Passover and Tabernacles, Ps. 118.26.

Matthew sets this 'lament over Jerusalem' outside the city itself, during Jesus' last week there, and so it looks forward to the final, eschatological and inescapable recognition of Jesus' lordship (Matt. 23.37–39). In Luke Jesus has yet to approach the city, and these words will be used when he does so on 'Palm Sunday' (19.38). However, this seems a rather banal fulfilment of the solemn *I tell you, you will not see me*, and Luke probably also looks beyond then to a final coming of Jesus. Yet this still leaves some ambiguity: is their final recognition of him as *the one who comes* (cf. 7.18–26) a promise of their inclusion or the belated acknowledgment by those now excluded (cf.13.25)? The ambiguity may be deliberate, for as with the prophets of old, including Jeremiah, messages of judgment and hope serve as a call to respond to God. Their response will determine the meaning of this prophecy.

Meals and the reversal of honour
14.1–24

Once again Jesus is invited to a *meal* by one of *the rulers of the Pharisees*: in fact the Pharisees did not have rulers, hence the REB's paraphrase *leading Pharisees*, but Luke may not have known this and is more interested in the way they represent status and power. Meals are a favourite setting for Luke for discussion and debate (5.29; 7.36; 11.37, see notes), and would have been familiar to his readers from the tradition of the 'symposium' in life and literature. Both the setting and much of the material are distinctive to Luke and illustrate well how his telling of the story of Jesus is shaped to fit the interests and expectations of his readers. In fact, a careful reading suggests that Luke has created a meal setting for some disparate material which is connected more by theme than by likely sequence of events. The topics of the discussion which follows, status and honour, would also be focussed naturally in the context of a meal, and for Luke's readers the way Jesus deals with them would include both familiar and more surprising elements.

First, however, the scene is interrupted by what appears to be an unrelated and slightly out-of-place incident. There is nothing to suggest that the *man suffering from dropsy,* or edema, was a Pharisaic plant, yet neither was he one of the guests. From Luke's point of view, he both balances the story of the woman in 13.10–17, with which there are several links, and brings the developing conflict out of the synagogue into the setting of *the house.* The issue is again that of healing on the sabbath, and Jesus' question whether *it is permitted* to do so could be seen as a challenge to their interpretation of the prohibition of work on the sabbath, similar to that in 6.9; but now, after those earlier exchanges, we are aware that it is not just a matter of debate over interpretation but of the total challenge presented by Jesus' ministry. Thus the healing of the man is only cursorily mentioned and he is *sent away* as of no further interest to the story; the climax is not the healing but Jesus' further challenge and their inability to answer it. The surprising conjunction of *a son or an ox* has led some manuscripts to substitute 'a donkey' for 'a son', while others have suggested an early confusion in the tradition; Matthew's account of the man with a withered hand has a similar justification referring only to a sheep which has fallen into a pit (Matt. 12.11). It is possible to find parallel debates in Jewish sources as to in what circumstances such a rescue could be effected on the sabbath, but Jesus is not only justifying his action, 'I am only doing what you would do – and how much more valuable than an ox is a man (or a son!)'; he is presenting them with a challenge – 'which one of you?' – and anyone who responded to that would be forced also to respond to all that Jesus was preaching and doing.

There follow two pieces of teaching – hardly *a parable* as we would understand it – the first to guests and the second to hosts, regarding appropriate attitudes to meals. In the world of the time meals were powerful indicators of status and honour: who was invited, where they were seated in relation to the host, and even the quality of the food they were served, were expressions of their status, while the whole system assumed a pattern of reciprocity. To assume your place within the seating hierarchy and then to be down-graded publicly in favour of another guest would bring shame, just as the reverse would bring honour, in a society where shame and honour were fundamental public values. Luke's advice, to invite honour rather than shame, seems like prudential wisdom which can be easily paralleled both in Graeco-Roman sources and in Jewish ones (Prov. 25.6–7). It is difficult to know whether we should look for any more profound meaning: the theme of reversal is a favourite of

Luke's, and the Magnificat already heralded the humiliation of the proud and raising of the lowly (1.52); Luke repeats the almost proverbial *'everyone who exalts himself will be humbled'* following the parable of the Pharisee and the tax-collector where the action of God in this reversal is more discernable (18.14). Luke may have seen such reversal as God's act in the final judgment, as explicitly in the promise of v.14, but it is perhaps more likely that he saw in such common wisdom a pointer to the values of Jesus and those demanded of the church (ctr. I Cor. 11.17–22).

Jesus' advice to *his host* would be more unexpected, for the norm was to invite those who were one's social equals or part of the same social network, which would also include dependents; the assumption was that they would *ask you back again* for this was what maintained the system; the refusal of an invitation or to reciprocate would bring shame. Here Jesus rejects that system of honour and shame, and of reciprocity: instead he urges that those be invited who would be totally unable to reciprocate, and in whose company the host would normally prefer not to be seen. It is true that in Graeco-Roman literature, alongside the dominant assumption that one should invite one's relatives and peers, there can also be heard the occasional criticism of the system. Jesus, however, here sets his alternative values within the sight of God; *the poor* and *the blind* are those to whom he came to promise release (4.18), while so to act is to be *'Blessed'* (cf. 6.20 and note), rather than *to find happiness* (REB), and carries with it the promise of future reward. *When the righteous rise from the dead* is probably just a common formula, although in origin it could reflect a belief that only the righteous would be raised, the wicked being left among the dead.

A banquet, particularly *a wedding feast* (v.8), could readily be seen as an anticipation of the kingdom, and so the next incident is linked by *one of the company* adding their own 'beatitude' for whoever *will sit at the feast* (lit. 'will eat bread') *in the kingdom of God*. As in 11.27–28, Jesus corrects what might be a superficially true but ultimately misleading pious exclamation. The parable which follows is rich in detail but fairly straightforward in its basic outline; Matthew has a similar parable (22.1–10) but both the context and many of the details are significantly different, suggesting that over the years parables changed in telling and in interpretation. It would probably be not unusual for *a man* to send *out . . . invitations* in advance and then to summon the guests when the time came. Presumably these people are those who belonged to the expected

115

circle of guests and at the very least their refusals would not only be rude but would bring shame to the host. His reaction is not to find other guests of appropriate status but to reject the whole system on which, as we have seen, hospitality was based; he orders his servant, or slave, to bring in the rejects of society, once again those who would never reciprocate and whose company would only bring the host, in the eyes of his peers, yet more shame. Given the number of poor in the ancient world the parable has already left the realm of any approximation to realism when it proves that *there was still room*. This only leads the *master* (or lord) to send his slave yet further afield; the dual purpose is to be achieved – a *house full* and the exclusion of all the original invited guests.

Given this broad outline, both the details and the meaning of the parable need further discussion. In a Graeco-Roman context and in the light of the previous teaching the parable could be seen as a vivid exhortation to Jesus' (or to Luke's) listeners to act likewise – to reject the conventions of society in recognition of their hollowness and to invite the dispossessed and needy. Yet there is clearly more to it than this: the excuses offered by those first invited may be loosely compared with those which according to Deut. 20 may properly prevent men in Israel from participating in war, or particularly in what is sometimes called the Holy War; now, however, such commitments – and, unlike Matthew, Luke even includes marriage – can no longer take precedence. Conversely, those finally invited include those who according to Lev. 21.17–20 were prohibited from 'drawing near' to God, a tradition we find continued in the Dead Sea Scrolls of those excluded from the community. Is this then the creation of the new community of the kingdom, where the urgency of the demand to respond brooks no excuses, and those who are welcomed are those who have long been excluded? The pious hope which provoked the parable is being radically restated. Yet Luke, again unlike Matthew, also adds a third group, those from *the highways and . . . the hedgerows*. It has been suggested that while *the poor* represent those in Israel to whom Jesus offered 'release', these anticipate the mission to the Gentiles which features so significantly in Acts. Thus while the initial pious hope also looked to the kingdom as an enjoyment to come the parable brings it radically into the present: the invitation has been issued and already some are making their excuses while those least expected are being brought in. The details, of course, should not be over-pressed, and it was an abuse of the parable when the command to *compel them to come in* was used to sanction any and every means of conversion or inquisition – there are many dangers in an over-literal reading of material not intended to be taken literally. Luke is more interested in the division between the excluded and those included than in any subdivision among the latter, and in the wider context of his Gospel the contrasting socio-economic status of the two groups must not be ignored. For Luke the proof of acceptance of Jesus' preaching of the kingdom must be shown in present social action, and there is an incontrovertible continuity between the social relations demanded now and the nature of the kingdom Jesus preached.

The challenge of discipleship
14.25–35

Once again attention turns from the Pharisees and the implied rejection of what they stand for, to the *crowds*, who are challenged to count the cost of following Jesus. In 9.23 the demand that a would-be disciple be prepared to *carry his cross* (see note) had a particular pathos after the prediction of Jesus' coming suffering. Here the emphasis is not on the readiness to sacrifice oneself and one's own immediate advantage, but on the renunciation if necessary of all family ties and obligations. As in the preceding parable, Luke, so often seen as the most humane and domestic of the Gospels, goes beyond the Matthean parallel (Matt. 10.37–38) by including even his *wife* among those who may have to be rejected – in his age it would not occur to Luke to consider the possibility of a disciple having to hate her husband! Within the polarized language of the biblical tradition to *hate* means not to prefer: discipleship of Jesus takes precedence over every other commitment or allegiance. In the history of the church this demand has often inspired the life-long renunciation of all family ties, while in the early church and elsewhere persecution has often made this choice between discipleship and family all too real. Already in Luke's time and context, in the conversion of 'households', it may have lost some of its immediacy, but it still has an essential place in the Gospel; it was not just that discipleship of Jesus could be dangerous, but that Jesus' understanding of the sovereign will of God radically challenged accepted values, and a life in conformity with that understanding must always be at odds with the wider values of society.

Thus discipleship is not a choice made on the spur of the moment or in a rush of enthusiasm: its demands need to be recognized and to

117

be prepared for; better to anticipate the cost of the whole enterprise than to be taken unawares after the initial more easy stages. While the preceding parable emphasizes the unexpected invitation to those least expecting it, this section stresses the demand involved in response. The parables which illustrate this could be seen again as prudential advice, applicable to a number of enterprises – do not start something you may not be able to finish. The themes of success in *building* and in *battle* also recall Prov. 24.3–6, where the source of success is Wisdom, not just common sense but conformity with God's ordering of the universe. Luke has taken this material and put it in the context of a decision for a commitment which overrides all other commitments. Yet in the final saying he ties this down to the realities of daily life, and to his favourite theme, *possessions*. Perhaps already in the experience of his church, these provided the biggest counter-pull to whole-hearted commitment; the earlier part of the chapter had already shown the day-to-day implications of putting aside possessions.

The final enigmatic saying about *salt* is similar to one found in Matt. 5.13 where the disciples are likened to salt, whose task is to flavour or to preserve the whole: if they lose that faculty all is lost, and they serve no useful purpose – the application here takes over from the illustration, for salt cannot *become tasteless*. In Luke both the saying and its meaning are enigmatic: it is not obvious why even 'good' salt would be used *on the land or on the dungheap*. The final exhortation for the one who *has ears to hear* to *hear*, i.e take heed and respond, acknowledges both the enigma and the seriousness of the warning (cf. 8.8). It may already have been a 'mysterious saying' when it came to Luke, for Mark has yet another, equally enigmatic, variation (Mark 9.49–50), but he probably understood it to underline the seriousness of a discipleship which has lost its commitment: consistency and perseverance are the ultimate test of authentic discipleship.

Parables of recovery of the lost
15.1–32

After Jesus' meal with a Pharisee in ch. 14 and his teaching on the invited guests, there is an unmistakeable irony when he is now condemned by the *Pharisees and scribes* as one who *welcomes sinners and eats with them*. In this way Luke returns to a central theme of the first part of Jesus' ministry, and his generalized *all the tax-collectors and sinners* may be modelled on those earlier, more specific occasions (5.30–32; 7.29–35; see pp.44 f.). Here the charge is not only that he *eats with them* but also that he *welcomes* them, perhaps as host – although on a journey Jesus could hardly entertain 'all' that group. In reply Jesus tells three parables which may be seen as a defence of that welcome, and so of Jesus' Gospel for the 'lost'. However, there is more to these parables than that, and it may be possible to distinguish between how Luke has used them here and what else they might have meant in the preaching of the church or of Jesus. Matthew has a version of the first one, the parable of the sheep (Matt. 18.12–14), but the fact that it comes alone and the very different way he uses it shows how Jesus' parables could be modified and re-applied in telling.

The first pair belong together, sharing a similar structure, language and theme. As elsewhere in Luke, one is about a man, who is relatively wealthy and belongs outside, the other about a woman, poor and confined to the house; this parallelism, but also the fact that Luke presupposes a male audience, comes clearly in the opening formulae, although obscured by the REB translation: *'which man of you has'* (v.4) . . . *'which woman has'* (v.8). The basic story in each case is clear, although spoilt when summarized, for the careful balancing of phrases invites the reader/hearer to watch the shepherd on his journey out and his joyful return home, or the woman as she searches and finds. Knowledge of the social and cultural context has led commentators to add further colour to the scenes, to comment on the risk in leaving *the ninety-nine in the wilderness*, on the burden of lifting a recalcitrant sheep *on his shoulders*, on the community context where *a hundred sheep* might belong to the wider family, or to speculate whether the woman's *ten silver coins* were part of her dowry, although the text does not say this and there is no contemporary evidence for a woman wearing her dowry jewelry. Such detail should not be over-pressed, and Jesus does not liken himself to either the shepherd or the woman – although if one is applied to him so should the other be – and the 'which of you' formula may be a challenge to them in the same way as it is in 14.5.

Two main elements may be drawn from the parables. The first is the effort extended in the search for what has been lost, purely because it is valuable to the shepherd or to the woman. The second is the joy in recovery, a joy shared with *friends* – in the Greek male for the shepherd, female for the woman – *and neighbours*. In each case

119

the final verse of the parable interprets this as *joy in heaven* or *among the angels of God*, both ways of speaking of God's presence, and as being over *one sinner who repents*. Here we may suspect that Luke is reflecting his own emphasis on repentance, as also at 5.32 (see note); in the parable neither the sheep nor the coin were responsible for their loss – the sheep did not stray but the man *loses* it as does the woman her coin. Similarly, neither the sheep nor the coin are responsible for their recovery; they are not models of repentance. Their passivity has been seen as pointing to the grace which searches for them, but perhaps this shows the danger of over-interpreting details which are a necessary part of the story: we might have then to explain the earlier carelessness of the owner/searcher in losing them! Similarly, the contrast with the *ninety-nine righteous* may be a comment added by Luke to fit the context he has given the story. The main focus of these parables is the proclamation of hope for the lost and the rejoicing of the kingdom.

The third parable, although picking up the themes of *lost and found* (vv.24, 32), is far more than a variation on the earlier two, and the profound influence it has had on literary and artistic imagination shows how difficult it is to limit to a single message. This is reflected by the different titles it has been given, each seeking to pinpoint the central focus of the story – 'the prodigal (or spendthrift) son', 'the lost son', 'the loving father', 'the two sons'. The first two of these proposed titles bring out the continuity from the earlier parables in the chapter, with 'prodigal' emphasizing that in this case the son is responsible for his 'lostness'. The third recognizes that the father, in his response to both his sons, far more than the sheep-owner or the woman, can be seen as in some way representing God. The last seeks to restore the final scene (vv.25–32) from being an insignificant appendix to the main story: the theme of two sons or brothers is a common one not only in the biblical tradition but also in many other cultures, while the contrast between two types of response is a frequent one in Jesus' parables (Luke 18.9–14; Matt. 25.1–13 and especially 21.28–32).

Once again sensitivity to the cultural and social context has added vivid colour to the parable, although we have to be careful in deciding how much of this would be apparent to Luke and his readers, or necessary for understanding the parable. Thus, a man could divide *his estate* between his heirs during his lifetime, but he would normally retain an interest in the produce and profits, so the land could not be sold by either the father, who had now willed it, or the heir. In asking his father to give him his *share of the property*, according to Deut. 21.15–17 a third, the *younger son* was pressurizing his father so to act; in turning *the whole of his share into cash* he would be acting as if his father were already dead. If this were part of his original intention it could be said that his request was tantamount to wishing his father were dead. However, in the parable itself there is no hint of disapproval towards that original request: the emphasis falls rather on his *leaving home* and squandering all he had *in dissolute living*: the details are left for the older son to supply – *running through your money with his women* (or *with prostitutes*) (v.30). The *distant country* means that he has left the Jewish setting of the parable, something confirmed by *the pigs* he was sent to mind: for a Jew such work showed the degradation into which he had sunk. There were several severe famines in the first century, and the situation where *the pods*, a form of carob, fed to animals might even be eaten by humans is not difficult to imagine; the implication is probably not that he would not or could not eat them but that they would not *fill his belly*.

As with the previous two parables the vivid detail and the emphasis on verbs of action, on what he does, invites the reader to follow the journey away from home as a sinking into despair. The turning point of the story in vv. 17–19 could be seen as a turning within the son. Yet this should not be over-emphasized: he did not repent but *came to his senses*; his reasoning is pragmatic – he could be eating rather than *starving to death* – even if he determines to acknowledge that he has *sinned against God* (lit. *heaven*) as well as against his father – an indication that the two should not be identified. His intention to seek re-admittance as one of his *father's hired servants*, rather than as a household slave, has been seen as pointing to his determination to remain independent and perhaps to earn the means to repay his debt; more probably it contrasts with the privileges and rights of a member of the family.

At this point a culturally-sensitive imagination may again enrich the story: 'the waiting father' – yet another proposed title of the parable – seeing his son while *still a long way off*; the indignity of a respectable man running *to meet* his son; the shock the gathered crowd – for little is private in the ancient village – would experience as instead of the expected and deserved rejection or rebuke they watched as the father *flung his arms around . . . and kissed* his son, not waiting for any words of explanation or self-abasement. Yet this is a story told and not an account of a real event which needs to be reconstructed from a brief report; while it is possible that the first hearers would mentally envisage these details, it is better to stay with the balder but no less powerful parable as handed and written down. The *servants* or *slaves* are instructed to treat him as a son of the family: *the best robe* would be a sign of status, either within the family or like that of an honoured guest, the *ring* perhaps a sign of authority, *and sandals* confirmation that he was not to be put to work. His prepared words of repentance, if that is what they are, are ignored, and it is not these which ensure his restoration but the independent act of his father. *The fatted calf* would be slaughtered only on major occasions and implies more than a family banquet, but it is a misreading to suppose that this is to ensure that the friends and neighbours who come as guests will be forced to recognize the son's restoration; this is *a feast* of celebration, as in the two earlier parables, and marks a climax to the story.

However, in contrast to the previous examples, a further scene is added, now focussing on *the elder son*. It is sometimes suggested that he also would have benefitted from the division of the estate, and that his implicit acceptance of this and his failure to reconcile the younger son at the beginning of the story already portray him in negative colours. This is to read into the story details which are nowhere suggested. The strong language of the REB translation in v.29 turns his reply into a retort, and makes him sound petulant as he claims to *have slaved* – the word might better be translated 'served' as in 'the servants' in v.22 – for his father and never to have *disobeyed his orders*; this encourages a negative characterization of the elder son which is not fully justified by the text. He refers to his brother as *this son of yours* (or simply, 'this your son') not because he is disassociating himself from them but because the story throughout speaks in terms of 'the son' and 'the father': only at the very end does he become, in the father's words, *your brother*, perhaps signalling the restoration of the family. His anger is not a public insubordination and dereliction of his duties as eldest son, and his absence until *the festivities* were well under way is part of the stage-management of story-telling. The elder son was justified in his claims, and whatever the legal situation after the division of the property, the story assumes that he has been and will be tied to the estate, owing his father the total obedience due in society at the time: he will be sole heir, and the words *you are always with me* are a promise as well as a responsibility. The eldest son is not as 'lost' as the younger; yet he has reacted with anger and refused to share in the celebration: thus his response provokes a reiteration of the climax of the parable – the inescapable joy at the restoration of the lost.

Luke may have seen in the elder son a model of the Pharisees, but if he did they are among those whose place is secure, just as in 5.31–32 they are among the healthy or righteous. Equally, there is no special merit in the younger son's decision to return: he does not earn his restoration but receives it by the independent will of the father. However, here the father does not go looking for the lost one. For this reason it is unwise to take this parable on its own as 'the gospel in the Gospel', and to make an immediate identification of the father with God (cf. vv. 18, 21 and note); there could be an element of 'if a human father could so act, how much more God' as in 11.11–13, although an alternative reading would be – 'Can you imagine an earthly father so acting! Well, God does, and so perhaps you need to rethink what "father" means.' Yet perhaps what this discussion and what the history of the interpretation and the preaching of the parable show is how the parables interact with readers in each situation revealing new possibilities of meaning: the parable does not explain itself but it makes possible new understandings, some-times by producing a sense of shock. Subsequent generations of Christian believers have seen in this parable their own story, or the story of the repentant believer; in Luke's context it may be rather more a justification to those who protested at Jesus' style of ministry and a challenge to them to acknowledge that *it is imperative to rejoice and celebrate*. On Jesus' lips the message may not have been so very different, but as with other parables, its primary message may have been a declaration of the offer of the kingdom: 'the poor are brought the good news and happy he who does not find a stumbling block' (7.22–23).

Riches and readiness for the kingdom
16.1–15

After the relative unity of theme and the directness of the preceding chapters, what follows appears both more disconnected and more obscure. Jesus teaches through a mixture of parables (a term not used), or tales, and brief sayings; since some of the material is also found, differently located, in Matthew while some is peculiar to Luke, he has probably strung this teaching together, often with only the loosest of connections. The audience is now Jesus' *disciples*, although the Pharisees are never far away (v.14), a pattern which continues to 18.31 through the remainder of Jesus' journey to Jerusalem. Thus the material seems both to offer a life-style for those who would be disciples and to set it against the alternative values which are represented by the Pharisees. There are several indications that the material has been used both before Luke and now by him to tackle questions which faced the early church, making it difficult to discover its original setting in the ministry of Jesus.

The story of the 'dishonest steward' is a good example of this. The introduction *there was a rich man* (cf. 12.16; 16.19) introduces a favourite theme of Luke's, even though it is his *steward* who is the focal character; we should probably assume that the latter was an agent of his master, with full oversight of the estate and business, and had authority to act on his master's behalf. The charge, presumably justified since he does not reject it, that he *was squandering the property* of his master provides a loose link with the son who did the same (15.13), although in this case presumably it was due to mismanagement or inefficiency. Dismissed from his post, he recognizes his inability to turn to manual labour, and the impossibility of turning to begging; such soliloquizing is characteristic of Lukan parables (cf. 12.17–19; 15.17–19; 18.4–5) and allows us to see not just what he does but the attitude of mind behind it. He has been instructed to *produce* the *accounts,* not as evidence but so that they can be passed on to his successor, and it is through these that he determines to ensure his future security, so that there *will be people* who will be indebted to him and who will offer him a job or a home. Exactly what this entails is not clear since neither the nature of *his master's* business nor the status of his *debtors* are explained; either money-lending, perhaps in the form of goods in kind, or land rental by which the tenants paid in produce would be possible. What the steward does is to renegotiate the sums due, presumably acting as if he still had the authority of his job. According to one explanation the sum stated on the bond or *account* was both the capital and the interest, which perhaps would constitute the steward's fee: what he does is strike out the interest component, in the case of the *olive oil,* calculated at 100%, in the case of the *wheat* at 25%; by cancelling his 'cut' he is not only offering them substantial savings since the volumes are large but also winning their gratitude, and, incidentally, conforming with Deut. 23.19–20. An alternative reading would understand him as cutting the fixed rent which he had earlier agreed, something which might be done by a generous landlord after a poor harvest or bad weather; although this might seem to be cheating his master yet further, it would win both him and his master friends!

Whether we should see him as suddenly honest, as continuing his dishonest practices, or just as calculating his advantage, depends in part on where the story finishes. The REB takes the first part of v.8 as the conclusion: if *the master applauded the . . . steward*, then presumably he has not been further defrauded, although he may have lost out on some profit or have been represented as acting with a generosity he had not intended. The last sentence in the verse must then be Jesus' comment recognizing both the steward and his master as among *the children of this world* who know well how to deal with their own kind.

An alternative is that since the word 'master' (also in vv.3, 5) may also be translated *'lord'*, it is Jesus who praised the steward, as happens in the similar 18.6: in both cases he was prepared to use a disreputable character to teach a serious lesson. However, in this case the second half of the verse would follow awkwardly, now reporting directly Jesus' comment, after the implied indirect comment in the first half, and before a fresh beginning in v.9. Since the story began by introducing the rich man, it is natural to end with him, and so the interpretation which has Jesus as 'the master' or 'lord' is probably less likely.

Taken on its own, the story is of a man who is faced with a crisis and, recognizing the urgency of the situation, acts with speed and foresight. As such it may be laid alongside other parts of Jesus' teaching which stress the urgency of the demand of the kingdom and the need to take action without delay but with due calculation (12.35–46, 57–59 (note); 14.28–32). However, the parable has been reinterpreted in new directions; on any reading the second half of v.8 connects more awkwardly than the REB's *'For'* betrays and perhaps represents a further stage in the telling. It makes a distinction between two groups of people, those who are guided by the ordinary values *of this world*, and those who belong to the *light*, presumably not 'of this world'. The imagery here, the formula *children of*, and the contrast between this world and another, or between light and darkness, echo the thought of Jewish literature of the period, particularly the community of the Dead Sea Scrolls which saw itself as separate from all other people. Thus with the addition of this verse, although the steward's dishonesty, if such it was, is hardly held up as an example to be imitated, his *astute . . . dealing with his own kind* is a provocation for the disciples, and perhaps for the church, to act with similar efficient deliberation, whether with their own kind or with the world.

V.9 offers a particular application of this, although the original intention may have been more general. That the parable was about a rich man and about the use of resources was incidental to its main point, but here it has become the main focus. Like the steward, the disciples are urged *to win friends* through their use of *worldly wealth*: the term here is literally *'mammon of dishonesty'* or *'unrighteousness'*, using a Hebrew or Aramaic term whose root meaning may have been 'something entrusted', a root which will become part of a word play in the following verses; wealth is not inherently unrighteous but Luke's formula, lost by the REB, acknowledges that it may become that. Just as the steward ensured for himself a home, so are they to ensure their reception *into a heavenly home* – the idea of 'dwelling places' in the life to come has other parallels (cf. John 14.2). How they are to do this is not explained, although it is natural to assume a reference to almsgiving as winning the friendship of the poor who might intercede or of the watching angels who might do the 'receiving'.

The further exhortations in vv.10–12 might seem to undermine the positive use of the parable: although surely wrongly, even some modern commentators have seen the original story as a negative example to be avoided, and a similar caution about the steward's example may have provoked these verses. The clauses are carefully balanced around three contrasts: *small matters* versus *great*; *the wealth of this world*, again *'unrighteous mammon'* (see above), versus *the wealth that is real* (cf. 12.33), and *what belongs to another*, perhaps again 'of the world' which is not the disciples' 'own', versus *anything of your own*. The rhetoric is clear even if the reference of the terms is less so – how is trustworthiness with 'unrighteous mammon' measured? The warning may in part be against any attempt to create a divorce between integrity of behaviour in daily living and the 'spiritual' nature of discipleship implied by the earlier description of them as 'children of light'; there is also an echo of the exhortations to trust-worthiness in 12.42–48 and 19.11–27 (cf.v.17), and it is easy to see how these words could be directed to those within the body of disciples or of the church.

If the preceding passages suggest that wealth can and must be properly used, a final saying warns against misunderstanding this. Matthew has this in almost exactly the same words in a different context (Matt. 6.24), perhaps indicating that Luke is constructing this discussion from diverse material. Here *Money* is again *'mammon'*, thus binding the passage together and looking back to the first use of the term in v.9; now, however, it is virtually personified and even without the epithet 'unrighteous' is given an almost demonic power, demanding an allegiance that is due to *God* alone. A dualism of contrasting powers and of contrasting choices has its roots in the Judaism of the period, with parallels again in the Dead Sea Scrolls. If, as has regularly been suggested, Luke's church included some who were wealthy, this saying would sound a stern warning.

It is therefore significant that Luke here introduces *the Pharisees* as the hitherto unnoticed observers of the debate. There is nothing in contemporary sources to confirm that they particularly *loved money*, and much to suggest that they were not among the wealthy classes; they have become for Luke the archetypal opponents and representatives of 'the establishment' which opposed Jesus, but if the preceding warning was partly directed at Luke's own community their mention here would be the more galling (cf. I Tim. 6.10). In fact the charge he lays against them, their desire to *impress others with* their *righteousness*, makes no reference to riches, unless it is implied that they spend on almsgiving only to win praise. God as one who *knows your hearts*, prosaically translated by the REB as *sees through you*, is a biblical theme (I Sam. 16.7; Acts 1.24) as too is the idea of what is an *abomination* (*detestable*) to God (Deut. 24.4; Dan. 9.27). It seems as if Luke has used a standard polemic to round off this section, and to give it a further rooting in a part of the Gospel which traces the increasing hostility Jesus faces.

Although the meaning and structure of this section are not always clear, it provides a fascinating insight into the use and reuse of the Gospel traditions within the life of the church. In different contexts the material has been differently interpreted, and has been balanced with other traditions, in an attempt to allow it to address new situations and to avoid misunderstanding.

The law, the prophets, and the good news of the kingdom
16.16–30

Again a single train of thought is not easy to detect through the sayings of vv.16–18, which have parallels in different places in Matthew (Matt. 11.12–13; 5.18, 32), and the parable or tale of the rich man and Lazarus, which is found in Luke alone. The references to the Law, or Moses, and the prophets which introduce and conclude this section may have prompted their association, while Luke may have seen a link between the Pharisees (vv.14–15) and the Law. The status of 'the Law' was the cause of intense debate and uncertainty in the early church which sought both to affirm it as the revelation of God and to justify a situation where Christians no longer treated it as binding in its entirety. Here Luke provides a partial answer by restricting *the Law and the prophets* to the period *until John*. The combination is a reminder that in Jewish thought 'the Law', or Torah, does not mean the legal formulations of the Old Testament but the whole of what modern scholarship calls 'the Pentateuch', the first five books of the 'Old Testament'; combined with 'the prophets' it could refer to the whole of (Jewish) scripture. John the Baptist, as elsewhere in Luke, is a bridge figure, the culmination of the time of preparation and the herald of the arrival of the fulfilment (cf. 1.5–25; 3.1–20; 7.18–35). That fulfilment has come in the proclamation of *the good news of the kingdom*: this could be taken merely as the announcement of the kingdom to come, but for Luke 'the good news' is already experienced as a reality in the ministry of Jesus. The picture of *everyone* forcing *a way in* uses the imagery of the kingdom as a physical realm under siege; it brings together the urgency of the demand (see above) and Jesus' invitation to 'the sinners', breaking down established barriers. *Forces* could also be translated *'is pressurized'*, recalling the compelling of the uninvited guests into the banquet (14.23).

Yet this understanding of Jesus as introducing the radically new can lead – and often has led – to the dismissal of God's past acts of revelation and of what has already been made known of God's nature and will through the scriptures. To do so is to reject the witness of Jesus' own life and the teaching of the early church. So Luke reaffirms in surprisingly unequivocal terms the continuing validity of the law, even down to the smallest stroke which distinguished *one letter* from another. It was, of course, part of Christian hope that *heaven and earth* would *come to an end*, so saying it *is easier* for this to happen may not merely be a hyperbolic way of asserting that validity, but a way of limiting it to the time before then, in which we continue to live. Yet the evidence of Acts (e.g. Acts 15) shows that Luke did not think that the Law with all its provisions must continue to be observed by all believers in the church. Possibly he meant that the Law would not *lose its force* as a pointer to Jesus (24.27, 44). More probably, and this is supported by Acts, he was not fully aware of the conflict the problem would generate, or had generated, in the early church (Gal. 4.21; 5.2–4); he may have taken for granted the relaxation of some of its provisions but have wanted to stand firm on the continuing validity of others, particularly those we might call 'moral rules'.

This would explain why he now adds the example of divorce and remarriage. The fact that Jesus' teaching on this was handed down in several different forms suggests that this was a very live concern in the early church (Matt. 5.31–2; 19.1–12; Mark 10.1–12; I Cor. 7.10–11). In his version here Luke does not appeal to God's intention in creation (Gen. 1.27; 2.24 = Mark 10.6–8), neither does he ask on what conditions, if any, divorce might be possible (cf. Matt. 5.31–2; 19.3, 9; Deut. 24.1–4). As was the norm in society at the time, he assumes that divorce is the act of the male partner (ctr. Mark 10.12): he *divorces*, she is *divorced*. However, the crucial step for him appears not to be the divorce but the act of remarrying: it is when a divorced man or woman is involved in remarriage that the man *commits adultery*. This reflects a different understanding from Jewish law according to which adultery is sexual intercourse with or by a married woman (Deut. 5.18; 22.22). By declaring remarriage adultery, Luke may be implicitly declaring divorce invalid: because the first marriage is in effect still operative, sexual relations with another person even within 'marriage' are adulterous.

Jesus' teaching as recorded in Matt. 19.1–12; Mark 10.1–12 sets him firmly within debates in first-century Judaism on the issue, while his reiteration of God's intention in creation can be understood as part of the agenda of the kingdom where human 'hardness of heart' (Mark 10.5) is overcome. This is not Luke's framework, as his omission of that incident indicates. Presumably he sees his version as exemplifying the continuing force of the Law, although he does not quote the Old Testament (ctr. Matt. 5.31). His choice of this particular example matches his model of discipleship where the disciple may even be called upon to leave his wife (14.20, 26; 18.29); it reflects an ascetic ideal which has always lived in tension within the church with an affirmation of family life and of the need to respond to the realities of human weakness.

The story which immediately follows is only linked with this debate when it returns to the witness of 'Moses and the prophets'. Once again it centres around one of Luke's favourite themes, wealth, introducing as its first character a nameless *rich man* – the popular 'Dives' is merely taken from the Latin word – and contrasting with him the only named person in a parable, *Lazarus*, the equivalent of Eleazar. Jesus may have been appealing to a popular tale for other parallels have been found, including in Egyptian literature, of the reversal of fortunes of a rich man and a beggar after death: in a tour of the underworld the former is seen in torment, the latter in the lap of luxury, warning against over-hasty envy of the rich; the theme of the return of a dead person with a message for the living also belongs to popular narrative. It is also probably part of popular piety that the individuals go immediately after death to their allotted places, both presumably in *Hades*, the 'Sheol' of the Old Testament, since they are in sight of one another; one part is a place of *torment* the other of blessing – the older and more literal '*in the bosom of Abraham*' captures the sense of honour and intimacy better than the REB's more prosaic *with Abraham*.

Although it is often assumed that the rich man is punished for his greed and apathy towards the poor *at his gate*, this is not stated, neither is he wrong to call *Abraham, my father* (cf. v.25). *Abraham* does not explain the rich man's fate as punishment neither does he refuse to send Lazarus to his aid because such punishment is his due; he merely reminds him that whereas *in* their *lifetime* the one had enjoyed *the good things*, the other *bad*, now conditions are reversed: Lazarus now enjoys the *consolation* which the rich enjoy in their life-time (= 6.24, 'time of happiness'). The extreme wealth of the one and abject poverty of the other, both exhibited in appearance (cf. Prov. 31.22) and food, living in closest conjunction with each other was, and is, part of the reality of present society. No doubt it was part of the hope of the poor that this inequality would be reversed in the age to come, and it is also part of Luke's vision that God's salvation 'means filling the hungry with good things and sending the rich away empty' (1.53; 6.20, 24). However, that vision only underlines the wrongness of the present inequalities; this parable does not say that the wealth of the rich man is morally neutral, any more than is the poverty of Lazarus, nor that it is only the former's use of his resources which is open to judgment. The vision of the future, whether in popular views of Hades or in Jesus' preaching of salva-tion, stands in judgment on the luxury of the rich in the face of the abjection of the poor.

Similarly, the warning to his *five brothers* is not merely for them to mend their ways – although for the first time a moral note is intro-duced in the hope *they will repent* – but to recognize their own situa-tion in the light of God's intention. *Moses and the prophets*, to whom they should have attended, are not sources of moral commands but proclaim a community ordered in accordance with God's will.

The parable itself spoke only of *someone from the dead* visiting them; in the final verse this is restated as *someone rising from the dead*, the formula which is regularly used of Jesus' resurrection. It seems likely that as the story was retold, a detail which was part of the popular narrative was reinterpreted in the light of faith in Jesus' resurrection. Even that could not be guaranteed to bring people to a new understanding. More important, and here the parable picks up the theme of v.17, scripture – *Moses and the prophets* – and the resurrection of Jesus must be understood in the light of each other and as confirming each other. They do not oppose each other – in later language Old and New Testament do not contradict each other; to fully hear God's call in one is to hear it in the other.

Luke's teaching on wealth is undoubtedly harsh; despite presentations of this Gospel as full of compassion and of accommodation to continuing daily life, there is a rigorous demand here which is part of the rigour of discipleship. It stands in tension with a picture of Jesus, and in Acts of Paul, who accepts and moves naturally within the welcome of the wealthy, perhaps reflecting the presence of such people in Luke's church. We may well wonder how Luke saw this rigorous demand as to be fulfilled within that church's life; however, to soften it out of the conviction that the church had to and did continue to live 'in the world' (cf. v.8), would be to lose sight of Luke's vision of 'the year of the Lord's favour' proclaimed by Jesus.

The responsibility of discipleship
17.1–11

Attention again reverts to the disciples and to their pattern of life The formal description in vv.5–6 of them as *the apostles*, a term] rarely uses in the Gospel (cf. 6.13; 9.10), and of Jesus as *the Lord* post-resurrection title, suggests that Luke is consciously wri from the perspective of the church and the concerns within it While in Jesus' ministry this teaching may have expressed hi cern for 'the lost' in society, in Luke's context *one of these li*' would probably refer to fellow believers, perhaps those in particular support. *Causes of stumbling* must refer to any' might cause such to give up on their faith and to fall away although the word originally meant 'a trap', the noun ha' semi-technical sense in Christian writing, not simply c or hurdle to overcome but of something leading to final failure or apostasy (cf. Rom. 9.33; 11.9). That there inevitably will be such things is simply accepted, and there is no attempt here to explain or to justify their existence; yet to be *the person through whom they come* is to carry a dreadful responsibility and to incur dire judgment expressed through the hyperbolic image of death by drowning, weighted with a heavy *millstone,* and though the prophetic cry of doom *woe betide* (cf. Isa. 3.9–13; Luke 6.24–26, translated 'alas').

The warning to *be on your guard* belongs in a setting of eschatalogical danger (21.34), and so serves as a fitting climax to vv.1–2 as in the REB, although it could also be taken, following the traditional verse numbering, as an introduction to the following exhortation. Here *your brother* is 'your fellow believer', and Luke recognizes that even within the community there may be conflict; reproof is proper, but whereas the Matthean parallel urges free forgiveness (Matt. 18.21–22), Luke, typically (cf. 15.7, 10 and note), looks for repentance. Such repentance is to be met with unqualified – *seven* is the proverbial number of completeness – forgiveness.

These questions of responsibility and forgiveness may have had in mind particularly those in leadership, and so *the apostles,* perhaps representing the leaders in the church, naturally ask for an *increase* to their *faith* to face such demands. Jesus' (*the Lord*) reply does not mean that at present they do not even have the smallest imaginable degree of faith but that it is the quality of faith which is decisive: faith such as that which Jesus demands would be sufficient to do the 'impossible'. Variations on this saying in the Gospels suggest that the issue of faith was a live one: Mark, followed by Matthew, speaks of the steadfast conviction that could tell a mountain to be thrown into the sea (Mark 11.22–23; Matt. 21.21; cf. also I Cor. 13.2); Matt. 17.20, like Luke, refers to the smallness of faith as the proverbial *mustard seed* and again has the mountain and the sea; Luke, by contrast, refers to a *mulberry,* or perhaps sycamore, *tree,* although, improbably, he also has it *planted in the sea.* However, whereas in the Markan and Matthean contexts faith is one that works miracles, in Luke it is the faith to live, and perhaps to lead, within the community. Faith does not seek to prove itself by spectacular wonderworking, but enables even the incredible demands of forgiveness to become possible.

It is therefore no accident that this request for faith is immediately followed by a call to obedience to 'the Lord'. Although the parable starts by likening the disciples to a master who *has a servant,* in fact it is with the servant, or slave, that they are to compare themselves. It is the slave's duty to do all the tasks assigned him, and having completed his labour in the field then to be ready to serve his master at table; he does not expect his master to treat him as an equal nor to offer him thanks – the parables rarely question the social *status quo!* So, the disciples, and perhaps in Luke's mind particularly those in leadership, are not to think they deserve special honour: they *have only done* what they were under obligation to do. They *deserve no credit*: this translation avoids the problem that the natural translation of the Greek, *'we are but useless'* or *'worthless'* (NRSV), seems to add an additional 'disqualification'; the point of the comparison is not their ability at the task but that they are but *slaves* whose very nature, as then understood, was to serve.

In this way the central section of the travel narrative has increasingly focussed on the demands of discipleship, demands which Luke surely saw as to be expressed within the life of the community even if anything that might be called 'church life' was far from uppermost in Jesus' preaching.

The Third Stage in the Journey to Jerusalem
17.11–18.30

The reminder that Jesus was on *his journey to Jerusalem* suggests we should see a new stage here (cf. 13.22), although there continues to be a mixture of healing, parable and teaching, and of groups within the audience, while there are also a number of continuities of theme from the previous sections. If only now was *he travelling through the borderlands of Samaria and Galilee* then Jesus would not have progressed very far since approaching a Samaritan village in 9.52; but the Greek here, literally '*through the midst of*', suggests that Luke had only a limited knowledge of the geography and that he was more concerned to provide an appropriate setting for the next healing with its mixed group of Jews and a Samaritan. After that, location will play no significant role until 18.31 when the approach to Jerusalem begins in deliberate and measured earnest.

The tenth leper
17.11–19

As just suggested, Luke has staged this miracle to make possible what for him is its most important point. It is found only in Luke and recalls the parable in 10.29–37 where again a Samaritan, in contrast to the Jewish priest and Levite, alone shows the right response. Although this is the only occasion in Luke when Jesus heals more than one person at once, there are some inevitable parallels with the earlier healing of a single leper (5.12–16). This time their remaining at a distance probably fulfils Lev. 13.46, while Jesus, as in 5.14, sends them to the priest in accordance with Lev. 13.49: that a Samaritan would not go to a priest in Jerusalem is a detail in which Luke would not be interested. Whereas on that earlier occasion the man was healed at Jesus' word, here it is only when they have left him that they *were made clean* – leprosy being viewed as much as a source of impurity as an illness (cf. 5.13). The focus of the story, however, is not on the healing but on the response and identity of one of the ten: *shouts of praise to God* are a favourite Lukan response to a miracle (cf. 5.25–6 and note), but this man also *turned back*; his *praise to God* is expressed in his obeisance and thanks to Jesus. The climax comes as Luke only now divulges his identity, *a Samaritan,* by the first century rejected as outside the people of God and often involved in reciprocal hostility (cf. 9.51–6 and note). Jesus' three questions hammer home the point: *all* were healed but the only one to return and give praise to God was *this foreigner* – the word used emphasizes his alien status within the religious structures which Jesus does not deny.

If as a Samaritan the man recalls the earlier parable, as a leper he perhaps recalls Naaman the Syrian (II Kings 5.1–19); in the sermon at Nazareth Jesus had used the example of Naaman to show how the promise of salvation would go to those outside the people of God who rejected it (4.24–27 and note). That theme was continued in 7.1–10 as well as in 10.25–37; although Jesus sends him *on* his *way,* this Samaritan prefigures the spread of the Gospel beyond the boundaries of Israel, something which was to happen after the death and departure of Jesus (cf. Acts 8.5–24).

Jesus' final words of dismissal, *your faith has cured you,* seem to confuse the story, for all ten were cured while the point has been to distinguish this one, who has not, in any case, shown particular faith so much as gratitude. It is possible to read into the ambiguity of 'cured', which can also mean *'saved'*, a suggestion that in his case alone the healing points to a deeper reality. More probably Luke is using a favourite formula (cf. 7.50 and note; 8.48; 18.42) to round off the story: thus the encounter moves from need to prayer, *take pity on us* (cf. 18.38–9), and then to praise and to dismissal – a model for Christian experience in times of need. Perhaps Luke saw how this healing could become a 'parable' in answer to the disciples' earlier request in v.5.

The surprise of the future
17.20–37

Luke has brought together here two very different sections of teaching, one directed to the Pharisees which is peculiar to Luke (vv.20–21), and the other (vv.22–37) to the disciples which contains some material found also in Matthew (especially Matt. 24.26–28, 37–41) and which anticipates a more extensive discussion in ch. 21 (see commentary). This contrast between the Pharisees and the disciples has become characteristic of Jesus' travel journey, while we have seen how the teaching to the disciples has also been directed by Luke at the continuing disciples within the church.

For Luke *the kingdom of God* does not belong to the unknown future; the dynamism of its presence was already to be experienced in the ministry of Jesus even if that did not exhaust its meaning (10.9, 11; 11.20). That *the Pharisees* should ask when it would *come* fits well an understanding of Jesus as a prophetic figure with a powerful message of warning, but it also fits Luke's picture of them as those who could not perceive the real meaning of Jesus' ministry. The REB translation suggests that their search for signs that would presage when *the kingdom of God comes* is futile. A better translation might be *'the kingdom of God does not come with observation'*: it is not a watchful and attentive scrutiny which ensures its presence, exemplified perhaps in the way that they have repeatedly been 'observing' him (6.7; 14.1; 20.20); neither can people triumphantly locate it, always somewhere else, *here* or *there*.

What Jesus declares is that *the kingdom of God is among you*: this is probably the best translation, for although the Greek would more naturally mean 'within you' there is nothing to suggest that Jesus, or Luke, saw the kingdom as a purely inward and spiritual reality, particularly not 'within' the Pharisees. Even so the meaning is ambiguous; 'among you' could mean present within you as a people, within Israel, or even present among this group gathered here, namely in Jesus himself; it could mean 'within your grasp', that if only they could but see they could reach out and experience for themselves its power. Although there is little other evidence for this use of the Greek preposition, something along these lines seems to be what is intended: the kingdom does not come by urgent human activity; it is there, to be experienced and to be acknowledged.

When Jesus goes on to talk to *the disciples* about *the days of the Son of Man* we should not think that Luke is identifying the coming of the kingdom with the coming of the Son of Man; in fact the opposite is true for he has separated them by audience and by imagery and language. Indeed he does not speak of the Son of Man 'coming' but being 'revealed' (v.30); this is a mystery which is a source of both hope and warning for the disciples as they face present and future, while 'the kingdom', at least in part, offers a way of understanding Jesus' ministry as it impacts on all who encounter him now.

By now it has become clear that the enigmatic title *Son of Man* binds together Jesus' ministry, the suffering and death he is 'bound' to undergo, and the vision of ultimate vindication for him and those who put their trust in him (see note on pp.42f. and the references there). This is particularly true in this passage and suggests that Luke has included this here as an integral part of his understanding of the nature of discipleship. It could be simply in the on-going tedium of the life of the church but more probably it would be under persecution that they would *long to see one of the days of the Son of Man*: the phrase is unusual since it implies a period of time in contrast to the sudden 'day' of vv.24, 30–31. It could nonetheless refer to that day or look back to the halcyon days of his earthly ministry; perhaps there is a deliberate ambiguity drawing attention only to the 'emptiness' of the then present, although this fits v.26, where the phrase is repeated, less comfortably.

As with the kingdom, claims to have (re)discovered the presence of the Son of Man are to be ignored, but not because it all the while is there to be experienced so much as because in the vindication of the future all the ambiguities of the present will be overcome. That vindication will be as unmistakeable as *a lightning flash* which leaves no part of the earth in darkness; yet such a hope should not lead to facile enthusiasm, for the vindication can only follow the *suffering* and rejection that Jesus as Son of Man must first undergo. The echo of the prediction in 9.22 prepares for the reminder that those who hope to share the vindication must also share the abasement (9.23–26).

The appeal to scriptural exemplars is not just as illustration, for the destruction of the habitable world by water *in the days of Noah* (Gen. 6.11–7.24) and of Sodom by fire *in the days of Lot* (Gen. 18.20–19.26) had become paradigms of God's judgment on an evil society, and of the deliverance of the righteous minority. Here the emphasis is on the heedlessness of those who *ate and drank*, continuing their normal activities, oblivious to the coming judgment. Here *the days of the Son of Man* must refer to the future, and the unusual plural is intended as a parallel to 'the days' of Noah or of Lot; the apparent unending flow of those 'days' is suddenly brought to a halt by the *day* when *Noah went into the ark* or *when Lot left Sodom*, as it will also be *when the Son of Man is revealed*. At that point it will be too late to take preventive or protective action: *Lot's wife*, who according to Gen. 19.26 turned back to look and became a pillar of salt, is now held up as a warning against wanting to hold on to some personal security, to grasp even then at one's *belongings*. However, this warning is not inspired only by the inescapable suddeness and uncertain distance of that future moment as it is in the parallel passages in Matt. 24.17–18 and Mark 13.15–16; it is the culmination of the continuing demand of disciple-ship that excludes any self-interest or self-seeking; the surrender of these in the present is the only way to sharing in the fullness of life.

If judgment is sudden, it is also divisive; the *two . . . in one bed* are probably men, since *one* and *the other* are masculine, and in typical Lukan pairing balance the *two women . . . grinding*, although the *night* accommodates the former more than the latter! It is not clear whether the one is *taken* for judgment or rescue, and *the other left* in safety or to be destroyed, neither on what principle the division is made. Instead the emphasis is that it will then be too late to try to be in the right place or on the right side; the choices that may be made now will no longer be open then. The disciples do not ask 'When?' as did the Pharisees, but *'Where?'*, an odd question which is met by an equally enigmatic answer. It is probably over-interpretation to turn *the carcass* into a metapor of the decay or corruption which will invite *the vultures* – technically 'eagles' but they were regularly confused – as a symbol of judgment; neither does this point to a less than uni-versal judgment directed only against those places or people who invite it, reducing the imagery in the preceding verses to hyperbole or 'myth'. It is a dramatic and ominous climax; however inaus-picious or disappointing the present may seem, vindication and judgment will be inevitable and unmistakeable.

The promise of vindication
18.1–8

The parable which follows acts as a further climax to the teaching on the future, and is clearly directed to the disciples, present and future. Like the 'parable of the unjust steward' (16.1–8), this *parable* also uses a less than reputable character, whose inward deliberations we over-hear, to point to God's activity, and it has been reinterpreted as it has been handed down. The basic story is clear, even if the pattern of justice envisioned is not. *A judge who had no fear of God or respect of man* is the very antithesis of an ideal judge, although corrupt judges are a theme of prophetic indictment (Micah 3.9–11; Amos 5.12); by contrast *a widow* is the model of those who need protection (Jer. 22.3). Here the judge gives *her justice* despite his character and inclinations, only to avoid being finally beaten down by her. Thus far the parable recalls that of the man who gives way to his friend's persistent bold-ness in 11.5–10: if even someone with no care or concern will respond, how much more, we have to presume, will God. This emphasis to the parable is brought out by the words of Jesus in v.6 drawing attention to the *unjust judge*'s motives: Jesus is here described as *the Lord*, the title used by the church who without this dominical reassurance may have hesitated to see God as represented by so disreputable a character.

However, v.7 then adds a further affirmation which directs the parable away from prayer in general to the cry to God for justice. 'To *give justice*' is taken out of the parable, where it is the action of a judge, to become the promised action of God in the final vindication of the faithful or the *chosen*; these are those who experience God's final salvation (Mark 13.20, 22, 27) and for Luke point to the disciples and the subsequent church who are called to *keep on praying*. Where the REB has *to whom he listens patiently*, a better translation would be *'and yet'* or *'although he delays over them'* – the NRSV's 'will he delay' is possible but grammatically more awkward: the experience of the early church, and one of which Luke is very aware, was that God's vindication did not come as soon as some expected. Such apparent delay should not lead them to *lose heart* or to give up crying out *night and day*, for it is certain that God will *give justice*. The addition of *soon enough* or 'speedily' may seem to undercut both the parable – for the judge did not act speedily – and the basic dilemma that it is being used to meet; although Luke in different ways, including in his account of the early church, meets that dilemma of the continuing life of the church and of discipleship, he does not want to dilute the confidence in God's culminating act of salvation but keeps it as the goal which defines discipleship. The final question thus turns away from anxieties about 'when?' or 'why not yet?' to the more immediate one which must face the disciples or the church: whether they use the imagery of God's vindication or that of the coming of *the Son of Man* as in the last part of ch. 17 (see notes), what matters for them is whether they maintain their faithfulness.

The parable is thus both about 'the unjust judge' and about 'the persistent widow'; the introduction that *they should keep on praying* points to the latter, but such refusal to lose heart is rooted in confidence in the faithfulness of God who is the antithesis of the judge. By placing the parable after the teaching at the end of ch. 17, Luke has implicitly redirected it from a general encouragement to faithful prayer to confidence in God's final vindication. Yet this shift is not as great as it may seem. Many of the themes in the parable are to be found in Sir. 35.14–26, which also moves from God as the judge in whom there is no partiality and who listens to the widow, to certain confidence that the Lord will not delay and will bring judgment and mercy. Prayer for justice in society and prayer for God's final salvation are inseparable from each other, and to yearn for one is to yearn for the other.

The lifting up of the humble
18.9–14

Like the preceding parable, this one is also found only in Luke, and works by contrasting two figures. Yet the connection with what precedes is weak and it may only have been linked by the theme of prayer, although here it is the prayer of two men in *the Temple* at Jerusalem, perhaps at one of the set hours of prayer, the third or ninth hour (i.e. 9 am or 3 pm). The depiction of *the Pharisee* and of *the tax-collector* as two opposing types does not come from any external evidence as to what these groups were really like; already in Luke's Gospel we have seen how they have become stereotypes of contrasting responses to Jesus' activity (see comments on pp.41 f., 44 f.). It is characteristic of a parable that such types should become even more of a caricature, for it is by caricature and contrast that parables work. Thus the Pharisee distances himself from *all the rest of humankind* whom he characterizes as thoroughly immoral in terms that Luke has already attributed to the Pharisees, *greedy* and *dishonest* (11.39, 42). His virtues, however, were proper ones and there is no suggestion that his claims were false: individual fasting, as opposed to communal fasting as on the Day of Atonement, seems to have become a feature of piety in first-century Judaism, and according to some texts was practised on Mondays and Thusdays; according to Deut. 14.22–23 tithes are due on the produce of land and animals, but here the Pharisee has extended this to *all that* he gets. It is not clear quite where the tax-collector is envisioned as standing; both the *distance* and his inability to adopt the normal attitude of prayer *to heaven* only emphasize his sense of lack of worth, and there is no suggestion that his evaluation of himself was wrong. Whether he *beat upon his breast* as a sign of active repentance or in despair (cf. 23.48) is not clear; but he acknowledges himself to be a *sinner*, a term Luke has already used of those to whom Jesus offers salvation (see p.37), and relies on God's forgiveness (not 'mercy' as in v.39)

The point of the parable is not that the tax-collector was *acquitted of his sins* (REB) because only he realized he had any: in the Greek there is no mention of 'sins' but the verb is the one which plays such an important role in Paul's thought and is traditionally translated '*justified*' where it emphasizes the creation of a right relationship with God. Yet even if Luke knew Paul's thought, he does not draw on it here and there is no contrast between faith and works; the tax-collector has *humbled himself* before God and so he has been restored to that right relationship by God. Nothing is said about the Pharisee: he thanked God that he was not like the tax-collector, and unlike the tax-collector he does not experience that restoration. He is the foil who emphasizes God's surprising reversal when 'the monarchs are brought down' and 'the lowly raised on high' (1.52). It is not so much that each gets what they deserve, but that God works in unexpected ways and does not reward always where men and women think reward is due: God is a God of the abased (cf. 14.11).

It is significant that Luke explains that this parable was directed *at those who were sure of their own goodness*; in view of the character of the Pharisee and their role elsewhere in the Gospel it is natural to think that the Pharisees were in mind. Yet Luke does not say this, and his more general phrasing suggests that he knew that such could be found elsewhere, perhaps even within his church. As elsewhere, he uses Jesus' challenge to the wealthy and self-confident to expose those failings within his own community (cf. 14; 16.14–15).

The kingdom and the challenge of discipleship
18.15–30

At this point Luke returns to the Markan outline which he left as Jesus began the journey to Jerusalem in 9.51. However, there is nothing in the text to indicate a new stage or setting, and we must assume that in Luke's eyes Jesus is still somewhere on that journey.

The incident of the bringing of the children is also found in Mark 10.13–16 (Matt. 19.13–15) but Luke refers to them as *babies*, a term he uses elsewhere (1.41, 44; 2.12, 16); this makes the following comparison rather more awkward since babies can neither come nor accept of their own free will! It is often pointed out that in the society of the time children were of little account, however dearly loved, and that in rebuking their bearers the disciples were only reflecting the common expectations of a teacher. In saying *the kingdom of God belongs to such as these* Jesus is not reserving the kingdom for children but using them as models of those who are disregarded or considered of little significance: thus the incident illustrates the final verse of the preceding parable, the exaltation of the humble. The imagery then moves to the relationship between 'accepting' and 'entering' the kingdom; there are many suggestions as to the meaning of *like a child*, some based on unrealistic idealizing of the innocence, passivity or ungrasping nature of children! Again the point seems rather that these are those who have no prior claim, who cannot presuppose their right to be there; they have no qualifications and nothing to offer, but it is they who will experience God's saving presence.

The incident has often been used in the church as an illustration of and sanction for infant baptism. While baptism was not one of Jesus' concerns during his ministry this interpretation may have been an early one. The command not to *try to stop them* uses the same language as Acts 8.36 and 10.47 where it precludes any objection that certain people, here because they were not Jewish, could not be baptized. However, unlike Mark and Matthew, Luke does not say that Jesus blessed or placed his hands upon them: *to touch* is very general. For Luke the incident says more about Jesus' affirmation of 'the humble' than specifically about children, although children were and may be important members of that group.

Their supposed insignificance contrasts with the status of Jesus' next encounter who is described without further explanation as *one of the rulers*. Although he asks the conditions by which he might *inherit* (better than *win*) *eternal life*, the meaning is the same as *to enter the kingdom of heaven* (cf. v.25). Jesus' rejection of the epithet *good* seems abrupt – and Matthew re-phrased it (Matt. 19.16–17); it is unlikely that Jesus is affirming his sinfulness, but he is using a conventional polite address to point to God as the giver of all good things – to be 'good' can also be to be a benefactor. In response to a similar earlier question Jesus had pointed to the law and to its summation in the double command of love of God and of neighbour (10.25–28); here he spells out *the commandments*, reaffirming their validity as expressions of the ultimate will of God. The ones he cites, in the traditional numbering the fifth to ninth of the ten commandments but in an order different from that in Deut. 5.16–20; Ex. 20.12–16, are those which deal with relations with other people.

When the man affirms his allegiance to these, Jesus replies there is only *one thing* he still lacks, but he demands two: first, that the man *sell everything . . . and give it to the poor*, and, secondly, that he *come and follow* him. The relationship between these and with the man's obedience to the commandments to which Jesus first pointed is not immediately clear. Was the 'one thing' still demanded discipleship, which incidentally would necessitate giving up his possessions, or was it the surrender of all he had, which incidentally would free him to follow Jesus. Was that demand made as an 'extra' only because he could claim to *have kept all these* since youth, for there is no suggestion that this was a false claim, or was it the real condition of eternal life from the beginning. Drawing out from this, according to Jesus or to Luke was the surrender of all possessions a demand made of all who would be disciples, or was it an 'extra' required only of some who would 'follow' in a particular way? In practice the latter has been the interpretation followed through most of the history of the church; in the circumstances of Jesus' ministry when the future course of events was far from clear it may not have been so obvious, while we have already seen how Luke both acknowledges the presence of the (comparatively) wealthy within the church and finds in it great danger. The greater value of *treasure in heaven* earned only by the giving of earthly treasure to the poor has been a special concern for him (12.33–34; 16.9–11). Here he describes the ruler as a *very rich man*, but he does not describe his reaction, unlike Mark 10.22 where he goes away (cf. Matt. 19.22); perhaps in leaving his response open Luke was inviting his readers to determine their own.

Neither Luke nor Jesus say it is only love or misuse of money which provide an obstacle to true discipleship. To be wealthy is itself a difficulty which can only be grasped by deliberate hyperbole: *a camel* was the largest animal familiar in Palestine, *the eye of a needle* a proverbially small hole. Suggestions that the latter was a tiny gate necessitating the removal of all unnecessary baggage are without foundation: the metaphor is of something which in human terms is *impossible*. Only *God* can make it *possible*, but what this means for the wealthy is left unsaid.

If the ruler, whose story is left unfinished, represents those who have to decide about the 'one thing', *Peter* represents those who have *left all* and followed Jesus. That 'all' means not only possessions but family; in fact, according to I Cor. 9.5 some of the apostles were accompanied by their wives, but for Luke discipleship demands surrender even of a *wife* (ctr. Mark 10.29; see Luke 14.20 and comment). Such surrender is *for the sake of the kingdom of God*: in the light of the previous incident Luke probably understands this as 'in order to be sure of entering it', but it could also mean 'in the cause of', perhaps in face of persecution or in order to preach. The ultimate reward is *eternal life*, which in this section Luke has used as an equivalent to the kingdom (cf. v.18) as participation in God's future salvation. It is contrasted with *this age*, where there is also a reward *many times over*: Luke does not specify this reward, certainly not as the multiple family of Mark 10.30 – he may have balked at 'wives many times over' – but he too may have believed that the renunciation of discipleship was more than compensated for in the life of the church.

It is characteristic of Luke that a parable which emphasizes the gratuitous nature of God's salvation should be followed by the harshest of demands of discipleship. The two belong together in a tension which cannot be resolved: on the one hand Luke is deeply aware that Jesus' ministry meant the overthrow of so many values and assumptions in society and the proclamation of a new order where God favoured the rejected and despised; on the other, he saw discipleship as no easy option but as demanding a total self-surrender which is not just emotional but involves one's very material and physical existence. He does not seek to harmonize these two aspects or to explain why they must co-exist; it is, however, important that Jesus' teaching on both takes place as he leads his disciples towards Jerusalem.

The Final Stage of the Journey to Jerusalem
18.31–19.27

So far the journey has only provided a loose but necessary framework for Jesus' teaching to the crowds, facing his opponents, and preparing his disciples. Now, on this last stage we are repeatedly reminded of Jesus' goal as he gets nearer and nearer to Jerusalem (18.31, 35; 19.1, 11). Each incident in this brief section is loaded with a significance which points beyond itself. At the same time there are important continuities from earlier material meaning that we should not see these stages in the journey as independent sections in the wider narrative.

Approaching Jericho
18.31–43

Through the travel narrative there have been hints that Jesus' closer band of disciples are being formed into a nucleus that was anticipated when he chose them as *the Twelve* (6.13; 9.1). It is to this group that he once again speaks of the goal of his journey *up to Jerusalem*. Predictions of his coming suffering in terms of *the Son of Man* had immediately preceded this journey (9.22; 43–45; see notes), and it is appropriate that they should be repeated as he comes to its end. On this occasion there are two new emphases: first, that what is to happen is in *fulfilment of what was written by the prophets*. This is a common conviction in Luke (24.27, 44–45; Acts 3.24; 10.43) and throughout the New Testament (I Cor. 15.3), although it was only later that they isolated particular passages and details; it was a way of affirming that all that happened fitted in with the continuing purposes of God. The second emphasis is that he would be *handed over to the Gentiles*, a clear reference to the Romans. Luke takes over this and the more specific details of the mockery, maltreatment and flogging from Mark 10.33–34, and it is in Mark, but not in Luke, that Jesus is mishandled by the Roman soldiers (Mark 15.16–20). While

Jesus may well have foreseen that his ministry could end in his death, such clearer details, including the involvement of the Romans, may have been read back into more vague anticipations.

As in 9.45 (cf. 24.13–25) the disciples fail to understand Jesus' words; this may in part be a later rationalization accompanying the insertion of more specific details, in order to explain the despair Jesus' death nonetheless provoked. The same divine activity which is at work in Jesus' death is also at work in preventing their understanding: God is the one who conceals.

However, sight can be given to those who do not see, and Luke follows this declaration of their 'blindness' with the healing of a blind man. In order to preserve this connection Luke has moved this healing to the approach *to Jericho*; in Mark, where the man is named as Bartimaeus, it takes place on the way out of Jericho (Mark 10.46–52), a setting not open to Luke who has a further incident to recount at Jericho, the story of Zacchaeus. In some ways Jesus' approach to Jericho, accompanied by *a crowd* who will shortly be giving *praise to God*, anticipates the entry to Jerusalem (19.28–40) and presents this last stage of the journey as a triumphal procession. *'Jesus of Nazareth'*, although not otherwise found in the Gospel, is a favourite designation in Acts (2.22; 3.6; 4.10 etc.), another hint that Luke may be looking forward to Jesus' presence in the church. Thus, hearing of his presence the man cries out in prayer *'have pity on me'* as did the lepers (cf. 17.13 and note), and shortly he will address Jesus as *'Lord'* or *'sir'*; first, however, he calls him *Son of David*, presumably a messianic, but not necessarily a political, title, although there is limited evidence of its use in Judaism prior to the New Testament. Like the disciples with the children earlier (18.15), some rebuked him, but he represents those for whom Jesus had come. Jesus not only restores his sight but declares *'your faith has healed you'*: once again (see 17.19 and note) there is a deliberate play on the ambiguity of the word which can also mean *'saved'*. *Instantly* healed, the man not only praises God, a routine response to a miracle in Luke (cf. 5.26 and note), but he also *followed Jesus*.

By these hints Luke takes the miracle and uses it as a response to the twelve's inability to understand in v.34. Yet as the man followed Jesus we are reminded of Peter's affirmation that they had left all to follow him and of Jesus' call to the rich ruler (18.28, 22); now this following is on the journey to Jerusalem with all that entails. Insistent prayer for mercy to one known as 'Lord', the assurance that faith brings salvation/healing, and the responsive praise to God are all themes which would resonate deeply in the life of the church. This is the last miracle that Luke recounts and he was surely aware of these deeper meanings; the miracle is not a mighty act tied to the past but a carrier of truths for the disciples of a later time.

Zacchaeus, a son of Abraham
19.1–11

Jesus' exultant procession continues *through the city* of Jericho, where another encounter reveals the true meaning and goal of his ministry. The story is only found in Luke, and in its vivid detail, particularly in Zacchaeus' need and efforts to climb *a sycamore tree*, it displays his narrative skill. Although Jericho was well situated for traffic and trade, and therefore for the levy of taxes, there is no other evidence of the post or responsibilities of a *superintendent of taxes*. The Greek is more literally '*a chief tax-collector*', and this, together with the description of him as *very rich*, makes him a representative of two favourite concerns of Luke. There is, perhaps, an intentional irony in that his name, *Zacchaeus*, means 'righteous' or 'upright', while the crowd dismiss him as *a sinner*. As we have seen, the linking of 'tax-collectors' with 'sinners', and the condemnation of Jesus for mixing with such, is a characteristic of the traditions about Jesus which Luke particularly develops (5.30; 15.1–2; 18.9–14), but which is far from obvious (see note on pp.42f.). 'Sinner' need not mean 'wicked' or 'immoral', and we should not conclude from the crowd's complaint that he was such.

Jesus' determination to *stay at* Zacchaeus' *house* is not explained, and imaginative attempts to psychologize Zacchaeus' state of mind miss the point. The twice repeated *today* points in a Lukan context to the presence of God's promised salvation (cf. 4.21; 5.26; 13.32–3); the *must* in Jesus' self-invitation is also a mark of almost divine necessity (cf. 9.22; 13.33). The conventional interpretation of this story has been that it is Jesus' gracious offer of himself which prompts Zacchaeus to repent of his past ways and to promise restitution. However, this may be to misunderstand the story: the REB's '*Here and now*' is an attempt to cover the fact that Zacchaeus does not say that he will give but that he does *give half* of what he has *to the poor* (not '*charity*' as in the REB); similarly he does, and not '*will*' as in the REB, *repay four times over* anyone he has *defrauded* (cf. Ex. 22.1); in grammatical terms the verbs are present, and what Zacchaeus is doing is protesting against the summary dismissal of his character by the crowd by affirming how he already behaves.

Jesus declares Zacchaeus to be *a son of Abraham* not because he has now repented – Luke who emphasizes this when he can (cf. 15.7) does not say it here; like the bent woman (13.16 and note), Zacchaeus, although dismissed by society's attitudes, already was heir to God's promises to Abraham no less than anyone else with whom Jesus might mix. The salvation hoped for in the past (1.69–71, 77) is a present reality when those traditionally despised are restored and given full recognition. Zacchaeus contrasts with that other 'very rich man', who, although he was one of the rulers, had still to be faced with the challenge of giving to the poor (18.22); he demonstrates that it is possible even for the rich to be saved (cf. 18.26), perhaps not by an impulsive and instant response but by a habitual attitude of giving and of recognizing that abuses do happen, deliberately or not, but can be set right.

The natural climax to Zacchaeus' story is in v.9, but v.10 is added as a generalizing statement to round off this final incident in Jesus' journey. In form it recalls 5.32 which declares Jesus' purpose, 'I have come', but instead uses the more enigmatic *Son of Man*; originally this may have been a self-effacing way of speaking of oneself, but in the development of Luke's narrative it now follows the predictions of his coming suffering (18.31) as well as the promise of vindication (17.30) as Son of Man, and binds them together with the activity of his ministry (cf. note on p.45f.). There is also an echo of Ezek. 34.16 – Jesus is fulfilling the promises of God *to seek the lost*, to care for those neglected by the religious structures of the day.

Faithfulness during the absence of the king
19.11–27

This parable marks the close of Jesus' journey to Jerusalem which has occupied the central part of the Gospel since 9.51. It is loosely connected to the story of Zacchaeus where Jesus declared that salvation had come 'today'; the parable is said to correct any misunderstanding that this meant that *the kingdom of God might dawn at any moment*. Such a misunderstanding is also provoked by Jesus' imminent arrival in *Jerusalem*; the first destination of anyone with messianic claims would be Jerusalem where God's sovereignty would surely first be manifested. Luke thus carefully distinguishes between the salvation experienced in Jesus' ministry and the final dawning of

God's kingdom, two moments held in tension as already in 17.20–21 (cf. 10.9–12; 11.20). As we shall see, because the parable deals with the behaviour of slaves in the absence of their master it also echoes the parables in 12.35–48; the significance and the demands of the present were a very real concern of the early Christians, and particularly for Luke who deals with the continuing life of the church. Thus the parable also responds to anxieties within the church as to whether and when 'the kingdom of God would dawn'.

A variation of the parable is also found in Matt. 25.14–30 in a different context. This suggests that the parable has been retold and reinterpreted in different settings and to meet different needs, which in turn have shaped it. As with other parables (see 16.1–8; 18.1–8) it is possible to trace these different elements and answers to different situations, although its original form and context in Jesus' ministry are no longer recoverable.

The basic core of the parable, which is shared with the Matthean form, is of a master who goes away leaving his slaves or *servants* with responsibility for *sums of money* with which to trade. In Luke there are *ten* such servants and each is given *ten pounds* (= REB 'sum of money'), considerably smaller in value than the Matthean 'talents'. On his return he summons them to give an account of their commission, although only three are described, a common pattern in parables (cf. 14.17–20; two in 16.5–7; there were only three initially in Matt. 25.15). The first two have gained a commendable rate of return, one at 100% and the other at 50%, and are rewarded, surprisingly – and here the story leaves the realms of probability – with control of an appropriate number of cities. The third, however, has done nothing, disobeying his original commission; his excuse, that his master was *a hard man*, liable to misappropriate things or to claim what was not his right, is not immediately clear. The slave could hardly have objected to the master exappropriating any profits since they were his due and the slave would have had no right to them. Neither has he misjudged his master's character, for the latter agrees to it – another, but less marked, case of the use of a less than exemplary character in a parable (cf. 16.1–8; 18.1–8); however, it seems unlikely that he was virtuously refusing to emulate his master since he describes his caution as due to fear. Possibly he feared the consequences of failure, which would explain why he should have taken the safer course of putting the *money on deposit* where it would have earned *interest*. The main emphasis is on his disobedience, contrasted with the obedience and reward of the others.

This is underlined when the first is awarded his 'pound', more a symbol for someone with ten pounds than a real benefit: that the second slave is here forgotten, and that we only now discover that the first has kept the ten pounds while the ten cities are ignored, is due to the attempt to bend the story to suit a moral given in v.26. It does not suit it well, for the point was not that the third slave *has nothing* but that he 'does nothing'; moreover, the moral sounds more like a comment attributed to Jesus, who said something similar in 8.18, than a natural justification in the circumstances by the nobleman. Since *his attendants* could also be translated *'those standing by'*, and *sir* by *'lord'*, we may wonder whether the audience of the parable have been caught up into it; it is they who baulk at the apparent inequality and it is Jesus who reiterates the principle that fruitfulness earns yet more reward, barrenness secures its own destruction.

As a stern warning about the proper fulfilment of responsibilities or use of gifts – not to be restricted to wealth – the parable could be directed either to the leadership within the Jewish people or to the disciples to whom 8.18 is addressed; within Luke's church it could be heard as directed to all Christians or particularly to those in leadership during the absence of their 'Lord', translated *sir* in the framework of the parable. In each case the moment of reckoning would also be differently understood, for the parable invites flexibility in its application.

However, the primary theme has been interwoven with a secondary one found only in Luke's version. The nobleman is absent in order to be *appointed king*, and it is *as king* that he returns, which explains why he can reward the *trustworthy* with the control of cities. His appointment is resisted by his *citizens*, not to be identified with the slaves: they seek to prevent it, but on his return they are put to death by him in punishment. This element in the story may have been based on events following the death in 4 BCE of Herod the Great: his son, Archelaus, went to Rome in the hope of being given the title 'king' held by his father; a delegation from Judaea opposed this and he was given the title of ethnarch, but on his return he took vengeance against his main opponents. The rejection of their rightful king must point to either the Jewish people or particularly to their leadership; it anticipates the rejection that Jesus will experience once he has entered Jerusalem, which he will shortly do as king (19.38–39). Positioning the parable before that event may be intended to prepare the reader for it or may mean the parable is a prophetic warning: if they do this, then judgment will surely follow. If Luke's readers saw in the parable their own experience, called to faith-fulness in the absence of Jesus, they may also have seen in Jewish unbelief a rejection of the king which would end in certain judgment.

This element in the parable, found only in Luke's version, demands some discussion of **Luke's attitude to the Jews**. To speak of Luke's attitude is to recognize that in this as in other respects the story of the Gospel is told through the prism of the concerns of the author and of the community among whom he wrote. Whereas Jesus and his first disciples were Jews and worked as one of a number of groups within the people as a whole, the Gospels were written at a time when the Christians were increasingly aware of their own separate identity and struggled to understand why the majority of the Jewish people had not believed in Jesus as Messiah, and what their continuing role was. This struggle has left its mark on most of the New Testament writings, including the Gospels; with Luke we can be particularly aware of it because he closes his second volume with an appeal to Isa. 6.9–10 as fulfilled in Jewish obduracy, and even earlier blames Jesus' death on the Jews, largely ignoring the fact that Jesus died from a penalty imposed by the Romans (Acts 2.23; 3.14; 10.39; 28.26–8). The analysis of 19.11–27 suggests that the parable of the slaves entrusted with money has been interwoven with a separate story of the punishment of the citizens who reject their king, and invites the question whether this second story has been added by Luke or an earlier tradition, or whether it existed separately as a parable by Jesus in a context and with a meaning now lost to us. In its present form, and if not for Luke's readers then certainly for later readers, it could suggest that the Jews who rejected Jesus would be punished without mercy, and this could then be applied not just to some present at the time of Jesus but to all the Jews during the absence of 'the King'. Other passages too could be read in a similar way (11.51; 13.5; 20.16 and see notes) and be taken as pointing to God's total rejection of Israel as the people of God. Although sometimes adopted, such a line of inter-pretation must be rejected as abhorrent to the biblical understand-ing of God's faithfulness and of God's ongoing purposes. Moreover, it does not seem that Luke intended such a generaliz-ing understanding of events and he is far from uniformly nega-tive about the Jewish response to Jesus. He begins the story of Jesus within the world of a traditional Jewish piety rooted in the

151

scriptures and in trust in God (1–2); however, there are premonitions of division from the start (2.34–5), and such division increasingly becomes the mark of Jesus' ministry. Much of the time the Pharisees represent hostility, the people are more supportive or are presented with the choice; this is a theme which will continue through the story of Jesus' time in Jerusalem, his arrest and death. Increasingly the leadership are set against 'the people' (cf. 20.6, 19 and notes) and it seems to be the former whom Luke holds particularly responsible (see 23.13). At the same time there are strong intimations that God's salvation will reach beyond the boundaries of Israel (4.16–30; 7.1–10; 14.16–24; 17.11–19 and notes), but this will only be realized in the time of the church, in Acts; Jesus' ministry is to those like the bent woman and Zacchaeus, daughters and sons of Abraham. It is not fully clear whether Luke saw Jesus' ministry and the preaching of the Gospel as establishing a new people of God, replacing the old or reconstituting and extending it (cf. 6.13), and it may be that he had not clearly identified this dilemma, which the early church continued to wrestle with.

The question needs also to be set alongside his attitude to Jerusalem; the destruction of Jerusalem in 70 CE probably made a deep impression on many Christians, and a number of passages in the Gospel would have acquired particular potency in its light (see below, pp.156–58). They could not know as we can that Judaism would continue a faithful and vibrant life through that and subsequent extreme distress. Modern interpretation and use of the New Testament is duty bound to recognize in penitence that Christian ideas about the punishment of the Jews for the rejection of Jesus have contributed to that extreme distress. If Luke, writing from his situation, made such ideas possible, the contemporary user of the Gospel must share rather in the celebration of the promise of peace to all in whom God delights.

Jesus in Jerusalem
19.28–21.38

The journey is now over as Jesus begins his *ascent to Jerusalem* where the rest of the Gospel will be staged; from now on timing and location become more important as an integral part of the narrative. Although Jerusalem will be the primary focus for the arrest, trial, death and resurrection of Jesus, Luke precedes these with a brief ministry by Jesus: there are no miracles, but Jesus teaches, with the leaders, the people and the disciples still forming the audience. Although this is a new stage in the Gospel it follows on closely from the parable in 19.11–27, which therefore offers a way of understanding what happens.

Jesus' entry into the Temple
19.28–48

The story of Jesus' entry to Jerusalem is found in all the Gospels, but each gives it a distinctive colouring (Matt. 21.1–9; Mark 11.1–10; John 12.28–38). It seems likely that the event has been invested with a significance which was not obvious at the time; certainly if it was but a week before Passover, as implied in the Synoptics, there would have been hundreds of pilgrims streaming into Jerusalem, and although it was normal to do so on foot, to ride on a donkey would not have been so extraordinary as to excite attention. As we shall see, the words cried out by those who surrounded Jesus come from Ps. 118, a psalm associated with Passover and also with Tabernacles; Matthew and John see a fulfilment of Zech. 9.9, but there is little evidence that this passage was understood as a reference to the Messiah in the time of Jesus, and Luke makes no allusion to it. It is therefore best to start from Luke's account of the event and to recognize what it would evoke for an attentive reader.

The route Jesus takes, via *Bethphage*, whose location is uncertain, and *Bethany at the Hill called 'of Olives'*, accords with an approach from Jericho, from the east; however, for some readers the repeated reference to the *mount of Olives* would recall Zech. 14.4 where it would be the scene of God's self-manifestation in eschatological judgment. Jesus' action shows foreknowledge and intention but not prior arrangement; he knows that they will find the *colt*, which has not *yet* been *ridden*, and so is suitable for a sacred purpose (cf. I Sam. 6.7). The donkey has *its owners* (= lords) who may object to its appropriation, but the *two disciples* are to answer '*Its* (not "the") *Master* (= lord) *needs it*' – Jesus is its true 'lord' at this moment. The appropriation of animals is a royal prerogative and to ride into the city on a donkey was a royal act (cf. II Sam. 18.9; 19.26; I Kings 1.33–40) even if in practice many others also did this. Other authors were to see a reference to Zech. 9.9 or Gen. 49.11 but Luke makes nothing of this. He does however focus attention on Jesus' journey and on the actions of the disciples, who provide *cloaks* on which Jesus sits.

Although the *people* offer him 'the red carpet treatment' as they lay *their cloaks on the road* – Luke knows nothing of (palm) branches (Mark 11.8) – it is *the whole company of his disciples* and not the accompanying crowd as in Mark and Matthew who shout their praises. It is not Jesus whom they acclaim but *God*, and their praises are in response to *the great things they had seen*: 'acts of power', the word here, have been a mark of Jesus' ministry since its beginning (4.14, 36; 5.17; 10.13), and praise to God has been the regular and proper response (5.25–6; 7.16; 13.13; 17.15, 18); so it is as disciples who have shared in that ministry that they can acclaim Jesus. Their words are taken from the pilgrimage Psalm 118.26, omitting the perhaps obscure 'Hosanna', but now '*the one who comes*', which earlier had been used as a somewhat ambiguous title of Jesus (7.19, see note), is defined more clearly as '*king*'. This is not a political acclamation, and Luke drops the Markan reference to 'the kingdom of our father David' (Mark 12.10). Instead '*in the name of the Lord*' goes as much with 'king' as with 'comes', while the final '*peace in heaven, glory in highest heaven*' probably stresses that this is no earthly kingship. Those words echo the cry of the angels in 2.14, but then they spoke of 'peace on earth'; since then that hope has had to face the harsh realism of the division Jesus must provoke (12.51), and peace remains a desired divine gift.

The *Pharisees* now make their last appearance in the Gospel, urging Jesus *to restrain* his *disciples*. His answer could mean that the celebration of the coming king is so imperative that it must be acclaimed by one means or the other, natural or supernatural. But the idea of *the stones* shouting *aloud* has a more ominous sound; in Hab. 2.11 the very stones of Jerusalem cry out in protest at the injustice and corruption, and judgment is bound to follow. If Jesus is not acclaimed with praise to God, then the judgment of an unresponsive city will surely come soon.

At this point Jesus does not enter the city as he does in Matthew and Mark; instead the assumption is that only now does he come *in sight of* it. Earlier, in 13.34–35 (see note), he had expressed his anguish over Jerusalem's recalcitrance and predicted the time when they would speak the words just cried by the disciples. Now, again in an incident found only in Luke, he weeps over the city which has not recognized *the way that leads to peace*. The formula is the same as that in 14.32 and so could refer to political and military peace, but it probably looks beyond that to the peace which the disciples acclaimed in v.38, an acclamation in which the city has not joined. *This day* thus refers to the day of Jesus' entry with all that it symbolizes, but it anticipates 'a day' to come: the formula 'on this/that day' is often used of coming judgment (cf. 17.30) and Jesus goes on to speak of *the time* of *your* (not *'God's'* as in the REB) *visitation*, a prophetic term for God's coming in judgment (Jer. 10.15; Isa. 10.3) or salvation. He foresees their coming destruction at the hands of their *enemies*; although the language of siege warfare and destruction is drawn from the prophets (Ezek. 4.1–2; Isa. 3.26; also Ps. 137.9), it was probably also enlivened by the realities of the Roman seige of Jerusalem which when Luke wrote was a recent memory. Implicity, if not explicitly, for Luke and his readers the destruction of the city followed inevitably from her failure to recognize 'the way that leads to peace'; while this might be a mundane recognition of the havoc caused by those groups who were committed to confontration with the Romans, it seems more likely that Luke saw in it God's hand at work (see further comment on pp.169f.).

Instead of entering the city of Jerusalem now, Jesus *went into the Temple*; although this is properly an artificial distinction for the Temple was part of the city, it is one which Luke makes. It is as if he has no continuing interest in the city over which Jesus has wept, and of whose coming destruction he will again speak in 23.27–31; instead his attention focusses on the Temple which will be the centre of Jesus' activity until the night of his arrest. Jesus' first act prepares for this continuing activity. Again the so-called 'cleansing of the Temple' features in each of the Gospels (Matt. 21.12–17; Mark 11.15–19; John 2.13–17), but the substantial differences between their accounts are compounded by John's placing of the event at the beginning of Jesus' ministry. Whatever the nature of Jesus' action it was not violent enough to provoke intervention by the Romans, who were usually particularly sensitive to any disturbances at Passover time. Although it has often been interpreted as a protest against the corruption of the system of selling animals for sacrifice, there is little supportive evidence of such corruption; instead, Jesus' action may have had a strongly prophetic character, symbolizing God's coming judgment on the Temple or on the sacrificial system (cf. Jer. 19.1–13). However, it is the way that Luke understands this event within the framework of Jesus arrival in Jerusalem which is of particular importance.

Luke's version lacks all the vivid colour of the Markan account; he says nothing about any money-changers and speaks only of 'those selling', *the traders*. The emphasis thus falls on Jesus' *words* as he drove them out. It was Jeremiah who spoke of the Temple as *a bandit's cave*, referring to the disobedience and moral injustice of those who worshipped there (Jer. 7.11): thus the words are words of judgment, not a description of the financial activities undertaken. The Temple's proper purpose is declared by God in the words of *scripture*, Isa. 56.7, but in Luke's version the Temple *shall be*, not 'shall be called', *a house of prayer*, and he omits the following words 'for all nations' (cf. Mark 11.17). Prayer for him is the central act even in the Temple (cf. 1.10; 18.10), and the Gospel closes with the disciples praising God in the Temple (24.53); however, despite his universalist interests, he knows that it will not be the Temple but the new community through Jesus which will be the focus of prayer for the Gentiles.

It is as if for Luke Jesus has made the Temple his own; from now on, *day by day*, he teaches there: 20.1, 9, 45; 21.38. It is not then surprising that the division which Jesus has provoked throughout his ministry should also be found here. The opposition are now described as *the chief priests . . . scribes* and *leading citizens*; Luke may not have had a clear identity of these groups but for him they represent the whole leadership, religious and political. For the moment their determination *to bring about his death* is hampered by the support of *the people*. The role of these two groups will continue to be at the centre of the events to follow.

It has become clear from this chapter that **Jerusalem and the Temple** play an important role in Luke's thought, transcending their historical and geographical significance. The Gospel account began with Zechariah in the Temple, and there was a continuing movement between home and Temple in the birth narratives, closing with Jesus' affirmation that he was bound to be in his Father's house (2.49); the Gospel will also close with the disciples in the Temple (24.53). In this incident Jesus has affirmed God's intention for the Temple and in the days leading up to his death he makes it the place where he teaches, as in Acts it is for the disciples also (Acts 3–4). The Temple is, and remains, a place of prayer (18.10; Acts 2.46; 3.1; 22.17). However, although in the birth narratives the Temple and Jerusalem seem almost identified (2.22, 42), through the course of the Gospel their relationship becomes much more ambivalent. Jerusalem has been the focus of Jesus' journey since 9.51 and the reader has been regularly reminded of this (13.22; 17.11; 18.31; 19.11); the first resurrection appearances will be in Jerusalem (24.33), and it is in Jerusalem that the disciples are to await the promised power, and from Jerusalem that they are to go out to the ends of the earth (Acts 1.4–8). Yet it is also in Jerusalem, the city which murders the prophets, that Jesus is bound to die (13.32–33): Jerusalem is almost bound to reject him although he weeps over the city in anguish – and it was the disciples and not the people who celebrated his arrival. There is a strong sense of the clouds of doom which hang over the city (13.35; 19.41–44; 23.28–31), a doom which follows inevitably on from that rejection. That doom is not some super-natural cataclysm but destruction in seige warfare, a destruction which Luke and his readers knew had been suffered in the war of 66–70 CE and which has coloured the language he uses (see further 21.20–24 and notes). Later Christian writers saw that destruction as divine judgment on the Jews' refusal to recognize Jesus; Luke does not do this for he distinguishes between the city and the various groups within it, and he also emphasizes Jesus' yearning for the city. Certainly there are moments in Jesus' teaching which could be taken as presaging the punishment of those who rejected Jesus (11.51; 13.5; 19.27; 20.16; see note on pp.151 f.), but the connection of these with the destruction of Jerusalem is not made explicit. Indeed, by separating the destruction of Jerusalem from the cosmic upheavals at the end of time in ch. 21, Luke may be offering a vision of hope for Jerusalem (21.24). Jerusalem is for Luke the representative city of the Jewish people, although it is not the only such city (cf. 10.13–15); the central yet

ambivalent role it plays reflects the ambivalence in Luke's understanding of the continuing place of 'unbelieving Israel' in God's
purposes. As we have already seen, this was a topic of profound
debate in the early church, and one which has rightly received
new understanding in more recent Christian thought.

The challenge of Jesus' authority
20.1–19

Jesus' ministry in Jerusalem is now centred *in the Temple* which
he has made his own. Luke has taken most of the material for
this period from Mark, but he has told it so as to bring out certain
emphases and to show continuities from the past. Thus Jesus continues the pattern of his earlier ministry, *teaching the people . . . and
telling them the good news* (cf. 4.18, 43); he is opposed by the leaders of
the people but the time when some at least showed him hospitality is
past. These leaders are no longer represented by the Pharisees but by
the chief priests and scribes and *elders*, those who in 9.22 were predicted
to be responsible for Jesus' death. This grouping probably stands for
the Jewish legislative council, the Sanhedrin, although it is unlikely
that Luke, or Mark whom he here follows, had a precise understanding of its composition.

The first confrontation focusses on the *authority* Jesus has
displayed; although in Mark (11.27–33) the reference is perhaps
particularly to Jesus' action in the Temple, in Luke it may rather
encompass his teaching which has been marked by 'authority'
from the start (4.32, 36, and see comment). Ultimately there is no
difference between the nature of Jesus' authority and its source, as
his reply makes clear; he answers with a counter-question, a familiar
technique in contemporary literature, not to delay his own answer
but because it will provide one, and more, for them.

Although we have no external evidence for the attitude of the
Jewish authorities to John the Baptist, within the Gospel they are
represented as rejecting him and therefore as rejecting 'God's
purpose' (7.29–30). In asking them whether *the baptism of John* was
from God or from man Jesus is implying that since they had not
acknowledged John they would hardly be likely to acknowledge
himself, for the two were bound together in the ongoing purposes of
God. Yet by 'eavesdropping' on their private deliberations, the true
motivation of these people who will later try Jesus is exposed: they

refuse to answer because they dare not admit to their rejection of a man whom *the people* regarded as *a prophet* (cf. 7.24–8 and notes). Therefore there is again a division between the leaders and the people, and in the scenes to follow much will depend on that relationship.

Although Jesus refuses to tell them *by what authority* he acts, his answer is implicit in his counter-question. He immediately goes on *to tell a parable*, again drawn from Mark (12.1–11), which makes it rather more explicit. The parable is told to *the people* but at its end *the scribes and chief priests* recognize that they are its butt, and so the division between the two is sustained. The parable is one which invites an allegorical interpretation, recognizing in its details precise equivalences of meaning. *A vineyard* was a familiar scriptural image for Israel, 'planted' by God, (Ps. 80.8–9; Isa. 27.2–5; Jer. 2.21), although Luke has omitted the fuller details of the planting which in the Markan form refer directly to Isa. 5.1–6. The lease of property by an absentee landlord to *tenants* who were bound to surrender a *share of the produce* was probably a familiar situation in Palestine in the first century although little is gained by trying to determine the legal details of the relationship: the meaning of the parable determines the course of events within it.

Three times, a regular number in stories (cf. 19.16–20), the owner *sent a servant to collect* what was his due and on each occasion *the tenants* abused them and *sent* them *away empty-handed*; Mark speaks of 'many others', some of whom are killed (Mark 12.5), seeing in these servants the prophets whom God sent to Israel, but Luke does not make this point, wanting rather to focus on the climax to *the owner's* (= *lord's*) dealings with his tenants. In 'the real world' his decision to *send his beloved son* (cf. 3.22) after the abuse of his servants might seem foolhardy, but within the parable his consideration, '*What am I to do*', an echo of Isa. 5.4, underlines God's forbearance and determination to offer yet another opportunity for a right response. Far more than servants, the son would carry the full authority and dignity of the father who sent him: to reject him would be to reject the father/owner. *The tenants'* response seeks only their own interest; on one level they hope that by killing *the heir* the vineyard might come by default to them – again, by what legal mechanism is unclear and irrelevant; on another, they thus seek to rid themselves finally of the rightful demands of the owner upon them. By flinging him *out of the vineyard* they show their utter rejection of him: that they then *kill him* 'outside' (ctr. Mark 12.8) probably is not a reference to the crucifixion of Jesus outside the city, which Luke does not seem to know (cf. 13.33 'in Jerusalem'), but only reinforces his isolation in death.

The parable does not end here. Jesus answers his own rhetorical question as to the inevitable response of *the owner of the vineyard* with the prediction of the punishment of *those tenants* by *death* and of the giving of *the vineyard to others*. If the vineyard is Israel and its 'lord' God, then the beloved son is obviously Jesus, God's final summons to Israel to obedience – a clear answer to the question as to his authority. Yet the point of the parable is not to focus on his sonship, and it would perhaps have been the early church rather than any in the ministry of Jesus who would have read more into the 'son' than a claim to finality. While the tenants might be the people of Israel who had failed to offer God their obedient response, here, at least in Luke's setting, they must be particularly the leaders who recognize themselves as the targets of the parable. In either case, and in contrast to Isa. 5.5–6, there is no reference to the destruction of the vineyard. The 'others' who will receive the vineyard are not further defined; it would be easy to take them to represent a 'new people', even including the Gentiles, although a better contrast would suggest alternative leaders whether from the people themselves or within that new people – a shift in the focus of the parable may have led to this ambiguity. However, this also is not developed, for then we would have to ask what if they too failed to give what was due; they rather emphasize the calamitous ending of the story for those who felt themselves secure in their tenancy.

The horrified response of those who *heard this* reinforces the message of judgment, but the *text of scripture*, Ps.118.22, which Jesus quotes in confirmation goes a step further; it speaks of the restoration of what had been *rejected* – the same word as in 9.22 – to become *the main corner-stone* which held together the whole building. This quotation, which is also found in Mark (12.10 = Matt. 21.42), may have been added in the retelling of the parable in order to show that the death of the son was not the end, making use of a psalm (Ps. 118) which the early Christians found a rich resource for understanding the story of Jesus (cf. 13.35; 19.38; Heb. 13.6).

This re-telling and re-interpretation goes a step further in Luke: whereas Mark and Matthew continue with the next verse of the psalm which speaks of the wonderful thing done by the Lord, Luke instead develops the imagery of *the stone* and of the judgment it will bring. The language is almost proverbial and recalls Simeon's warning in 2.34–5 but it may also be drawn from other scriptural passages: in Isa. 8.14 the Lord becomes a stone or rock over which Israel may stumble, while in Dan. 2.34–5, 44–45 a stone in Nebuchadnezzar's dream is interpreted as God's kingdom which crushes all other kingdoms. It was in this way that the early Christians linked passages from the scriptures because they shared certain terms or ideas, and used them to interpret the Christian message, often regardless of their original context or meaning (cf. I Peter 2.4–8; Rom. 9.32–3). Here in Luke it means that the final note is one of threat and not of hope as in Mark. As we have seen, it is a threat which *the scribes and chief priests* recognize as directed against themselves, but once again (cf. 20.6) their fear of *the people* forces them to inaction.

Further challenges to Jesus: the authority of God
20.19–44

Still following Mark (12.13–17,18–27), Luke continues with two further challenges to Jesus. The first, in response to the parable of the vineyard is, even more clearly than in Mark, an attempt by *the chief priests and scribes* to trap Jesus; their intention is already to hand Jesus over to the Roman *authority* – perhaps for Luke an ironic contrast with the valid authority of Jesus which was challenged earlier (20.1–8). This means that the political charges laid against Jesus before Pilate in 23.2 can then be recognized as spurious and as the resort of those driven to use *agents* who pretend to be righteous (cf. 18.9).

The political role of Christianity in relation to the state is a significant concern for Luke, who alone records the charges in 23.2, and is developed particularly in Acts; this incident already gives a partial answer to the problem although the issue here is a highly specific one. It was an intrinsic part of Roman control that the Jews were required to pay a tribute tax *to the Roman emperor*, and it is this rather than taxes in general which is in mind. For some Jews this was not just an acknowledgment of the resented Roman supremacy but was an implicit denial of the sole lordship of God, particularly as the coins used would have given the emperor the epithet 'son of the divine Augustus'; the census carried out when Judaea had become a Roman province had provoked a violent response for that very reason (see 2.1–3 and comments). The flattering preface to the question thus recognizes Jesus as one who teaches what *God requires*, and who should adjudicate not on whether such tribute is just but on whether it is *permitted*, lawful in the light of God's will enshrined in scripture. Yet Jesus does not answer by appeal to scripture but in their own terms, for implicit in *their trick* was that Jesus would be forced either to deny God's sole authority or to lay himself open to the charge of treason.

The *silver piece* or denarius used to pay the tax would have been inscribed with the *head* of the emperor or 'Caesar', at the time Tiberius – an afront to those who rejected any human representation – and his *inscription*, including the unacceptable epithet 'divus'. It is unlikely that Jesus is simply saying that the coin *belongs to* the emperor which, since he authorized its minting, was technically correct, and cannot be withheld from him. The coinage represented the authority and the benefits of the empire in which they participated; this is the sphere which pertains to the emperor and which has its proper claims. However, Jesus immediately continues '*pay . . . to God what belongs to God*'. The relation between these two parts of Jesus' answer has generated a centuries-long debate about the relationship between the demands of the state (*Caesar*) and those of God. Was Jesus saying that each has a separate and independent sphere and that what God requires is that both be accorded their due obedience; or in immediately speaking of 'what belongs to God' does Jesus reduce the claims of the emperor to nothing, for everything belongs to God; is he dismissing such concerns, urging them rather to set their minds on the kingdom (12.29–31); or is he both opposing any refusal 'in God's name' to pay tribute and reminding them that they are bound to give God what is due (cf. 20.10) – indeed they belong to God, for they bear God's image, and are bound to offer to God themselves? The first, although an important tradition in Christian political thought, does not seem to cohere with other aspects of Jesus' teaching. Yet his answer, like his parables, does more to provoke reflection than to provide clear guidelines, and the issue rightly has continued to challenge the church not least when the demands of the state have seemed to conflict with or to claim greater authority than the demands of God. (Cf. also Rom. 13.1–7; I Peter 2.13–17 which do little to solve these dilemmas.)

Now that Jesus has silenced them, a further challenge is posed from a very different quarter. Little is known about the *Sadducees* outside the Gospels and Acts and the information reported by the first-century Jewish historian Josephus; here they are generally contrasted with the Pharisees (Acts 23.7–8), and it seems likely that they were of considerably greater importance than the few surviving references suggest. They are widely agreed to have been associated with the priesthood, perhaps claiming some continuity with Zadok the priest (I Kings 1.32–40), but also to have included many of the lay aristocracy; they were, according to Josephus, more conservative than the Pharisees and rejected many of the oral traditions of interpretation to which the latter gave such importance. It may have been this conservatism which led them to *deny . . . a resurrection*, for this belief only developed in the two or three centuries before the time of Jesus and is barely represented in the Hebrew scriptures (Dan. 12.2–3,13). Their question seeks both to expose through scripture the vacuity of that belief, which Jesus is presumed to share, and to test his skill in scriptural interpretation. Thus they draw their example not from contemporary practice, about which we know little, but from the Levirate law as described in Deut. 25.5–10: according to this law, which was designed to prevent a man's line from dying out, if a man died childless – originally without a son – it was the duty of his brother to *marry the widow* in the hope that she would bear a child to carry the first husband's name (cf. Gen. 38.8).

The picture of a widow being handed down through *seven brothers* is a 'reductio ad absurdum' and mocks the assumption that human relationships are maintained in the resurrection life. Jesus' answer presupposes that the purpose of marriage is procreation: because people *are . . . subject to death*, marriage is necessary in *this world* in order to ensure some form of continuity. Since mortality does not belong to *the other world*, neither do marital relationships; to be *like angels*, a rare word, is presumably to be free from the constraints of sexuality. Yet resurrection is not for all, but only for those who are *judged worthy* and, in a comment added only by Luke, it is these, and not all humankind, who are, or will be, *children* (lit. 'sons') *of God*. Jesus then adds an argument also drawn from scripture, in fact from the uncontestable *Moses himself*, to support the idea of resurrection; in Ex. 3.6 God is revealed at *the burning bush as the God of Abraham . . . of Isaac . . . of Jacob*. Since God speaks in the present, and cannot be defined as *God of the dead*, these too must be living. This does not mean that they never died, nor that they were in some sense immortal, an idea which would imply a distinction between their mortal physical body and immortal 'soul'; rather, despite death, they live: resurrection here is not reserved for some future but distant date but is already a reality for God. The REB's translation of the final argument, found only in Luke, *'in his sight all are alive'*, is misleading; the point is that as God is the source of life, so *in* and through a relationship with God *all live* – although quite how broadly Luke intends that 'all' which might seem to contradict the earlier restriction is not clear. Interestingly, a very similar argument with a similar conclusion that the patriarchs 'live to God' is found in IV Macc 7.19, probably written during the first or second century. This incident well represents the fluidity and variety in belief regarding the resurrection at this period.

Surprisingly, this response earns the approval of *the scribes* who would have shared the belief in the resurrection. Yet the final note is that Jesus has now effectively silenced all who sought to challenge him. We should not assume that these were the only controversies in which Jesus engaged nor even that they happened as and in the order described. Rather, Mark, and following him Matthew and Luke, have used these to present Jesus as victorious over all types of opposition; Jesus' own authority has been demonstrated and he has declared God's total claim on men and women in life and in death. Jesus now takes the initiative and challenges his hearers to grapple in full seriousness with the question of authority. However, although it seems that Luke understands this final encounter as pointing to the true nature of Jesus' authority, its original meaning is rather more obscure.

The question he poses assumes that *the Messiah* was popularly identified as *David's son*; it also accepts, as did most people of the time, that David spoke the psalms, in this case Ps. 110.1, which according to some modern scholarship probably is somewhat later than the time of David, and accepts further that the second 'Lord' in the psalm is a reference to the Messiah. Thus according to this interpretation God (= *the Lord*) addresses the Messiah, whom David describes as *my Lord*. Surely David would not call someone who was his son – dependent on and derivative from him – 'Lord'? This does not mean that the Messiah is not a descendant of David, something which Luke did believe of Jesus (cf. 1.27, 32; 3.32 and comments); rather, that relationship does not provide a final or adequate way of understanding him. There is little evidence that in the Jewish thought of Jesus' day Ps. 110 was widely referred to the Messiah, or even that *the Messiah* and *Son of David* were technical terms; they were, however, so used in early Christianity. It is certainly possible that Jesus made some of these links but it may be that the passage also reflects concerns in the early church about Jesus' relationship with David. For Luke, as for Mark (12.35–37) before him, the demonstration provides a fitting climax to Jesus' ability to outwit his opposition and points unmistakeably to the true source of his authority.

Jesus' condemnation of the scribes
   20.45–21.4

Although Jesus has silenced those who oppose him, he further distances himself from them as he warns both *all the people* and *his disciples* against *the scribes*. Luke included a similar attack, there against both Pharisees and lawyers, in 11.39–53 (see comments), yet now he makes it clear that such conflict was as true of Jesus' ministry in Jerusalem as it was in Galilee. At the same time, by making the disciples the primary audience Luke may be directing an implicit warning to those who sought leadership within his own church. As with the earlier polemic this blanket condemnation must be understood as polemical rhetoric and not as a description of what the scribes, or even necessarily some of them, were like. Despite claims to do so, we cannot certainly identify either the *long robes* or *the chief seats in synagogues*; these, together with respectful greetings and *places of honour* (cf. 14.7–8), indicate ostentation and vainglory, as too do the *long prayers* which are dismissed as a pretence. How they *eat up the property of widows* is less certain – perhaps by maladministration or by extortionate charges through their activity as lawyers, or perhaps by sponging off the credulous or by persuading excessive charitable giving from those who were pious but could least afford it. Again, this is language of polemic rather than of careful description, and serves mainly to strengthen the prediction of severe judgment.

The cameo incident which follows illustrates these charges, although Luke, characteristically, contrasts the *poor widow* with the *rich*. The *temple treasury* refers to the receptacles placed in the outer court to collect the various offerings of the people. One interpretation of Jesus' words would be that Jesus sets the widow as an ideal example: she has given *all*, and it is this which God requires. This would certainly fit in with Jesus' other teaching about wealth in this Gospel (cf. 18.22), better than the slightly 'more comfortable' interpretations which speak of a gift needing 'to cost something for the giver' or of 'the spirit rather than the amount': Jesus' says nothing about the spirit of any of the givers here. Yet an alternative interpretation would be that Jesus' words are spoken in lament: what she has done in giving away *all she had to live on* only illustrates the rapacity of the scribes; she is their victim and proof of the corruption of the system. Such a reading provides a dismal but natural conclusion to these encounters. There may be an element of truth in both interpretations; in Luke those who are victims of the religious establishment are at the same time those who are readily responsive to God's offer and demand. Even in the Temple there are those who 'give to God what belongs to God'.

Preparation for the end
21.5–38

Although Luke sees Jesus' ministry in Jerusalem as a time of teaching (cf. 20.1), the only example he gives, besides the controversies of ch. 20, is this long, and in some ways non-typical, preview of 'all that is coming' (v.36). A preview of this kind, particularly when it deals with events on a cosmic scale, with heavenly as well as terrestrial upheavals, with the prospect of suffering and the confidence of ultimate victory, and when it is couched in allusive and ambiguous terms dependent on the revelation to or by someone with insight into the divine plans, belongs to a type of thought and literature known as apocalyptic; in so far as it deals with the things to do with 'the end' it may also be called eschatological. This pattern of thinking seems to have developed and flourished during the two centuries before and after the birth of Jesus and undoubtedly would have been part of the thought world of his time. Both Matthew (23.1–36) and Luke follow Mark (13.1–37) in setting an apocalyptic discourse by Jesus at the end of his ministry; this follows a literary convention whereby similar material comes at the end of the prophetic books (cf. Mal. 4.1–5; Zech. 12–14); it also fits the 'testament' pattern found in other literature of this period where a teacher or father in the face of his coming death or departure warns his dependents of what is to come.

Both Matthew and Luke make significant changes to the Markan discourse, in part because they needed to interpret it in the light of their own understanding of the events they were living through and of their expectations for the future. Luke in particular reshapes the pattern of events to come, although it seems unlikely that he had any other written sources to guide him than Mark. We should expect that Mark also retold the discourse in the light of his own understanding, although in his case we cannot know in what form it came to him. This means that it is not possible to recreate Jesus' own preaching on the subject, whether given on one or more occasions. Luke's version shows how such teaching lived on in the church, and how a church which was facing a longer period of continuing existence than at first perhaps had been expected, found meaning in the vision of the final working out of God's plan.

Luke leaves the audience of this preview unclear; as in 20.45 the setting is public, provoked when *some people* remark on the famed beauty of the Temple buildings, but the true audience must be the disciples, then and future, whom Jesus addresses throughout as 'you'. Unlike Mark (13.3), Jesus does not leave the Temple and after the initial warning in v.6 it slips out of the concerns of the sermon (see comment on 21.20, below); although he foresees the time when *they will all be thrown down*, Jesus does not reject the Temple but will continue to teach there (v.38). However, those who hear his prediction rightly understand its deeper significance, already implied by the sonorous *the time will come*; the Temple was the place where God had chosen to dwell and its destruction would surely herald divine judgment or intervention. The *sign* that they ask for would be one of the anticipated signals of that coming intervention (cf. 11.29; 12. 54–9).

However, Jesus dismisses both any concentration on the fate of the Temple and any expectation of an imminent 'finale'. Instead, in what follows he speaks more of the slow but certain pattern which they must first live through, and his concern is not with providing a clear timetable but with encouraging the disciples in their faithfulness during all that is to come. Vv.8–9 give an immediate answer to their question, and it is that *the end does not follow at once. Wars and insurrections*, such as Luke and his readers would have lived through by the last quarter of the first century, are inevitable and not the first stages in the final cosmic conflict which was a feature of much apocalyptic thought. The threat of being *misled* also belonged to such patterns of thinking (cf. I John 2.18; 4.2; Acts 20.30); here such deception might be occasioned by claimants to Jesus' authority or even to his person: however, if *I am he* means 'I am Jesus returned', this must be a later Christian expression presupposing belief in a 'second coming'. We do not know of such claimants in the first century, and it seems unlikely that those who had known Jesus would be misled; yet during the unsettled years leading up to and including the Jewish revolt of 66–70 CE there were a number of 'charismatic figures' in Palestine who claimed a 'messianic' authority. The threefold warning, not to be misled, not to *follow* false claimants to divine authority or messengers of the imminent end, and that the end is not yet, leads to what they are to do and how they are to understand what happens.

It is not clear whether *nation going to war against nation* refers back to the wars and insurrections of v.9: certainly the first century did witness *severe earthquakes, famines and plagues*, while in the history-writing of the period the sighting of *terrors* and great portents regularly accompanied momentous events such as the destruction of the Temple. Therefore, despite the vivid language, these need not be supra-natural disturbances. However, it seems likely that these events still lie in the future even for Luke's readers, for they must first face what happens *before all this*. In Acts the early Christians face persecution at the hands of the Jewish authorities and of kings; Paul in particular is opposed by *synagogues*, thrown *in prison*, and brought before *kings and governors* (Acts 16.23; 17.1–5; 24–26). How representative his experiences were is not known, although Nero's persecution of the Christians in Rome was notorious. Synagogues had limited powers of jurisdiction, and then only over their fellow Jews. This is not a historical record so much as a way of emphasizing the comprehensive opposition they will face for their *allegiance* to Jesus; discipleship was to be placed above all family ties (14.26; 18.29), and it is in persecution that that choice bears its bitterest fruit, betrayal even by family and *friends*. Yet all this means that to be persecuted is not something unexpected or extraordinary, but fits entirely into the pattern of things; at the same time it belongs to the dissolution of order and to the breakdown of a world which is driving a course apart from God.

To *testify* is to act as a witness, and persecution is here the supreme opportunity to give witness: it is no accident that the Greek word for a witness, 'martyr', came to be used of one who witnessed in and by death. Yet here comes the first note of assurance; the disciples will not be on their own at that point and need not be anxious about planning a full *defence* in advance. Jesus himself will be the source of all they say, inspiring their *words* and empowering them with *wisdom* (see on 7.35); the similar encouragement in 12.11–12 spoke of the inspiration of the Holy Spirit, as does the Markan parallel here (Mark 13.11), but here in Luke the emphasis is that just as they are arraigned for their *allegiance* to Jesus, so it is Jesus who is faithful to them. *Some of them will be put to death,* and so it would be wrong to take over-literally the assurance that *no opponent* will be able to *refute* them, or that *not a hair of* their *head will be lost* (cf. 12.7; I Sam. 14.45); Luke may be spiritualizing here – not physical but spiritual safe-keeping is promised – but such exaggerated optimism is in character (cf. Acts 16.25–28; 27.21–25), and may owe its origin to his confidence in Jesus' victory and presence. In reality the early Christians, and others since, recognized that death often did follow the most steadfast and inspired testimony, and indeed saw death as the seal of that testimony. A firmer note is sounded by the exhortation to stand firm with the promise that it will bring true *life*: earlier in the Gospel (9.23–25) this path of suffering leading to life had been demanded of anyone who would be a disciple, for it is the path taken by Jesus himself.

Yet even persecution fits only into the sweep of events and does not herald the eschatological opposition to God. At this point Mark speaks allusively and ominously of 'the desolating sacrilege' (13.14), an allusion to Dan. 9.27 which conjures up the almost supra-natural opposition to God, and thereafter his preview presses on with urgency and speed to the final dénouement (Mark 13.14–27). Luke departs radically from this scheme, showing how the early church was compelled to reinterpret the relationship between current events and visionary hope. He instead 'forsees' events on the plane of history, the *armies* encircling *Jerusalem*; even then these point not to a final climax but only to the nearness of *her devastation*. Yet those who might hope in God's protection of the city (cf. Ps. 46.5) are misguided, for the situation would be hopeless. In time of war it would be natural to take refuge from the countryside in the security of a walled city, but so certain is defeat that it will be better to *take to the hills*, even for those already *in the city*. War is always hardest on *women* and *children*, and so it would prove to be, and as always in defeat there would be wholesale slaughter and the enforced capture into slavery of the survivors.

All these would be the standard features of siege warfare, but the language is also coloured by the Old Testament depictions of the defeat of Jerusalem (Jer. 21.7; Ezek. 32.9, 20; Ezra 9.7); more immediately, Luke's readers would recognize the horrific conditions of the recent Roman seige of Jerusalem and of her final fall, and it seems likely that Luke's rewriting of his Markan original deliberately evoked that disaster. For those who struggled to make sense of the destruction of Jerusalem within God's plan, Luke was placing it within the sequence of historical events and denying that it was a sign of the imminent end. At the same time he does interpret it; it is not simply a disastrous military failure but is the time of *retribution*, of judgment, just as the prophets had understood the earlier defeats (cf. Hos. 9.7; Deut. 32.35). For the prophets these were judgment against corruption and faithlessness, for Luke presumably for their rejection of Jesus and perhaps of the disciples, although this is not spelled out (cf. 19.41–44). It is not an unforeseen calamity but the fulfilment of *all that stands written*: the earlier prophecies are now being reinterpreted of this new disaster. Luke also sees Jesus' death as fulfilling all that was written (18.31; 24.44), and so he may be incorporating the destruction of the city into the pattern of the rejection and death of Jesus. This means that the prediction is not, like the warnings of earlier prophets, directed to the city as a call for repentance: the passage is addressed to the disciples to help them understand what *they see*.

Later Christian writers would develop this theme and explicitly interpret this defeat, and the subsequent further defeat of the Jews under Bar Kochba by Rome in the second century, as God's punishment of the Jews for rejecting Jesus, and as evidence that God had turned from them to a new people. Such an interpretation also made possible the utterly unacceptable view that any Jewish suffering was merited and was divine punishment. This development has deeply corrupted some Christian attitudes to God's people, the Jews. Although Luke may have seemed to take an initial step in this direction he does not sanction the later developments. He speaks only of the city and not of the whole people: in v.23 *judgment* might better be translated 'wrath' and emphasizes more the horror of what they suffer. Moreover, Luke even seems to remove the Temple, which was implied in the Markan version (Mark 13.14), from the picture. He recognizes the sheer horror of a devastation which strikes even the vulnerable and gives it a place after the suffering also undergone by the disciples.

The devastation of Jerusalem is for Luke the act of *the Gentiles* who will trample it *underfoot*, a further prophetic reference (Zech. 12.3); they will have their appointed time or *day*. This does not mean that Jerusalem will then be restored: Luke does not share Paul's vision of the salvation of Israel once the full number of the Gentiles have come in (Rom. 11.25–26). It is not even stated that their 'time' is the time for the conversion of the Gentiles; in this chapter it belongs only to a scheme where each event or period has its allotted span.

The time of the Gentiles thus has no distinguishing characteristics and there are no indications how long it will last. This would be the period in which Luke's readers were living and so their only certainty would be that the events to be described in vv.25–28 lay somewhere in the future. Here the imagery shifts from the 'historical' to the supra-historical. As we have already seen (v.11), *portents* did belong to the description of significant historical events, but here the language has gone beyond that. These are cosmic events affecting both the 'heavenly bodies' and those on earth, and they echo the Old Testament imagery of God's judgment (Isa. 13.10–13; 24.19–20; 34.4); although sea travel was an integral part of the Mediterranean world, within the Old Testament tradition *the roar . . . of the sea* could be a symbol of the chaos which threatened human security (Ps. 46.3). These events are not necessarily anticipated literally: they represent the collapse or dissolution of the order which God had established in creation; they are a figurative way – and there is no other way – of envisaging the end of created existence as we experience it. For Luke they have no interest in themselves for they serve only to herald the climax.

This climax comes in imagery drawn from Dan. 7.13–14: there, in a sequence of visions, the one like a human being who came to God represented those who had withstood suffering and oppression. In Jewish interpretation of that passage, and in the Christian tradition, that figure became significant in his own right as *the Son of Man*. Here in Luke his coming is no longer to God but to those whom he will judge or vindicate. We have seen how this title is used by Jesus in the Gospels in different ways; if Jesus did originally reinterpret the Daniel passage in the way it is used here, it would not have been obvious to his hearers that he was referring to himself, although undoubtedly this is how Luke understands it. By following the sequence of the Gospel as readers we have come to see that the one who suffers is also the one who vindicates and who judges (see comment on pp.42f. and 17.20–30 and comments). Luke also indicates this by changing the cloud*s* of Daniel (and Mark 13.26) to *a cloud*, anticipating Jesus' ascension in Acts 1.9 which is but a prelude to his return.

Thus while others may *faint with terror*, the disciples are to wait in confidence, for the coming of the Son of Man ensures the ultimate vindication of those who as disciples have remained faithful. Their *liberation* can also be translated '*redemption*'; here for Luke it is not redemption from sin through Jesus' death (cf. I Cor. 1.30; Eph. 1.7; Heb. 9.15) but the promised future vindication which lies beyond the suffering of present discipleship.

The *parable* Jesus tells reinforces the reliable sequence of all he has forseen, as predictable as the sequence of the seasons. Here the nearness of the Son of Man is replaced by the nearness of the *kingdom of God* (ctr. Mark 13.29). Usually Luke keeps these concepts separate (cf. 17.20–25 and comments, above); in his Gospel the 'kingdom of God' is a more flexible term, both yet to come and the reality of God's sovereignty already experienced, particularly through the activity of Jesus. Here he uses it with future force to direct attention away from the Son of Man to God, for ultimately it must be God's kingdom which is the final consummation of all things.

Throughout this chapter Jesus has been addressing his words to *you*; as we have seen, although not explicitly identified this must be the disciples, present and future, who are called to faithfulness. However, that flexibility becomes rather more strained in the difficult promise of v.32 that *the present generation* would not pass away until it had seen *it all*. The 'all' must in the context refer to the whole sweep of events and not just the persecution or the devastation of Jerusalem. Yet addressed to Jesus' disciples this would be patently untrue, and even Luke knew of the death of some (Acts 12.2). There is little evidence that 'generation' could refer to the Jewish people or to humankind, neither of which make much sense in the context. It has been suggested that 'this generation' is used in apocalyptic literature to refer to the final generation, the people of the end time, although such solemn words, marked by the weighty *Truly I tell you*, can hardly be saying only that the final generation will indeed be the final generation. Similar prophecies are found in Mark 9.1 and Matt. 10.23; it may be that they reflect the early conviction, perhaps held by Jesus himself, that the end was imminent, within their lifetime. For all their difficulty, as a solemn promise they may have been preserved even through the passage of time; how Luke understands them is not clear and that means we cannot be sure whether he thought the end would come within the lifetime of his own readers. Perhaps he saw them as a solemn affirmation of the truth and of the serious relevance of this sermon; the assurance of the end and the anticipation of its completion are not a fantasy to be dismissed or seen as irrelevant in the pressures of daily living, for they shape and condition the steadfastness demanded of disciples.

The further assurance that Jesus' *words will never pass away* reinforces the solemnity. Taken literally one might wonder what value these words of Jesus would have once *heaven and earth* had passed away; in 16.17 Jesus had said something similar of the Law, which also proved not easy to interpret. Out of its context the saying points to the abiding authority of Jesus, transcending the conditions of his earthly ministry; yet the difficulty of understanding the preceding verse shows that this does not mean that Jesus' words can be repeated in a literalistic fashion without interpretation. Luke has engaged in such interpretation but still feels able to claim these words to sanction what he has done.

In keeping with the way he has focussed this discourse on the disciples, Luke concludes with an exhortation not found in Mark or Matthew. In the seductive ordinariness of daily living and the apparent unending pattern of life there was a danger that Christians would lose the sense of urgency and expectation that the belief in an imminent end had produced. For Luke the point of this teaching is not so that people begin marking off a programme but that they live in readiness. Whether *dissipation and drunkenness* is meant literally or is a metaphor for an attitude which is heedless of the call to discipleship matters little; Luke sees the choice as between an outlook which is conditioned by the ordinary *cares* of daily life (cf. 12.29), and one which is focussed on the pattern of discipleship he has traced throughout the Gospel. He recognizes that this is no easy path and so demands prayer *for strength; what is coming* whether seen as persecution and betrayal, as the devastations of history, or as the uncertain 'day of the Gentiles', is but a prelude. Those who can *stand in the presence of the Son of Man* are those who have no need to fear him as judge.

Luke clearly found it imperative to retain this passage of Jesus' teaching, but he also found it necessary to reinterpret it. He has also done this by including related material elsewhere in the Gospel (12.11–12; 17.20–37), so that it does not become an esoteric but irrelevant passage which is easily passed over. It seems likely that he still retained an expectation that all would be resolved in the not-too-distant future. As time has passed many have found it increasingly difficult to use this material. It has to be admitted that it cannot provide a total interpretation of life in the world. The apocalyptic world-view tends to be negative about this world and society, setting it in a simple contrast with God and God's coming kingdom; it is less likely to see signs of God's kingdom already at work or to recognize the presence of love and life and truth in human society. Yet it does grasp firmly the sense of God's lordship over the patterns of history and offers a confident hope in the working out of God's purposes. The imagery it uses may not speak so evocatively to a modern generation as it did to those whose understanding was shaped by the 'Old Testament'. Understood as a programme to be applied to contemporary events it can be abused and focus more on judgment than on liberation (but cf. v.28). Yet Luke rightly recognized that to do away with this material entirely would be to lose an essential element in the Gospel, an element which still needs restating.

With this Luke draws Jesus' public *teaching* ministry in Jerusalem to a close. Without any indication of the span of time he leaves a picture of Jesus at home and uncontested *in the Temple*; it is there alone that he teaches so that *the city* does not even provide a resting place for him at night. *The people* still flock to listen to him: as yet he has lost none of his popularity. Yet the reference to *Olivet* not only recalls the beginning of this period in 19.29, 37 but also anticipates Jesus' going there 'as usual' on the night he was betrayed (22.39); it is perhaps assumed that he spends his time there in prayer as he will then, and for readers who know that next stage in the story it carries a warning that this time of open ministry will come to an end.

Passion and Resurrection
22.1–24.53

It seems likely that the account of Jesus' death and resurrection was the first part of his story to be told as a continuous narrative; it would have been necessary both as the central part of Christian preaching and to explain 'the scandal' of belief in someone who had been crucified (I Cor. 1.23). Yet this already means that the story was told not as an objective historical report but from the standpoint of faith that Jesus was indeed Christ and Son of God, that his death was part of God's purposes and efficacious for humankind, and that the climax was his resurrection. More particularly, although in their bare outline the Gospel accounts follow similar lines, there are considerable differences between them, reflecting their own under-standing of the significance of these events. We cannot therefore go to any one of the Gospels, and even less to an amalgam of them, as if they could provide a factual record. The question of the difficulties of a historical reconstruction of the events surrounding Jesus' death is one that will continually arise, although our main emphasis will be on Luke's interpretation of what has been the implicit goal of his Gospel since 9.51 and indeed since the promise of the birth of Jesus.

Plot and betrayal
22.1–6

It is fundamental to early Christian tradition, and reaffirmed in later Jewish tradition, that Jesus died at Passover time. The *Passover* was the annual celebration commemorating the deliverance of the people of Israel from Egypt; it was the major pilgrimage festival of the year for it was only in Jerusalem, in the Temple, that the Passover lamb could be slaughtered, late in the afternoon of 14 Nisan. The lamb would then be eaten in family and similar groups within the city soon after sunset, which in Jewish terms heralded the beginning of a new day, 15 Nisan. *The festival of Unleavened Bread* was a week-long

harvest festival immediately following Passover: Luke's identification of the two is an oversimplification, although an understandable
one.

Luke does not explain why the nearness of the festival period
should particularly provoke *the chief priests and the scribes* to seek
Jesus' death; in practical terms the crowd was always volatile at
Passover time and any messianic disturbance would be the more
dangerous, but perhaps he also sees an implicit connection between
these religious festivals and the dominance of the religious leadership – hence the introduction in the next scene of the *temple guards*.
However, their cautionary inaction also reintroduces the implicit
tension between the leadership and *the people* which has been a
thread through Jesus' ministry and particularly that in Jerusalem
(20.19, 45f.).

That, despite their hesitation, Jesus was 'done *away with*' was
according to all the Gospels due to *Judas* who agreed to *betray* Jesus
to them; the horror this provoked in the early Christian mind is
shown by the regular reminder that Judas was *one of the Twelve*, a
member of the innermost group chosen by Jesus himself. Although
subsequent interpreters have tried to understand Judas' reasons for
what he did, the Gospels give no information about this. However,
Luke does offer one interpretation by pointing to *Satan* entering into
Judas. After Jesus' temptation 'the devil departed' (4.13); now he re-
enters the scene, although all of Jesus' ministry should be seen
as a victorious battle against his power (10.18; 11.18; 13.16). John
similarly speaks of Satan entering Judas (John 13.2, 27), one of a
number of links between Luke and John, but neither evangelist
thereby excuses Judas for his action; the agreement to *pay him a sum
of money* makes his act the more ignominious and does not mean his
only reasons were for monetary gain. Precisely what *he agreed* to do
is unclear, although it might be to disclose where Jesus could be
found alone (see vv.47–48), but the emphasis in the Greek is more
that he 'handed him over' than that he 'betrayed' him.

The Last Supper: the meal
22.7–20

Thus far in the Gospel Jesus has taught and acted, but his actions
have chiefly been those of miracle and of association, particularly in
meals, with particular groups. There now follows a further meal, but
his only associates are the apostles, and it becomes the scene of

actions of extraordinary significance and power. This meal is not only recorded in each of the Synoptic Gospels but also by Paul in I Cor. 11.23–25, probably written earlier than any of the Gospels; as Paul shows, some form of re-enacting 'the lord's supper' and of repeating Jesus' words had become part of the liturgical life of the early church (I Cor. 11.20–34). It seems likely that such liturgical practice has influenced the language of the Gospel accounts and explains the differences between them.

For Luke the meal is a Passover meal, although he is wrong in identifying the day when the *Passover lambs* were *slaughtered* (14 Nisan) with *'the day' of Unleavened Bread*, which was, as we have seen, a week-long festival following Passover. In this dating, which follows that of Mark (and Matthew), he differs from John for whom the Passover only begins after Jesus' death (John 18.28, 39; 19.14): for John Jesus' final meal is not a Passover meal, neither does he record any interpretative actions over the meal. How this contradiction is to be resolved and why it has arisen has been the subject of much debate; the balance of opinion favours the synoptic presentation of the meal as a Passover meal, but the issue is by no means closed.

As with the entry into Jerusalem (19.29), two of Jesus disciples, here named as Peter and John, future leaders in the early church (Acts 3–4), act as his agents in making the necessary preparations – procuring a lamb, sacrificing it within the Temple courts and roasting it, and preparing the other elements of the meal. The emphasis here, as it will be in all that follows, is on Jesus' initiative: he sends before they ask (ctr. Mark 14.12). In what follows we should not wonder whether the *man . . . carrying a water jar*, presumably normally a woman's task although there is no explicit evidence for this, was a pre-arranged signal; again, and as in 19.30–32, it is Jesus' foreknowledge which is most important. Rooms would have been at a premium in Jerusalem where the meal had to be eaten, and it is still possible that their use of *'The Teacher'* means that *the householder* was a disciple, but Luke is less interested in practicalities than in Jesus' intentions which govern all that follows.

The Passover meal recalled the deliverance from Egypt, offered the participants the opportunity to reclaim that experience as their own, and by the time of Jesus also looked forward in anticipation of the final deliverance in God's kingdom. The provisions of Ex. 12.1–14; Num. 9.1–14 and Deut. 16.1–8 had been developed and formalized over time so that the meal had a clear structure, in which the recalling of the past deliverance and the interpretation of the elements of the meal, particularly the lamb, unleavened bread, and bitter herbs, played an integral part. In what follows Jesus both affirms and reinterprets the Passover symbols; the solemnity of the occasion is signalled by the words *when the hour came*, and by calling those present no longer 'disciples' but *the apostles* (cf. 6.13; 24.10), Luke acknowledges its significance for the establishment of the future community or church.

By sharing in the eating of *this Passover*, probably a specific reference to the lamb which was sometimes so called, they would be bound together with Jesus in all that it symbolized of the people redeemed by God; the unusually forceful language in which Jesus expresses his longing shows how important this continuity with God's past acts is for Luke's understanding of Jesus. He did not fear that his imminent *death* might forestall the meal; rather his death would be seen in its true meaning in the light of the shared Passover: the word translated *death*, or better '*suffering*', sounds similar in Greek to the word for *Passover*. Just as we have seen how there is a tension between the kingdom manifest in Jesus' ministry and its full expression in the future, so there is a tension between Jesus' sharing now with his disciples and the awaited *fulfilment in the kingdom of God*. Luke and his church would see themselves as living between those two defining moments, Jesus' death and the time of fulfilment; the Passover which already looked both to the past and to the future deliverance expressed this tension and gained a new level of meaning through it.

Giving thanks over and sharing wine at three, or later four, moments during the meal was also an integral part of the Passover celebration. Jesus offers it to his disciples, and this time it is less clear whether he also partook of it. Sharing in the *cup* they are bound together and dependent on what Jesus gives; once again the tension between the present, so laden with meaning and yet incomplete, and the coming *fulfilment* dominates Jesus' words. The coming *kingdom of God* is not some distant moment of no immediate relevance: it gives meaning to the present but also acts as a reminder that the present is not complete in itself.

The *bread* eaten in the Passover meal would be the unleavened bread which reminded them of the haste in which they left Egypt (Deut. 16.3). Once Jesus has given *thanks* – the Greek word is the origin of the later term 'eucharist', thanksgiving – *he broke it*, the usual action in a meal. Yet this time his *words* invest it with new meaning, no longer a reference to the Passover but to himself. It is often pointed out that although there is a word for *is* in Greek, in the Aramaic in which Jesus would certainly have spoken there need be none: *'This . . . my body'*, the relationship between them certain but undefined. The bread and Jesus' body are being brought together to be understood one in the light of the other, but this openness leaves unspecified precisely how. To stress the 'is' on the one hand, or to replace it, or its absence in Aramaic, with 'symbolizes' on the other may be to look for a 'mathematical' meaning which ignores the power of the total moment: the breaking, Jesus' giving of it, and perhaps the eating which is implied but not stated, are all part of 'This'. His 'body' would be Jesus himself, but in the light of Jesus' death – and almost certainly the first time that Jesus' words and actions were recounted was after his death – it could only evoke his body broken on the cross. In what sense Jesus' own words at that Passover meal were spoken in anticipation of his death and, if so, how far those present would have understood it, is of course unknown to us.

Thus Jesus has made three solemn utterances, concerning the Passover (lamb), concerning the cup, and concerning the bread. It would be possible to structure these in different ways, as a Passover saying followed by a close pair regarding cup and bread, or as a Passover pair, lamb and cup, both looking to future fulfilment, followed by a single saying regarding the bread as Jesus' body; a third structure seems preferable, that the sayings move from that which refers exclusively to the Passover, to the transitional saying concerning the cup which both repeats the Passover symbolism and implies the new community who share it, and finally to the saying over the bread which completes the transformation of reference from Passover to Jesus, without denying the continuing significance of the former.

What is striking about this sequence, particularly for those familiar with the other accounts or with Christian liturgy, is the absence of any explicit interpretation of either bread/body or cup in the light of Jesus' death and its meaning. Equally remarkable is the absence of any injunction to repeat what Jesus has said and done, although Luke knew of the breaking of the bread by the early church (Acts 2.46); indeed there is no reference at all to Jesus' blood, and if the cup is seen as part of a new symbolism for the new community, the order – cup followed by bread – reverses that found in the other NT sources.

Some of these problems would be removed if we were to follow

179

the text printed as a footnote in the REB, adding to v.19 an interpretation of the body *given for you*, with the command *to do this*, and following it with a parallel offering and interpretation of the cup in v.20. This, often known as 'the longer text', is very well attested in the manuscript tradition but has been relegated to a footnote by the REB on the grounds that if Luke had written vv.19b-20 it is difficult to imagine why they would have been excluded in some manuscripts. Moreover, the additions are close to, although not identical with, the wording in I Cor. 11.24–25, suggesting that they may have been borrowed from there when early readers or scribes found Luke's 'shorter text' deficient.

How finely balanced the question is is shown by the NRSV having chosen to print the longer text, indicating the shorter alternative in a footnote. If Luke did write this longer text his understanding of Jesus' death would be richer; bread/body and cup are given or poured out 'for you', for the disciples (ctr. Mark 14.24 'for many'), although how they benefit from it is not explained (ctr. Matt. 26.28 'for the forgiveness of sins'). The cup points to but is not identified (ctr. Mark 14.24 'This is') with Jesus' *blood, poured out* in death; there is a reference back to the covenant at Mt Sinai sealed with the blood of sacrifice (Ex. 24.1–8, more clearly alluded to by Mark 14.24), but also one forward to *the new covenant* promised by Jeremiah (Jer. 31.31), an allusion also made by I Cor. 11.25 but not by Mark or Matthew. The injunction over the bread to *do this as a memorial* (cf. I Cor. 11.24) picks up an important Passover theme, for that celebration was both to recall the decisive past event and to make it a reality for those in the present (Deut. 16.3).

Whichever form of Luke's text was original, the other must have been developed very quickly so that both survived; it may be that both forms circulated almost from the beginning, particularly if the celebration was held in Luke's church. This variation even in the text of Luke, and the further variations between our other sources, show how important this event was for the early church, and how rich was the interpretation of it. It should not matter that we cannot certainly recover Jesus' original words and intentions, although attempts have been made, usually favouring the simplest possible form; throughout the Gospel story, and particularly in the events of his Passion, Jesus' words and actions lived through the faith of the church, a faith which did not blindly repeat but which reinterpreted them in the light of their own new understanding of what that faith meant.

The Last Supper: teaching the disciples
22.21–38

Unlike Mark and Matthew, Luke follows the supper with Jesus teaching his disciples in preparation for what they will encounter in the immediate and more distant future. This is also the case in John (14–17), although with very different content, and both follow a common literary pattern of farewell instruction by a teacher to his disciples; it has also been one of Luke's characteristics to set Jesus' teaching at a meal during his ministry (cf. ch. 14).

The opening words are a solemn prophecy of Jesus' imminent betrayal. Mark and Matthew place this before the meal, but in setting it here Luke emphasizes the horror that Jesus' *betrayer* should be someone who had shared this deeply symbolic meal with him at *the table*. As we have seen, attributing Judas' action to Satan (v.3) does not absolve Judas, but neither does it mean that Jesus is the helpless victim of human and diabolic treachery. Even as Jesus has been travelling to Jerusalem since 9.51, so now he *is going a way* determined for him by God; this too does not absolve Judas, meaning that he is a pawn in a divine purpose, for he has chosen the path of opposition to God and stands under judgment (cf. 6.24). There is a dilemma here in the relationship between divine purpose which is secure and human freedom of action: Luke affirms both, and so affirms Judas' responsibility for his choice, but he does not attempt to resolve the inevitable tension between them. While *Son of Man* could be not a title but a way of saying 'I', the build up in its use which we have traced through the Gospel points to the one bound to suffer and certain to vindicate those who remain faithful to him (see comment on pp.42f.).

The perplexity of the disciples as to the identity of the betrayer is a sombre warning that even among the chosen apostasy is possible. It may seem historically unlikely that the disciples would at this moment begin *a dispute* as to their relative superiority; Luke, however, introduces this here, although the Markan parallel comes earlier in the ministry (Mark 10.42–45), because his theme is the vocation of the apostles in the future beyond Jesus' death. *Benefactor* was a title of honour given not only to those who made financial endowments to the city or people but also to rulers whose exercise of *authority* might be seen or lauded as bringing prosperity and security; Jesus does not condemn this, for it is the normal role of *kings to lord it over their subjects*.

What Jesus calls for is not a reversal of roles: *the greatest* will still be this, and so will *the one who rules.* However, Jesus offers a new pattern of leadership: those who are in positions of authority are to bear themselves as those without authority. Serving, which for Luke has a primarily domestic setting, has been a repeated theme in the Gospel, particularly by women (4.39; 8.3; 10.40). Jesus does not deny that that role is the more menial (cf. 12.37; 17.8), but now he defines himself in the same terms: he is not *'like a servant'* as in the REB, for this is not the word Luke uses, but *as one who serves.* In the context this refers to what Jesus has done through the meal, offering them the bread and cup; yet the meaning cannot be limited to the context, for in these words Jesus defines his whole relationship with the apostles while not in any way detracting from his sole authority of which he will immediately speak.

Jesus is not speaking of himself in relation to all of humanity but *among* them; he is a pattern to be followed by them, but he also defines them as those whom he serves. In this way they are bound together with him and so also with each other. This unity reaches back into his ministry: in Luke the disciples will not desert Jesus at his arrest and it is assumed that they *have stood firmly by* him throughout his ministry; as it now nears its climax that ministry is shaped by what lies ahead as *times of trial,* that is a time of conflict with the forces of opposition to God (cf. 11.4). Beyond that lies a vindication which is already guaranteed, for God as *Father* has already *entrusted* to Jesus a *kingdom*: here the kingdom belongs to the future but is a present certainty. The disciples will share in that vindication for Jesus makes the same commitment to them: sharing in his kingdom is symbolized by the common image of a banquet (cf. Isa. 25.6). Yet even more is promised them: Jewish hope looked to the ingathering of the twelve tribes in the eschatological future, and the twelve apostles will represent and rule (rather than 'judge' in the sense of condemn) those tribes.

Matthew has a slightly different form of this promise in another context (Matt. 19.28). It may be that Jesus' choice of twelve 'apostles' already symbolically represented the twelve tribes of Israel whose 'ingathering' he hoped to inaugurate in some way (cf. p.69). For Luke, however, this promise may not so much offer a message of hope for Israel who will participate in Jesus' reign, as point to a 'new' or 'reformed' Israel, including the Gentiles who come into the church in Acts.

Now Jesus' attention reverts to the challenge of the immediate future which marks the apex of conflict with the powers of evil. In 3.17 the separation of *wheat* from chaff was the act of the coming judge, here it has been claimed by *Satan* as the faithfulness of the disciples will be put to the test most stringently. As in Job 1.6–12 Satan here acts only with divine permission, and he is countered by the power of Jesus' intercessory prayer. *Simon*, here marked out for future leadership, is to be the source of renewed hope and *strength* for his fellow disciples, but he can only be so if he first repents and recommits himself. Yet he neither recognizes that he depends solely on the prayer of Jesus, nor that he too will need renewal. In Acts 5.18 Peter is put into *prison* and later tradition told of his going to *death* for his faith, but that came later and not *with* Jesus; his confidence in his own preparedness would first be undermined by his failure even to acknowledge that he knew Jesus.

Although it is often assumed that *cock . . . crow* refers to a fixed time in the Roman division of the night, there is no parallel to this formulation and it may be that Jesus refers to the sudden and unexpected cry of the bird which will catch Simon unawares and expose his over-confidence. For later readers for whom the choice when faced with persecution was to confess or to deny, this prediction of Peter's behaviour, soon to be fulfilled (vv.54–60), would be an ominous reminder of their own weakness and dependence on Jesus (cf.21.14–15).

Jesus' final warning now to all his apostles is perhaps the most difficult passage in this chapter – some would say in the Gospel! It looks back to the sending out of the twelve in 9.1–6 and more closely to that of the seventy-two in 10.1–12 (cf. 10.4) – Luke is not concerned about such conflation. Then *without purse or pack* they were able to fulfil their task of preaching and healing without obstacle or need. Now they face a radically different situation. The precise translation of the Greek is not clear but the overall import is: they will need not only *purse . . . and . . . pack* but even a *sword*; indeed so urgent is the latter that anyone without one should even *sell his cloak to buy one*. If meant literally does this refer to the violence of Jesus' arrest in which he implicitly sanctions their self-defence. The ensuing events seem to contradict this (22.49–53), although some have seen here a remnant of an earlier tradition in which Jesus was more involved in active resistance to the authorities, Jewish or Roman, than most surviving sources suggest. Or does it look forward to their future missionary activity when they will face opposition and aggression and even death: this solution would then provoke the question whether Jesus here advocates armed self-defence or is only using this vivid language to symbolize the danger in which they will live. Clearly each of these interpretations has important consequences for the attitude of future Christians to the use of arms in defence of themselves or of the Gospel.

A further possibility is suggested by the quotation of *scripture* which follows – fulfilment of scripture in Jesus' death is an important theme for Luke. The verse comes from Isa. 53.12, a rare explicit quotation from the so-called (fourth) suffering servant song (Isa. 52.13–53.12) which is often claimed to have been a primary source of Jesus' own self-understanding but of which the Gospels make little if any use in understanding his death. *Transgressors* are more prosaically 'the lawless', as one of whom Jesus was treated and in whose company he was crucified (23.32–3); in speaking of the need for a sword was Jesus ironically refering to the way he would be arrested? In contradiction to all he stood for he would be treated as an armed insurrectionist, but he is not seriously advocating that they should adopt such a style. So, according to this view, when they eagerly declare they already *have two swords here* – a surprising piece of information which for some supports the picture of 'Jesus the resistance-fighter' – he wearily dismisses their misunderstanding, *'Enough* of that!' Although they do not desert him, the scene at his arrest (vv.49–51) reinforces the sense that he alone understands and chooses the path he takes. This interpretation probably fits Luke's general attitude to Jesus and to relations with state power most naturally, but the passage remains enigmatic and Luke may have retained it from his tradition because of the way it prepares for what follows.

Jesus at the mount of Olives
22.39–53

From now on Jesus stands alone; he takes the initiative as he *made his way* (cf. v.22), but although *the disciples followed*, better than the REB's *accompanied*, him their role is largely one of misunderstanding and failure. That Jesus went *as usual to the mount of Olives* may explain why Judas knew where to find him, but more importantly it marks all of Jesus' Jerusalem ministry and not just this night as a time of prayer (cf. 21.37). Unlike Mark and Matthew, Luke does not name the place Gethsemane, neither does he separate Peter, James and John to watch with Jesus (Mark 14.33–34). *His disciples* are to *pray* for

themselves, that they do not have to face the ultimate *test* or eschatological conflict encapsulated in Jesus' coming death: this is an echo of
the Lord's Prayer (11.4, cf. 22.28) so that each passage illuminates the
other and would emphasize the value of prayer for the early
Christians in their situation.

Jesus' own prayer, with the address *'Father'*, may also echo the
Lord's Prayer, but only if Luke or his sources also knew the longer
'Matthean' form; his own in 11.2–4 does not ask that God's *will . . . be
done*. In the Hebrew Bible the *cup* can be a symbol both of destiny
(Ps. 11.6; 16.5) and also of divine wrath (Ps. 75.8; Isa. 51.17); although
this does not mean that Jesus suffered God's judgmental anger, his
death could be seen not just as his personal destiny but as his entering into the judgment which was part of the ultimate test or conflict.
Jesus makes his prayer only once in Luke, thus softening the sense of
anguished inner conflict suggested by Mark's three-fold prayer, and
emphasizing his commitment to God's will.

Countering this 'softening' is the vivid scene of Jesus' extreme
anguish of spirit, and the succour brought him by *an angel from heaven*.
However, as indicated by the footnote in the REB, a number of early
and significant manuscripts omit this scene, and it is bracketed by
the NRSV. Angels as divine messengers are part of Luke's narrative
style (1.11, 26; Acts 5.19), but the verses do interrupt a natural flow
from v.42 to v.45; if they were originally part of Luke's text it is con-
ceivable that scribes found them incompatible with their own more
exalted view of Jesus and omitted them, yet it is equally possible that
they were an independent tradition which became incorporated
here at a later stage to add more drama to Luke's otherwise more
emotionless scene.

As Jesus returns to *his disciples* the emphasis is on the contrast
between his self-commitment and their failure even to pray for their
own need in the coming *test*. By attributing their sleep to exhaustion
from *grief*, perhaps psychologically improbable, Luke may be excusing them. The implication of course is that there was no one to
witness Jesus' own prayer and experience. The scene has been reconstructed by the early church or Gospel writers and reflects their own
understanding of Jesus, of his relation to God, and of the meaning
of his death. For them this is what surely he would have said and
done, and for later readers it offers both a key to understanding all
that follows and a model for Christian disciples in their own times of
testing.

The arrest immediately follows, *while he was still speaking*, and so must be seen as the answer to Jesus' own prayer and the moment for which he was preparing his disciples. Again the horror that *Judas was one of the Twelve* is repeated, but Jesus retains the initiative, being the first to speak, so that we are left unsure whether Judas did in fact *kiss* Jesus. The *kiss* was a sign of greeting and fellowship, and it is Jesus who identifies what he is doing as an act of betrayal or 'handing over'; again *the Son of Man* could be a way of saying 'me', 'this person here', but in the broader context of Luke's use of the term it has a much deeper meaning (cf. v.22). Thus Jesus identifies himself, but not merely as 'Jesus of Nazareth', nor as a robber (v.52), but as 'Son of Man' who is bound to die.

In v.39 those with Jesus were designated 'disciples', here they are *his followers*; presumably only the Twelve are meant but they are no longer called such for the emphasis is on their conduct and not on their future status. If we have rightly interpreted the dialogue in vv.35–38, they now display their misunderstanding in using the *swords* they had then claimed. Luke agrees with John (18.10) in identifying the *ear* cut off as *his right*, perhaps following a natural tendency for tradition to become more specific. Jesus' response is not simply to reject the use of violence, but, again taking the initiative, to heal – whether by restoring the ear or healing the wound is not Luke's concern.

Although earlier (v.47) described as *a crowd*, those arresting him are now more explicitly identified as *the chief priests, the temple guards, and the elders*. Only John (18.3) suggests that Roman forces may have been involved; undoubtedly there is a tendency in the Gospels to increasingly focus the blame on the Jewish authorities, and whereas in Mark 14.43 those who arrest him are only sent by these authorities, Luke, less convincingly, has them present. Thus in Luke Jesus can challenge them before they will challenge him (vv.66–71). By recalling how *day after day* he was with them *in the Temple*, Jesus looks back to the ministry in Jerusalem which Luke explicitly located there (19.47; 21.37); the reader knows that they had not raised *a hand against* him, although they had sought to trap him, and that Jesus had successfully answered all their challenges. A *robber* might also be one who used violence in the cause of resistance, and Jesus clearly disassociates himself from such, even if not everyone at the time or since has done so.

Although Jesus has taken the initiative, his arrest was earlier implicitly identified with the time of testing and conflict with evil; in language reminiscent of that favoured by John (John 13.1; 12.35), it is now their *hour*. Throughout his ministry Jesus had exercised 'authority' (4.32, 36), but now is the time for the *'authority'* (= REB *reigns*) of *darkness*; although for Luke Jesus' death is in fulfilment of scripture and accords with God's will, it is nonetheless the work of the forces of evil and all that opposes God.

Peter's denial
22.54–65

Luke's account of the events surrounding Jesus' trial is rather different from that of Mark. In particular, while the latter has an initial trial by 'the whole Sanhedrin' at night, something which was contrary to correct procedure as later laid down, Luke only has this the following day. This need not mean that he had a different source, for there is little in his account that could not come from a rewriting of Mark's version; how much of the events leading up to Jesus' condemnation by Pilate was known to the earliest Christians is uncertain, and it may be that they reconstructed them with the help of their own convictions about Jesus and about his death.

In Luke, then, Jesus is merely kept under guard in the house of *the high priest*, whom other sources identify as Caiaphas. In contrast to Mark (14.50) and Matthew (26.56) the disciples do not flee, but *Peter* alone *followed*. *The courtyard* could also be a hall; we should perhaps envisage that Jesus was also being kept there since v.61 does not say that he had only just come in at that moment. The narrative of Peter's three-fold denial is told in vivid detail; the presence of the story in all the Gospels, and the fact that no one in the later church would invent such an incident to Peter's discredit, witness to its authenticity. In the later church to deny being *with him* or *of them* was tantamount to apostasy, the most heinous of sins, so it is unlikely that the story was retold in order to comfort those who did so. It was rather a stark reminder that even Peter failed, and that Jesus remained alone in his faithfulness. Yet all happens according to his foreknowledge, and the crowing of the cock confirms the fulfilment of his prediction in v.34. It is not this, however, which provokes Peter to remorse but the moment when *the Lord turned and looked* at him; Jesus is spoken of here as the one whom the church acknowledged as 'the Lord', and *'the word of the Lord'*, obscured by the REB's translation *'the Lord's words'*, recalls the language used of the prophets' proclamation of God's word. Thus Jesus' word is as authoritative and as sure of fulfilment as God's; in this context we should also remember Jesus' earlier injunction that Peter (Simon), once he had repented, was to strengthen the others (v.32).

In sharp contrast to the recognition of Jesus as 'the Lord' whose word is authoritative stands the treatment he receives by those *guarding* him. This abuse is totally unprovoked whereas in Mark it is placed after Jesus' condemnation by the sanhedrin (Mark 14.65); there their demand that he prophesy might make some sense, here its irony is only evident to the reader who recognizes that Jesus has just shown himself as prophet, and more than prophet, for 'the word of the Lord' is his own word. Thus Luke has ordered the events of which he knew through the tradition so as to point to the deeper ironies and truths at play.

Jesus before the sanhedrin
22.66–71

Whereas Mark, followed by Matthew, reports only a cursory meeting of the sanhedrin the following morning, in Luke this constitutes the only occasion when Jesus is brought before them. Moreover this is no formal trial and there are no witnesses, true or false, (ctr. Mark 14.55–9). It is not clear that Luke fully understood who constituted the sanhedrin or *Council*, which he may see as a place 'into', rather than a body, *'before'* which Jesus *was brought*. In practice the sanhedrin was a body limited by number, whose membership and powers in this period are not entirely certain; there were others, not part of it, who also exercised influence. In bringing together *the elders . . . chief priests, and scribes* Luke wishes to indicate the entire ruling establishment of the Jews, and in identifying the first named as *of the people*, he may be implicating them also.

Luke uses the occasion to express what for him are the central elements in acknowledgment or rejection of Jesus. First that he is *the Messiah*: as elsewhere in the Gospels this is the term others seek to apply to Jesus but which Jesus does not use of himself, perhaps conforming to historical reality. His equivocal answer does not reject the label but may recognize its ambiguities, for the early Christians used it of Jesus only by inscribing it with their own understanding. The term Jesus introduces, again as elsewhere in the Gospels, is *Son of Man*. As we have seen, it is used to indicate the obscurity as well as the authority of Jesus' earthly ministry, to identify him as the one bound to die in fulfilment of scripture, and to express the conviction that he would also bring vindication and judgment (pp.42f.). Here the last element alone is evoked, echoing the vision of Dan. 7.13 but coloured by Ps. 110.1; *seated at the right hand of Almighty God* would mean that the Son of Man was acknowledged and given authority by God: this is no distant hope but *from now on*, not even beyond the resurrection and ascension but so certain that it is already true.

Their response, implying that he is claiming to be *the Son of God*, again reflects Christian convictions, although again Jesus' reply is carefully ambiguous, neither affirming nor denying the title. It is anticipated by the allusion to Ps. 110.1 which speaks of divine sonship, but in Jewish circles 'Messiah' and 'Son of Man' were not identical concepts, nor were 'Son of Man' and 'Son of God', and while there is limited evidence that 'Son of God' might refer to the Messiah it need not be so limited. Moreover, the use of none of these titles was blasphemous, the conclusion that is drawn in Mark (14.64), but not in Luke; Luke's Gentile readers may have found the term 'blasphemy' meaningless, but by omitting the charge Luke leaves it uncertain what they *have heard . . . from his own lips* and why this means they need no *further evidence*.

Thus Luke's account of the trial – and here he is following and developing the earlier Markan tradition – leaves the essential points unclear. There is no obvious connection with Jesus' ministry, neither with what he has said and done nor with the controversies in which he was engaged. The issues or titles named in his 'interrogation' reflect Christian faith more than convincing charges that might provoke his condemnation. There will also be a similar lack of coherence with the charges they lay before Pilate (23.2–5). This is not because the Jewish authorities did act inconsistently and incoherently; the early Christians were convinced that Jesus died because he was whom Christians believed him to be, Messiah, Son of God; they were also convinced that he died because the Jewish authorities had rejected him and had been the main movers in his condemnation. The trial scenes reflect these convictions. The questions of the charges under which Jesus was condemned and the relative roles of the Jewish and Roman authorities are much debated with no universally agreed conclusions. For the modern interpreter it is important to distinguish between the 'historical' question 'why?' and the 'theological' answer given by the Gospel writers.

Jesus before Pilate and Herod
23.1–25

What they take as Jesus' testimony against himself immediately leads them to bring him *before Pilate* (see on 3.1); Luke emphasizes that this is the unanimous decision and responsibility of *the whole assembly*, the entire Jewish leadership as he understands it. It is then the more surprising that the charges they bring are not those of their earlier questions but overtly political ones. Although it is sometimes assumed that they felt Pilate would have little time for abstruse religious debate, the Jews were permitted to organize their internal affairs according to their law; even if, as John states (18.31), capital punishment could only be passed by Pilate, they need only have demonstrated that he merited it (John 19.7). While Luke has shown that Jesus was rejected by the Jewish authorities for what Christians knew to be true, he also wants to show that he was crucified by the Romans on patently false grounds. The attentive reader knows that there has been little evidence over the last chapters of Jesus *subverting our nation*; certainly he did not oppose *the payment of taxes to Caesar*, although they had tried to trap him into this (20.19–26), and the closest to *claiming to be . . . a king* came in the cry of the crowds with the crucial addition 'in the name of the Lord' (19.38).

Pilate, surprisingly, ignores the first two charges and takes up only the last, asking Jesus directly not whether he claims to be but whether he is *the king of the Jews*. The Gospels agree that this was the charge under which Jesus died (v.38), and here most scholars agree lies the historical nucleus of the grounds on which Jesus was put to death. Such a claim, inevitably understood as a challenge to Roman rule, would have to be taken seriously by any Roman governor, and Jesus would not be the first, nor the last, to die for such pretensions. Whether the charge was based on particular actions or claims of Jesus, or relied on a (deliberate) reinterpretation of the ambivalent term *Messiah* remains a matter of debate.

Jesus' reply, as it was to the Council (22.67), is probably a guarded refusal to affirm or to deny the term. At least from Luke's point of view, Jesus could neither reject it nor accept it as probably understood by Pilate; yet there is also an irony in that Pilate, the representative of Roman power, should be the one to make the confession '*You are the King of the Jews!*' – his words can also be read as a statement since the question is only indicated by punctuation and context. Again surprisingly, Pilate does not pursue this equivocation but makes the first of three declarations of Jesus' innocence (cf. vv.14–15; 22). Luke is less interested in the historical probabilities of Pilate's cross-examination of Jesus than in wanting to reassure his readers that Jesus was not found guilty by the Roman authorities.

At this moment *the crowd* is also brought into the scene, although it is unclear where this is taking place; they will also be present in v.13, for Luke did not want to deny the responsibility of the Jewish people even if he lays most weight on that of the leadership. However, it is probably only the latter who respond by introducing a new element in the picture, Jesus' *teaching*. *All over Judaea* probably refers not to the province or southern territory but to the entire area inhabited by Jews, including *Galilee*. This understanding of the extent of Jesus' influence is typically Lukan (4.44; 5.17; 7.17; cf. Acts 10.37); despite the presence of 'the crowds' it reaffirms Jesus' influence over *the people* and further isolates the leadership.

It also serves to introduce a new scene which is only found in Luke's Gospel. He assumes that as a *Galilean* Jesus came under the *jurisdiction* of *Herod* Antipas (cf. 3.1), and so could properly be tried before him. There are no certain parallels to this procedure, and it seems unlikely that Pilate would surrender all authority to a neighbouring local ruler, particularly one with whom he had *a feud*, and it is unclear how he would act if they had come to conflicting conclusions. However, although some have suggested that Luke is trying to create a fulfilment of Ps. 2.2, 'kings . . . and rulers . . . against his anointed', there is no explicit scriptural allusion here (cf. Acts 4.25). That Herod should be *in Jerusalem* at Passover time is likely, and that he was involved in some way is not impossible, although Luke's account of the events before Herod in vv.8–11 could be constructed from existing tradition and shows little real knowledge of what went on. For Luke the incident provides yet another opportunity to implicate *the chief priests and scribes* as those most involved in accusing Jesus, and to reaffirm that but for them Jesus would have been found innocent (v.15). Moreover, within Luke's Gospel Herod has already played a rather ominous role (cf. 3.19; 9.7–9; 13.31), and despite the fact that *he was greatly pleased* to see Jesus we might expect little positive of him. Indeed, by subjecting Jesus to *contempt and ridicule* he allies himself with the Jewish authorities who had done the same without just cause (22.63–65); it seems that Luke has transferred this mockery from that inflicted by the Roman soldiers in Mark (Mark 15.16–20; Matt. 27.27–31). There is also an element of irony that Jesus should be an agent of reconciliation between these two men even when being tried for his life.

The third and final scene presses home further the main points already made. Pilate again finds Jesus innocent of the *charge* brought against him, and is confirmed in this by Herod. Now, most clearly, it is not only *the chief priests and councillors*, or 'rulers', but also the *people* who are implicated in all that follows. That Pilate should *propose to flog* a man he had found innocent seems both unjust and improbable: perhaps he too must be shown to be tainted by injustice in the face of Jesus' innocence. Yet the responsibility of those who cry for Jesus' death is the strongest theme. Unlike Mark (15.6–11; cf. Matt. 27.15–20), Luke does not mention Pilate's (unparalleled and improbable) custom of releasing a prisoner of their choice at Passover time; therefore their unexplained demand that a man imprisoned *for insurrection and murder* be *set free* and that Jesus, who has been found innocent, be crucified is the more perverse and horrific, as too is Pilate's compliance with it. Nothing more is known of *Barabbas* nor of the grounds on which he was released; his name could be translated 'son of the father', but the Gospel writers do not make anything of the irony of this, and the name is not an unusual one.

Jesus was crucified, a Roman penalty famed for its barbarous cruelty. That the crowd cry not just '*Away with him*' but '*Crucify him*' anticipates and presupposes the means by which Jesus dies. The Roman authorities alone could pass that sentence and inflict that penalty, and it is this fact which prevents any attempt to absolve them of responsibility and place it all on the Jewish leaders. Yet this is what Luke attempts to do when he says that Pilate *decided that they should have their way*, and that he *gave Jesus over to their will*. The first does not fit with the Roman governors' attitude to their subjects in general, and with Pilate's in particular, as we know it from other sources; the second cannot be literally true. Luke reflects a move, found also elsewhere in the New Testament and other early Christian writers, to absolve as far as possible the Romans, and to place all the blame on the Jews; this in part was a consequence of the early Christians' need for good relations with the state authorities and their experience of the refusal by most of the Jewish people to acknowledge Jesus as Messiah. Truth is now better served by seeking to unravel the uncertain process by which Jesus came to die a Roman death, and by refusing to perpetuate the claim that 'the Jews' crucified him.

Jesus led to execution
23.26–31

Since his arrest Jesus has been both the centre of attention and activity and yet also the victim of the activity of others as he has been *brought* from place to place (22.54, 66; 23.1, [7, 11] 14). Once more he is *led away*, the sequence from v.25 would suggest by the Jews or their leaders, although we have seen this to be historically false. Two incidents help set this in a wider context. In the first incident Jesus does not, as was standard, carry his own *cross* – probably the cross-beam on which he would be hung; instead it is given to *a man called Simon from Cyrene* to carry. Mark further identifies Simon by his sons, suggesting they were known to the Markan community (Mark 15.21); Luke, for whom the connection means nothing, drops this but instead emphasizes that Simon is made to *carry the cross behind Jesus*. Thus he becomes an unwitting model of the demand of discipleship Jesus had made in 9.23 (cf. 14.27).

Next, in an incident only recounted by Luke, Jesus is *followed by great numbers of* (the) *people*: although the people were joined with their leaders in v.13 and by implication in what followed, here they are again separated from them (cf. vv.35, 48 and comment), perhaps holding open at least for them the possibility of repentance. Significant among them are *women who mourned and lamented*. These women are not those who watch in v.49, who were his followers from Galilee; these are *daughters of Jerusalem*, representatives of the city and sharers in the challenge made to it and in its fate (see pp.156–58). Earlier, in 21.23 (see p.169) Jesus had acknowledged the particular hardship that women and children would suffer in the disaster Jerusalem would face; he repeats this as he envisages a time when to be *barren*, often in the biblical tradition seen as divine punishment, and not, as usual, to have born *a child*, would be seen as a blessing (= *Happy*). The words of Hos. 10.8, there spoken of Israel's shame and destruction for her unfaithfulness, would be invoked as people longed for speedy oblivion in the face of untold horrors. The words are allusive but are clearly an oracle of judgment aimed not at these women alone but at Jerusalem. Jesus does not reject their compassion but redirects it for those who think that this is the worst that can happen. He finishes with a proverbial saying which contrasts the *green wood* with the *dry*; dry wood is much more susceptible to burning than green so the sense may be, 'If this is what happens to one who least merits it – the death of an innocent man – what will

193

happen to those who do?' There may alternatively be a contrast between the spring or the beginning of the process and when it is fully ripe. In either case, the emphasis is on what will surely come upon them: the connection between that and Jesus' death may be implicit but it is far from explicit, and the mood is not one of condemnation but of compassion.

The crucifixion
23.32–49

The place of crucifixion was perhaps *called The Skull* because of its shape, although the exact location is no longer certain. Yet generally Luke is less interested in the 'objective' details; unlike Mark's more 'objective' description (Mark 15.25–26), he is silent about the time and mentions the superscription which declared Jesus' 'crime' only later in an aside (v.38), although we have seen that this, that Jesus (was) claimed to be *the king of the Jews,* is one of the core elements in the story. Jesus is *led out to execution with two others,* perhaps recalling how before his death he had spoken of the fulfilment in him of Isa. 53.12 (22.37), although here they are *criminals* and not 'lawless' (transgressors) as in the Isaiah passage. There are echoes of various other scriptural passages in the account of the crucifixion which follows, particularly of Ps. 22.8, 18; 31.5; 69.21: the early Christians saw in these psalms an anticipation of what Jesus underwent and they retold the events through their language. Often in the psalms the speaker is the innocent victim of suffering and abuse, and able only to put faith in God; to the early Christians these psalms could be seen as encapsulating the experience of Jesus beyond all others, and so they help give shape to the long hours of the crucifixion. For Luke, therefore, the whole account focusses on Jesus.

Jesus' initial words of forgiveness are found in Luke alone, and in fact only in certain manuscripts as indicated by the REB footnote. They are spoken not of the soldiers who technically would have performed the crucifixion, nor of the other two criminals who have just been mentioned, but of the Jews. Despite the impression of the narrative so far that the Jewish authorities acted in full awareness, Acts 3.17 also attributes to them ignorance of the real meaning of their actions. Therefore, it is not easy to decide between the two possible explanations for the absence of v.34 in some major manuscripts: the prayer may have been original to Luke's Gospel, for it is consonant with his thought, but have been omitted by scribe(s) who balked at the forgiveness for the Jews; alternatively it may not have been written by Luke but have been added by scribe(s) who felt that if Stephen could forgive (Acts 7.60), then so could Jesus. The wording is not identical to that of Stephen, and it is possible that, as with 22.19–20, this is an early independent saying which has found a fortuitous home here.

Luke next carefully distinguishes between the different groups present and their response to Jesus. *The people* are now passive and only stand *looking*. By contrast (ctr. Mark 15.29), it is *their rulers* who mock him both as *God's Messiah* and as *his Chosen*: at the transfiguration the divine voice had declared Jesus to be 'my Chosen' and commanded them to 'listen to him' (9.35). The soldiers, who would have been Roman, had the right to cast *lots* for his clothes; Luke leaves his earlier pattern of excusing the Romans by having them also join *in the mockery* – this could suggest that he thought of them as Jewish although their words, *'king of the Jews'* would be more convincing on foreign lips. The *offering of sour wine* is presumably also meant in mockery and not to alleviate Jesus' discomfort (ctr. Mark 15.35–36). The third voice comes from *one of the criminals* and returns to the taunting confession *'Are not you the Messiah?'* The common theme in this mockery is the challenge *'save yourself'*; the three-fold pattern, and the introductory *'if this is . . . if you are'* recall Jesus' temptation by the devil (4.3–12). The details may be different but the underlying theme is the same: Jesus is indeed God's Messiah, the Chosen One, and even, rightly understood, their King, and he has *saved others*, but to save himself would be to negate all this.

The third voice, however, is balanced by another one which comes in Luke's Gospel alone. For him the two men, as so often in this Gospel, invite a contrast between them. Although often called 'the penitent thief' this is not what he expresses: rather, how can those who share the *same sentence* join in mockery? More than that, they, by the standards of the time, have earned their punishment, while Jesus *has done nothing wrong*. Thus the theme of Jesus' innocence, which dominated his trial before Pilate, is recalled and set in sharp contrast to the abuse he has endured.

Yet the man then goes beyond that to an implicit acknowledgment that Jesus is indeed king, and is to enter into his *royal power* or kingdom (rather than REB's *throne*). In the psalms the cry to God to 'remember' is a cry for help and deliverance (Ps. 74.2, 18, 22), and so the man now asks in faith that Jesus *remember* him and bring him to share in the deliverance of the kingdom. This prayer could look forward to the final judgment, but Jesus' answer speaks of *today*. With this word he had inaugurated his ministry as the time of salvation (4.21, see comment), and so it is appropriate that in his death he makes the same offer. Originally *Paradise*, a Persian loanword, had been used of the garden in Eden, but it had come to be used of the abode of the blessed among the dead. We should not press Jesus' words here to ask whether he (or Luke) thinks of salvation following immediately upon death rather than at the end of time in the eschatological age: the emphasis of the 'today' is not one of time but of the certainty of the salvation present in Jesus – as it had been in his ministry so now is it in his death.

So far the scene of the crucifixion has been one of the human response to Jesus, in rejection or in faith. Now the stage becomes a cosmic one as supernatural *darkness* falls *over the whole earth* (= REB *land*). This is not an eclipse, for being Passover it was full moon; the failure of *the sun's light* and this darkness point to the apparent triumph of evil. In Mark (15.38) the tearing of *the curtain of the Temple*, probably that which separated the Holy of Holies from the inner sanctuary, follows Jesus' death and probably symbolizes the new access to God it has won. For Luke it is another ominous and supernatural sign which precedes Jesus' death; it is unlikely that it presages the destruction of the Temple for Luke continues to give the Temple a role (see p.157) and thinks more of the destruction of the city of Jerusalem. Instead it provides an awesome moment for Jesus himself to commit himself to God.

It is noteworthy that whereas for Mark Jesus' last audible words are the much debated 'cry of dereliction' (15.34), Luke ignores this, presumably deliberately if he knew Mark; instead Jesus' last words, replacing the inarticulate cry of Mark 15.37, are those of confident faith as spoken by the 'righteous sufferer' in Ps. 31.6, prefaced by the characteristic *father* (22.42). Luke throughout has stressed that Jesus' death is in accordance with God's will and has been Jesus' deliberate goal, and his dying words set the seal on this certainty. For the psalmist '*my spirit*' meant 'myself', and this is probably what the Lukan Jesus means also, although we should not forget that it has been 'in the power of the spirit' (4.14) that he has conducted all his ministry.

The scene closes with those who see *what had happened*: this might refer to Jesus' manner of dying or to the supernatural signs of the previous hours, but it would probably be wrong to seek too much precision. *The centurion*, a Roman, who would have been guarding the crosses, responds as do those throughout the Gospel who recognize the mighty acts of God in Jesus, by giving *praise* to *God* (2.20; 7.16; 13.13; 17.15; 18.43). His words, however, are nothing more than we might expect of a Gentile at this stage in the story: he does not acknowledge Jesus as 'Son of God' as in Mark (15.39), but as a *man* who was *beyond all doubt . . . innocent*. Thus he reaffirms once again that in the eyes of the Romans Jesus was indeed innocent; but for Luke's readers the term *innocent* or *'righteous'* would align Jesus with all who put their trust in God and could rely on God's final vindication (cf. 1.6; 2.15; 14.14). In contrast to him is *the crowd*, who have come as for a *spectacle*; their response is to return home *beating their breasts*. Luke does not elaborate this further and we are left to wonder whether they have been moved to belated repentance or to recognition of the truth implicit in Jesus' words to the women in vv.28–31 and of the judgment that awaits them. Thus Luke leaves unresolved whether there is still hope for the people of Jerusalem and Judaea.

Finally there are *his friends*: if their *standing at a distance* is intended to echo Ps. 38.11 then they are being judged more as having failed in support than as having remained faithful. With them are *the women who had accompanied him from Galilee*; they will be mentioned again in 23.55 and introduce the story of the empty tomb in 24 (see comments). In this way they provide a continuity of witness, for they *watched it all*, from his death to his burial and then to the empty tomb. It is a continuity which reaches back to his earliest ministry for they had been described first in 8.2–3 (see comments). It is a remarkable characteristic of the Gospel narratives that it is not Jesus' closest disciples but women who provide this continuity of witness, although in subordinating them to 'his friends' Luke may already be qualifying the more independent role given them in Mark (15.40–41).

The burial of Jesus
23.49–56

The impression has been that the opposition to Jesus within *the Council* was unanimous, but now Luke acknowledges that this was not so in the person of *Joseph* who came from the small village of *Arimathaea*, not far from Jerusalem. As someone who was *good and upright* – the same word as 'innocent' in v.47 – he joins the ranks of those like Zechariah and Elizabeth (1.6), Simeon (2.25), and Anna (2.36), who were earnestly hoping for God's speedy intervention and rule: as we saw then, it is among such as these that Luke sees hope for Israel.

Most criminals would end up in the common graves in which the poor were also buried, without any record of their individual identity and resting place. Joseph's action saves the *body of Jesus* from this fate and thus makes possible the discovery of his resurrection. There were many tombs *cut out of the rock* around Jerusalem, in which the body would be laid, on a horizantal shelf or the floor. An unused one would presumably be owned by Joseph for his own or his family's use, but for the early Christians it would be particularly fitting that Jesus should be buried alone in a new tomb. *The sabbath* would begin at sunset, and so only the preliminary stages of preparation for burial are performed, although in the hot climate there would be little purpose in delaying the application of *spices and perfumes*: Luke emphasizes that Jesus' closest followers did observe the sabbath rest. It is, however, with *the women* that the story ends, and again we are reminded of their role as witnesses, first *from Galilee*, and now of the identity of the tomb and of the fact that Jesus' *body was laid in it*. Luke is careful to exclude any suggestion that the claims of an empty tomb rested on lack of certainty about what happened in the confusion and haste of the Friday evening.

In the way he has presented the Passion narrative Luke has expressed something of his understanding of **the death of Jesus**. None of the evangelists could simply record the event which was both the centre of their faith and yet for outsiders a major obstacle to accepting Jesus as God's agent, his ignominious death at Roman hands. The primary theme in this understanding is that Jesus' death was in accordance with God's will; this is expressed first by saying that he, particularly as Son of Man, was bound to suffer – there is a divine necessity about it (9.22; 17.25; 24.7, 26). Secondly, his death fulfils the scriptures – a theme which will be particularly important in the next chapter (18.31; 24.26, 44). At this stage particular scriptures do not play a significant role; even Isa. 53 is only quoted of the company in which Jesus was crucified and not of the effect of his suffering (22.37, see comment). These two themes stress that Jesus' death was not an unexpected disaster soon to be rectified by the resurrection. As we have seen, the dominance of the Journey to Jerusalem since 9.51 means that Jesus' coming death there provides an interpretative framework for much of his ministry and particularly for his teaching about discipleship. This does not only mean that Jesus is a model to be followed, an exemplar of the martyr or murdered prophet, although this is certainly present. For Luke discipleship is to be understood in the light of Jesus' death, and despite his much-lauded compassion, Luke's standards for the disciples are particularly stringent. To a church living through the continuing rhythm of time, Luke offers the stern reminder that the kingdom can only follow on from the suffering. There are also other continuities with the ministry of Jesus, even though these do not figure strongly in the express charges laid against him. His association with 'sinners', highlighted in that Isaiah quotation, is carried through to the reponse made to him by one of the thieves and by Jesus' gracious promise to him. The conflict with Satan, heralded in the temptations, reaches a climax in the death (see comment on 22.3, above).

Yet a more theological interpretation of Jesus' death is lacking. Luke omits Jesus' saying which interprets his death as 'a ransom for many' (Mark 10.45), and in 21.28 'redemption', a related term, is the awaited eschatological vindication. Similarly, he also omits the cry of dereliction (Mark 15.45) which at least hints at the alienation from God which identification with humankind entails (see comment on 23.46, above). If the 'shorter' text of the Last Supper is original, Luke also omits the other covenant and soteriological themes which Mark and Matthew express through the words of institution (see comment on 22.19–20, above). Moreover, throughout his account of Jesus' ministry, Luke makes it clear that it is there that salvation is encountered and experienced. Forgiveness is offered in response to repentance, a Lukan emphasis (see 15.7; 24.47). The 'today' of 4.21, which is repeatedly echoed through the Gospel, offers salvation in the present, and this certainty has also become an integral part in Luke's understanding of the kingdom (see 17.21 and comment). Moreover, for Luke, Jesus' death is not itself the climax, neither can it be described, as it is by John, as Jesus' exaltation. His 'departure' or Exodus (9.31) and his 'going up' (9.51) which he must accomplish at Jerusalem will only be achieved in ch.24; there is some truth that for Luke the suffering is a necessary prelude to his 'entering upon his glory' (24.26). Other moments of extreme duress also lie in the future, not only for the disciples but particularly for Jerusalem, to whose devastation the Lukan Jesus returns more than once. In part Luke may see this as inevitably following on from the Jewish rejection of Jesus, but it does not lose its drama for that (see p.170). The peace promised at Jesus' birth (2.14) remains a path to be chosen, or more often to be rejected (14.32; 19.38, 44), and certainly Luke has no superficial optimism that with Jesus, or even with his death, all conflict and evil are ended – even if it enables the reconciliation of a Pilate and a Herod (23.12).

That last unexpected twist shows that Luke's understanding of Jesus' death is far from simple, and would in any case have to be augmented by the more explicit reflections in the preaching in Acts. Yet it is also distinctive, so that in reading Luke's account of the death of Jesus we must hear not only how but also why, for him, it happened.

The women at the tomb
23.56–24.12

Each of the Gospels commences their final chapter with the discovery of the empty tomb. In practice this means that Matthew and Luke follow Mark, although they go beyond him by continuing with appearances by the risen Jesus: for Mark, the earliest Gospel, the empty tomb and the declaration 'he has been raised' is all that needs to, and perhaps all that could, be told (Mark 16.1–8). The other early record of these events is given by Paul as the tradition he both received and passed on, in I Cor. 15.3–8; he says nothing about the empty tomb but cites only a series of appearances, last among which was that to himself. This suggests that the empty tomb tradition and the appearance tradition(s) were originally independent of each other, although which was earliest is still debated. However, in the three later Gospels they have been brought together, particularly in Matthew and John where Jesus appears to the (or a) women (woman) near the recently discovered empty tomb (Matt. 28.9–10; John 20.11–17). Luke does not go so far, but he too retells the story of that discovery, which he has drawn from Mark, in order to express something of his understanding of the event and its meaning.

It is natural to think of a major hiatus or dislocation between the Friday of Jesus' death and the Sunday of the resurrection, just as there must be a hiatus between the death, which can be described, and the resurrection, which cannot but which belongs to the language of faith. Although the chapter division encourages such a separation, Luke's account denies it. The last part of 23.56 and the first verse of ch.24 together form a single sentence, so that while *on the sabbath* the women *rested, . . . on the first day of the week they came*. In this way he maintains the continuity of the women's witness and of the story of Jesus' 'departure'.

Although the Jewish day began at sunset with the deepening gloom, by *'very early'* Luke thinks of a Roman day and of the early hours of the Sunday. He had not mentioned the great stone used to seal the tomb in Mark 15.46 and therefore need not envisage the women only belatedly realizing the problems it would pose for them (Mark 16.3), perhaps finding that unconvincing. Instead he focusses on the women's experience as a chain of discovery and response. *They found . . . the stone . . . rolled away*, but *did not find the body*, which in 23.55 they had seen laid there. In naming it the body *of the Lord Jesus* Luke is already using the language of Christian faith (cf. I Cor. 11.23; II Cor. 4.14), although there is some slight textual evidence that this may be a later addition (see NRSV). The *two men* are not simply seen by them (ctr. Mark 16.5 where there is only one), something which some might ascribe to hallucination, but actually *stood by them*, although their *dazzling garments* clearly identify them as angelic beings (cf. Acts 10.3, 22, 30). The women respond with the fear (= REB *terrified*) appropriate to such a visitation (cf. 1.12, 30; 2.9–10; Acts 10.4), and bow down in awe and worship – the REB's *eyes cast down* is too tame and too coy.

The angels do not announce Jesus' resurrection, at least according to what is probably the best text (see REB footnote and ctr. Mark 16.6), for in Luke this is something which Jesus had promised and which the disciples will come to declare as their own confession (v.34). Instead, in words reminiscent of Jesus' own reply to the Sadducees in 20.38, they merely affirm that *one who is alive* is hardly to be sought *among the dead*; as on that earlier occasion, what could be a proverbial truth gains powerful meaning because it is applied to one assumed to be among the dead. It is to Jesus' words that the angels point the women, to what he had already said about all that awaited *the Son of Man* (9.22; 18.33); as the chapter continues it will become clear that resurrection faith depends on responding to the words both of scripture and of Jesus himself. Once again the reader is reminded that nothing has taken place without the foreknowledge and active commitment of Jesus himself.

While the emphasis may now lie on the final clause, that he *must rise again on the third day*, that certainty is inseparable from and meaningless apart from his handing over and death, which, in contrast to the more general language of the earlier predictions, can now

201

be specified as to *be crucified*. The resurrection of Jesus can only be proclaimed as part of the whole message of his death, of its divine necessity, of his role as Son of Man.

In Mark's account the angel proclaims that Jesus is going ahead of them to Galilee (Mark 16.7; 14.28). In Luke's rewriting of that message *Galilee* is retained only as the scene of Jesus' earlier prophecy. As we shall see, while Galilee was the starting point of Jesus' ministry, for Luke Jesus' appearances are all in Jerusalem and it is there that the disciples will receive power and from there that the Gospel will go out (see p.209 and ctr. Matt. 28.7, 16–20). It is in this and other ways that the evangelists tie the proclamation of the resurrection to the on-going life of the church as they knew it, so that we have no access to a resurrection belief which is not at the same time a foundation of the church, or one part of the church.

In both Mark and Matthew the women are commissioned to tell the disciples, a commission reinforced in Matthew, as also in John to Mary Magdalene, by Jesus himself. Luke omits this, thus, despite his supposed sympathy for women, denying them that primary role in the proclamation of the resurrection. They do indeed report *everything*, although in a curious duplication it is not clear whether this is to *the eleven and* presumably a number of *others*, or only to *the apostles*, so named as representatives of the future church (see 9.10; 17.5; 22.14). They are met with disbelief, for in Luke's account belief in the risen Jesus can only come from a direct encounter with him, and not from hearing of an empty tomb (vv.22–24). Only later will those commissioned be able to proclaim the resurrection from their own witness (v.48), and the women are invisible among them. If v.12 (REB footnote, and see on vv.24, 34)) is original, the women's testimony is even confirmed by *Peter* himself, although it may have been added to account for those later verses and in imitation of John 20.6–10.

Only at the end of the story does Luke name these women who have provided the continuity since 23.49. There they were described as having accompanied him from Galilee, a reference back to 8.1–3. Of the women there named *Mary of Magdala* and *Joanna* are repeated, but Susanna is replaced by *Mary the mother of James*, whom Luke probably drew from Mark 16.1. They will now disappear from his story, even in Acts, and so from any certain role in the early history of the church – a strange fate for those accredited with the first discovery of the empty tomb.

The road to Emmaus
24.13–35

Without Mark to guide him, Luke, like Matthew, now draws on independent tradition, recasting it so that it can also convey the meaning of the resurrection for those who come later. This story is not otherwise known – Mark 16.12–13 from the later longer ending is probably dependent on Luke – neither is the only named participant, *Cleopas*; this, and the failure to provide a name for his companion, some have suggested his wife, point to the authenticity of the tradition: the tendency would be to ascribe appearances to those who were later important in the church and to supply appropriate names to anonymous traditions. The location of *Emmaus* is also uncertain, and for Luke it is of no interest in itself for at the end of the story they will not stay there but immediately return to *Jerusalem* from where they had set out.

In outline the story follows a familiar pattern of the stranger whom the audience, reader or hearer knows to be the one whose absence the unwitting participants are lamenting. The failure to recognize the risen Jesus also features in John 20.14; in part this may be due to (reflection on) the nature of the resurrection body (I Cor. 15.35–41), but it is also demanded by the drama of the narrative which, as we shall see, has a certain artificiality in its retelling. Luke does not say what *prevented them from recognizing him*, nor that it was God, but their blindness followed by the opening of their eyes (v.31) recalls the disciples' earlier failure to understand Jesus' declaration of his coming death which was followed by the healing of the blind man (18.34–43, see comments).

Cleopas' reply to the stranger's comment might well sound abrupt but it clears the way for him to elaborate. His summary of *what has happened* sounds at first like a summary of the Gospel or of early Christian preaching (cf. Acts 10.36–39), but this only underlines where it falls short (ctr. Acts 10.40–43): *the third day* introduces not the message of vindication and the offer of salvation, but empty bewilderment. That the *women . . . failed to find his body* is on its own not the foundation of the Gospel or of faith, and is too easily dismissed as *a vision*, even when corroborated by others, for what matters is that *him they did not see* – a particular irony for the reader/hearer who knows that the speaker is even now seeing him! In smaller details too Cleopas' account reveals its inadequacy as a statement of the gospel: *a prophet* and *liberator of Israel* are ways in which Jesus is understood in Luke (7.16; 9.8; 1.33; 2.25), but by now he has been shown to be much more than that (cf. 22.67–70).

Therefore Luke has used Cleopas' words to express his own understanding, something which may also be seen in the contrast between *the whole people* and the *chief priests and rulers*, who, although they *handed him over*, are still said themselves to have *crucified him* (cf. p.192). Yet there are inconsistencies which may also suggest that he is using an earlier tradition: in his account the *angels* did not (in the better text) say Jesus *was alive*, while he has not described a further visit by *some* among the disciples. Perhaps it was this which led to the introduction of such a declaration by the angels (v.5) and to the visit by Peter in v.12 (see v.34 below).

For Luke, however, it is Jesus who alone can reveal himself and make sense of his death, and this is more important than the historical improbability of the stranger who had just affected ignorance now being able to explain everything without betraying his identity: only the reader knows that everything he says *referred to himself*. The appeal to *all that the prophets said* (cf. 18.31) and to the necessity or inevitability of suffering (cf. 9.22) are themes Luke has already emphasized, but now the one to suffer can be acknowledged no longer as the 'Son of Man', a title Luke does not use in this chapter, but openly as *the Messiah* (cf. v.46): the ambiguities of the earlier predictions have now given way to the foundation of faith in Jesus as Messiah. Yet suffering is here the preface to his *entering upon his glory*; the wording leaves it ambiguous whether Jesus has already entered or has yet to do so, but this may reflect the early belief that Jesus was only fully made Messiah by God's act after his death (cf. Acts 2.36). It was also part of early Christian belief that not only the prophets, but *the whole of scripture* including the Law, represented by Moses, pointed to Jesus (cf. also v.44).

The final scene of their encounter with Jesus is equally laden with significance. Pressed to *stay with them* he immediately and surprisingly acts as host *at table*. His actions in taking the *bread*, saying a *blessing*, breaking and offering it are those of an ordinary meal, but inevitably recall the feeding of the five thousand (9.16) and more importantly the last supper (22.19a). This is not a symbolic meal nor a 'eucharist'; it is a real meal but Jesus' actions transform it so that it becomes a vehicle of deeper meaning. Luke's readers may well have thought of it as they thought of the 'breaking of bread' in the early church as a routine event transfigured by its association with Jesus (Acts 2.42, 46; 20.7,11).

Jesus disappears as mysteriously as he had appeared, another common feature of the appearance traditions (cf. v.36), but only after they have *recognized him*. The purpose of the event has been for Jesus to reveal himself but, as their response shows, Jesus does not only reveal himself through direct encounter. First they recall their experience *on the road* or *'way'*, which in Acts becomes the name of the new Christian movement (Acts 9.2; 19.9, 23). There, in retrospect – in the interests of the dramatic structure it could not be otherwise – *the scriptures* had received new meaning as the source of certainty and hope through their interpretation by Jesus himself: for Luke Jesus is the source of and the authority behind the new understanding of the scriptures, and it is in them and in that understanding that his living presence could be encountered.

Next, ignoring that evening had long since come (v.29), they return *to Jerusalem*: on one level this is to tell the other disciples, on another it is because for Luke it is in Jerusalem that the news of the resurrection must first be proclaimed and from there that the gospel must go out. Yet once again the foundation of the resurrection message will not come from the report of others but from Jesus' self-revelation. Even before they speak they are met with the confession *'The Lord has risen'*: the confession can be made because *he has appeared to Simon*. That the future leader of the apostles should have experienced a resurrection appearance should be no surprise; what is surprising is that no detailed account was either preserved or created. However, the mere mention is enough to recall Jesus' words in 22.31–2 to *Simon*: now, surely, he has been 'restored' and can fulfil his commission – it is this link back to Jesus' earlier promise that a later scribe has missed in inserting a fruitless visit to the empty tomb by Peter (v.12).

Only in response to this can the two report *what had happened* on *'the* way' (= REB *their journey*) and that Jesus was known to them *in the breaking of the bread*. While this could simply be a summary of the meal they had shared, the term is that used of the Christian shared meal in Acts (see above and cf. I Cor. 10.16). For later Christians this, and the exposition of scripture, would be the primary ways in which they experienced the presence of Jesus among them. Through this narrative Luke has both affirmed that experience and rooted it in the self-revelation of Jesus himself. All Christian worship, study of the scriptures, and experience rests on Jesus who makes himself known through them; his risen presence in this way is not tied to the first generation. Yet equally they rest on the experience of the first disciples which alone makes possible the confession, 'The Lord is risen'.

Commission and departure
24.36–53

Each of the Gospels ends in a way which makes it clear that the story of Jesus is not now finished: there is an openess to the future which embraces the reader, even in the mysterious and ambiguous closing of Mark (16.8). Both the task of the church and the experience of its members are guaranteed by the risen Jesus – and here each of the evangelists may have been speaking of his own community as a microcosm of the wider church.

To emphasize this, and that the crucified Jesus and the risen Jesus cannot be separated, Luke compresses all the events into a single day – in contrast to his account in Acts 1.3. Therefore it is still on the first evening *as they were talking* that Jesus appears to the whole group. Once again faith will rest not on the report of others alone but on Jesus' self-revelation: despite their recent assurance (v.34), their reaction to Jesus' sudden presence is one of fear and awe (cf. v.5) as before a supernatural being (*'spirit'*) or *ghost*, and even of disbelief, which will only be dispelled by Jesus himself bringing them understanding and joy.

The sudden appearance of Jesus, *standing among them*, their *doubts* which he perceives, and his demonstration of his *hands and feet*, presumably marked by the nails although these were not mentioned in the crucifixion account, all recall the stories in John 20.19–29. In a number of manuscripts the links are strengthened by Jesus' greeting, 'Peace be with you', and by his explicitly showing his hands and feet (REB footnote to vv.36, 39–40; cf. John 20.19–20). While these additions may have been made by a scribe familiar with the Johannine story, it is equally possible that they are original and come from a common underlying tradition: the use of *fish*, more natural in Galilee than Jerusalem, points in the same direction (cf. John 21.5,9). The physical reality of Jesus' resurrection body was an important part of early Christian apologetic against charges of hallucination or against the rejection of God's total involvement in human bodiliness. Once again a meal is involved but here it only establishes that Jesus has *flesh and bones*: although different accounts vary on this (cf. Gen 19.3), it is assumed here that supernatural beings do not eat or digest.

More important than the fact of the resurrection of Jesus is its meaning, which Jesus alone can interpret. He does so by recalling his *words* (= REB *'what I meant by saying'*) and *the scriptures*; the main focus of his ministry, *while* he *was still with* them, is now not the miracles but what he said, which itself only points back to scripture. At the same time *scripture* is now understood only as pointing forward to Jesus. Luke does not refer to particular passages but to the whole of scripture. At this time *the law of Moses*, or in modern terms the 'pentateuch', and *the prophets* were firmly recognized as authoritative; the remaining books, usually known as 'the writings' may still have been given less authority and seen as a not-yet-closed collection, and it is unclear whether by the *psalms* Luke intends only the book of that name or other 'writings' also. Understood in their original setting only in the prophets are there any passages – and even here very few – which anticipate a coming deliverer; the term *Messiah* is not used technically for this hoped-for-figure and nowhere are his *sufferings* or *rising* foretold. Convinced that Jesus was indeed God's promised deliverer and that all that had happened *was bound* to do so, in accordance with God's will, the early Christians were equally convinced that it must be 'according to the scriptures' (cf. I Cor. 15.3). Only subsequently did they begin to isolate particular passages, often by ignoring their original meaning and context. Luke represents the earlier conviction, but his comprehensive wording anticipates how 'the Old Testament' would come to be interpreted entirely as foretelling not only Jesus' death and resurrection but as pointing to every detail of his and of the church's life and experience.

Modern study is now much more concerned to recognize the meaning of the writings of the **Old Testament** in their own right, as literary units and as records of and responses to particular historical settings. To do this is to affirm their own testimony that they bear to God's working through the history of the people of Israel and to the people's experience of and response to God. Jesus himself understood God and his own mission in the light of that history and experience, and Luke too, particularly in the infancy narratives, has shown how Jesus must be understood in continuity with Israel's past. Luke is representative of the general early Christian attitude which treated the whole of the scriptures as prophetic of Jesus, and, in time, of the church. Contemporary reading of the Old Testament will recognize the difference between how passages were understood in their original setting, and the use Christians made of them in the conviction that all

God's activity was one and that it found its climax in the person of Jesus.

For Luke this meaning of scripture is not self-evident but is dependent both on Jesus' explanation and on *their minds* being *opened*, the same verb as in v.31. For him it is with Jesus' authority that the church uses scripture in the way it does, but this does not work as a self-evident proof but only for those already among the disciples who are given the gift of understanding. Scripture is not only the foundation for understanding all that has happened to Jesus but also for the church's proclamation. It was one part of prophetic hope that 'the word of the Lord would go out from Jerusalem' (Isa. 2.3), but here this is reinterpreted in terms of Luke's understanding of the gospel as *repentance* and *forgiveness of sins* (1.77; 3.3; 5.32; Acts 2.38; 5.31; 10.42). These are made possible through Jesus' authority and power, represented by *his name*, but are not specifically tied to his death (see p.199).

Although Luke started by fixing the story of Jesus firmly within Israel's hope of redemption, there have been from the start hints that this hope is to be offered universally (see 2.31–2), a theme which will control the story told in Acts. Although during Jesus' ministry a Gentile like the centurion could only express his faith and receive blessing at a distance (7.1–10), now in the time of the church the proclamation is to be made *to all nations*; this will not be through default or chance events, as might appear, but rests on the authority of Jesus and of scripture. In reality the conflicts which beset the church over the inclusion of non-Jews suggests that there was no explicit command of Jesus to which they could appeal (cf. Acts 15 and Paul's letters, especially to the Galatians and Romans); Jesus' own anticipations regarding the future and his attitude to Gentiles are far from certain. In putting this injunction on the lips of Jesus in this way Luke is expressing the faith that this expansion was part of God's intention through scripture and made possible through Jesus. At the same time it is to begin *from Jerusalem*: Luke does not forget or deny the origins of the Gospel, and although we have seen that his understanding of the continuing place of Jerusalem and the Temple is not fully worked out (pp.156–58), Jerusalem will be where the Gospel ends, as it began.

The initiative lies with Jesus, in accordance with scripture; the task of the disciples is named last for it is dependent on this. That task is to be *witnesses*, those who authenticate the proclamation and who make it known. This theme too will continue in Acts (cf. Acts 1.8,22; 2.32; 10.39 etc.) where it is the primary mark of an apostle; it is also the foundation on which the Gospel rests (see 1.2 and comment). The disciples are given no other authority and no other task than this; in this sense they are as in 1.2 'servants of the Gospel'.

For Luke these will be the foundations of the church: the study and exposition of scripture, the proclamation of repentance and forgiveness, the universal mission, and the testimony of the apostles. They are founded on the words of Jesus as the risen one, and so are an inseparable part of faith in Jesus as risen: there is here no experience of the risen Jesus without commission, and so this final scene includes all the earlier actors. Yet they will also be part of a new stage in God's activity; so, just as Jesus was *armed with power* at the beginning of his ministry (4.14), they too must be. Here this power is not identified as the spirit but only as God's *promise* (cf. Isa. 32.15); the effect is to bind together Jesus, as sender, and God, *'my Father'*, as promiser, which anticipates the later development of the understanding of God in binitarian, but not yet trinitarian, terms.

Their commission is sealed by Jesus' blessing, a prayer for divine favour as much as a commission. The scene is remarkably restrained, concluding only with his departure, and no hint that this was final: it is probably a later scribe who, finding that a lack, has added a clarifying reference to his ascension (REB footnote). For reasons that are only partly clear Luke tells a different story here than that which opens Acts, where Jesus only after forty days leaves them with the more apocalyptic 'scenery' of cloud, ascension to heaven, and angelic interpreters. Perhaps he did find that a more powerful inauguration to the story of the church. Here all has happened within a single day – although the approaching evening of v.29 has now been extended even to include the walk out to *Bethany* and the disciples' return. In this way Jesus' 'entering upon his glory' (v.26) becomes a single process of rising and departure, a fitting climax to his journey to his 'taking up' at Jerusalem (9.51 and comment), and to the Gospel story.

The story ends as it began, in Jerusalem and in the Temple (see above and p.157). Only now (ctr. vv.4–5,17,37,41) are they filled with the *great joy* (= REB *full of joy*) which was promised in the beginning (2.10); now they too respond by *praising God* as in 1.64; 2.28 (cf. 2.13,20 using a different verb). By echoing his beginning in the ending Luke invites the reader to see how the promises inherent in the birth narratives have now found their fulfilment and their proper response – a response in which all should join.

Index of Main Themes